Lark in the Morning

Lark
in the
Morning

*The Verses
of the
Troubadours*

A Bilingual Edition

EDITED BY
ROBERT KEHEW

TRANSLATED BY
EZRA POUND,
W. D. SNODGRASS,
& ROBERT KEHEW

THE UNIVERSITY OF CHICAGO PRESS
CHICAGO & LONDON

The University of Chicago Press, Chicago 60637
The University of Chicago Press, Ltd., London
© 2005 by The University of Chicago
All rights reserved. Published 2005
Printed in the United States of America
16 15 14 13 12 11 10 09 08 07   2 3 4 5 6
ISBN: 0-226-42932-6 (cloth)
ISBN: 0-226-42933-4 (paper)

LIBRARY OF CONGRESS CATALOGING-IN-PUBLICATION DATA

Lark in the morning : the verses of the troubadours / edited by
    Robert Kehew ; translated by Ezra Pound, W.D. Snodgrass,
    & Robert Kehew. — A bilingual ed.
        p.   cm.
    Includes bibliographical references and index.
    ISBN 0-226-42932-6 (cloth : alk. paper)
    1. Provençal poetry.   2. Provençal poetry—Translations into
English.   3. Troubadours.   I. Kehew, Robert.   II. Pound, Ezra,
1885–1972.   III. Snodgrass, W. D. (William De Witt), 1926–   IV. Title.

PC3365.E3L37 2005
849'.1008—dc22   2005000956

♾ The paper used in this publication meets the minimum requirements
of the American National Standard for Information Sciences—
Permanence of Paper for Printed Library Materials, ANSI z39.48-1992.

To my mother &
the memory of my father

CONTENTS

Song did not again awake until the Provençal viol aroused it.
—Ezra Pound, *Spirit of Romance,* 21

As we explore the vast field of English letters, sometimes we encounter a
form—a sonnet or an ode, a villanelle or a sestina—to which poets turn re-
peatedly and whose usage continues back through generations until it dis-
appears in the mists of the past. When was that form first used, we may ask?
When was a sestina not a template but just an original poem whose unusu-
ally felicitous arrangement of meter and rhyme invited later emulation? If
we seek to penetrate the mists and to trace that form back to its earliest ap-
pearance, we most likely will find ourselves standing at one of two headwa-
ters—times when poetic practice was unusually fecund. On the one hand
we may travel back in time through Rome to find ourselves in classical
Greece, seated at the feet of a Pindar. Or we may follow the route back past
the Elizabethans, past Chaucer, to cross the English Channel into medieval
Europe. If we continue back, brushing past the *rondeaux* and the *canzoni,*
we will find ourselves in southern France. And there, in the twelfth and thir-
teen centuries, we will encounter the troubadours.

As we will see, the troubadours exerted a strong, albeit indirect, influ-
ence on English letters; yet it has been difficult for the English reader to get
much of a sense of their work. One cannot expect the general reader to be
conversant in Old Occitan, the troubadours' tongue. Moreover, from
Chaucer to the present, there has been no collection of sufficient scope to be
called an anthology of the troubadours' poems in translations that attempt
to respect the verse forms of the originals. There have been anthologies of
prose translations prepared to exacting academic standards, and collections
of *vers libre* versions, and even small groupings of formal verse translations.
But the present work is the first to gather translations that allow the English
reader to appreciate something of the formal effects of the originals.

Readerly enjoyment thus is one motive for the present work, and a suffi-
cient one: beauty is its own justification. Yet poetic translation has served
and still could serve an even more vital function in the development of
English literature. *Influence* means a flowing in, and so the inpouring of
translated works often revitalizes a culture's literature. Where would English

letters be without the translation of the *Romance of the Rose* in which Chaucer himself probably had a hand, without Wyatt's Petrarch, Golding's *Metamorphoses,* various respectable runs at Homer and Dante, Pound's Chinese poems, and so on? The likely answer: impoverished. While a skeptic might argue that the age has long passed when poetic translation could greatly influence English literature, that position pretends to a knowledge of the nonsequential future that no one possesses. In a similar way, a critic in the 1850s might have claimed that the King James Bible no longer could exert a fresh impact on contemporary letters—but that would have been before the advent of Walt Whitman.

Such are the motives for compiling the present anthology. Which, though, of the 460-odd troubadours whom we know by name should be represented? Which of the 2,500-some poems that have come down to us should be included? Several rules guided this selection. First, I wanted to represent the major troubadours. This selection, for the most part, is not radical: it generally respects the wisdom built up over the centuries as to which troubadours merit attention. With one major exception: I have broadened the sampling of women troubadours in comparison with previous general anthologies. The present anthology showcases three women troubadours, out of a total of some twenty *trobairitz* who are known to us by name as the authors of extant poems.[1]

Second, I wanted to represent the major troubadours *adequately.* A single popular work may not provide much insight into a composer's overall output—think about trying to draw conclusions about Leonard Bernstein's oeuvre after listening only to *West Side Story*—and so for each major poet I tried to offer at least two poems, and in certain cases as many as six.

While highlighting the major troubadours, I wanted to suggest at the same time the sweep of the entire troubadour accomplishment. I therefore selected lyrics from all periods during the two centuries when the troubadours wrote, including certain poems that are of interest mainly from an historic, rather than a purely artistic, perspective. I also included examples of nearly all of the major (as well as a sprinkling of the minor) poetic forms cultivated by the makers of song.

Happily, these basic rules allowed me to include most of the troubadour translations prepared by my fellow translators and poetic superiors, Ezra Pound and W. D. Snodgrass. The poems that attracted their attention are also, for the most part, of general interest. Regretfully, however, I was not able to use all of their fine work. My upper limit of six poems per troubadour eliminated several of Pound's courageous runs at Arnaut Daniel and one of Snodgrass's translations of Bernart de Ventadorn's poems. Further, a decision to include only complete or near-complete translations ruled out a number of Poundian snippets. Finally, the focus on major troubadours excluded limpid translations by both Pound and Snodgrass of anonymous works. I did, however, bend my rules enough to admit Pound's translation of a poem by the obscure Peire Bremon lo Tort.

Dealing with troubadour melodies offered a trickier challenge. Melodies survive for about a tenth of the extant troubadour poems, which are in fact song lyrics. The troubadours set down their melodies using a rudimentary form of musical notation that indicates the pitch of notes but not other qualities such as rhythm or duration. Undaunted by the challenge, both Pound and Snodgrass have transcribed melodies for modern use—an exercise that necessarily involves a certain amount of artistic license. Further, in several cases where an appealing lyric has lost its original melody, Snodgrass has gone so far as to "borrow" a melody from another troubadour song, creating *contrafacta*. But despite the existence of transcribed melodies for a number of poems (although not always with scholarly blessing), as an anthologist I had to ask myself whether their inclusion, which could add substantially to page length and book price, would be of proportionate interest to the majority of the intended audience. While the present volume contains no melodies, readers interested in perusing Snodgrass's transcriptions of troubadour melodies may turn to the Internet.[2]

One advantage of focusing on the known, major troubadours is that this practice allows one to better frame their work in a historic and artistic context—an aid to appreciation. To this end, the book proceeds as follows. First, an introduction sets the stage. Then come a series of chapters on individual troubadours, generally arranged in chronological order. Each chapter opens with an excerpt from a medieval biography of the troubadour in question. These biographies—known as either *vidas* ("lives" of the troubadours) or *razos* ("commentaries" on individual songs)—were set down in the thirteenth and fourteenth centuries. The earliest apparently flowed from the pen of one Uc de Saint-Circ, a cleric, *joglar* (performer), and troubadour in his own right, who lived in Montpellier around 1220. Based largely on loose gossip and the patter used by the troubadours' *joglars* to warm up their audiences, these biographies are as colorful and charming as they are, in many cases, wildly inaccurate. Beginning each chapter in this way is a nod to the earliest troubadour anthologists of the Middle Ages: their handsome illuminated *chansonniers* (songbooks) often introduced poems, penned in black, with miniature biographies set down in rubric (red).[3]

Following these medieval excerpts, I in my own way try to warm up the audience. In each chapter I offer a more accurate (if less charming) *vida* of the troubadour in question, along with the occasional contemporary *razo* on the poems selected.

The poems themselves make up the bulk of each chapter, with English translation saluting the Occitan originals across the page. While the original texts will be of interest mainly to students of Old Occitan, the general reader who speaks a contemporary Romance language may well gather some insight from the troubadours' expressions of *joi* and sighs of *alas* in their original tongue.

Matching up translations with originals in this way was not always a straightforward task. For any single troubadour song, various versions in Occitan often exist: a poem that surfaces in one *chansonnier* may reappear with variations in another. Further, there are various critical editions that scholars have prepared over the past 150 years. While I knew or was able to ascertain at first hand the base texts relied upon by Snodgrass and myself, information was spottier in the case of Pound. I endeavored to include the critical edition that Pound was known to have used, or else the closest approximation possible, bearing in mind that Pound sometimes worked directly from the *chansonniers.*

It should be noted that the critically edited texts in Old Occitan represented in the present anthology span roughly a century of troubadour scholarship. In accordance with accepted scholarly practice, I have made no attempt to standardize editorial conventions for the versions used.[4] The minor exception to this rule is the decision to capitalize the first letter of the first word in each line. In this and in other ways (for example, in the spelling of troubadour names), I have taken as a guide Akehurst and Davis's impressive *Handbook of the Troubadours,* a touchstone of recent troubadour scholarship.

Perusal of the English versions reminds one that translation, particularly for those who translate into verse but for others as well, is an inexact science, an impure art. Even those who translate poetry into prose, who thus are freed to hone in on one aspect of the original text—namely, meaning—and to let other qualities go by the board, will admit that capturing the sense originally intended by the author with full fidelity is a near-unattainable challenge. One either does not know or else cannot completely replicate all the overtones of significance that reverberate in the original work. At the same time, many words that we use today have accumulated a set of connotations that are, in the context of translating an eight-hundred-year-old poem, anachronistic.

The translator who aspires to create a work of art in English that reflects something of the original's formal, metrical aspects while at the same time clearly conveying its meaning faces an even more daunting challenge. To begin with, the foundations of prosody differ from language to language. Poems written in Old Occitan adhere to strict patterns regarding the number of syllables per line. Most traditional English poetry, on the other hand, is accentual-syllabic: poets count both stresses and syllables. This dual emphasis leads to greater flexibility as to the precise number of syllables per line than in a purely syllabic system. A further difference between the two languages is that Old Occitan, like other Romance languages and in contrast to English, is rich in words that rhyme. This circumstance allowed the Occitanian poets to construct ever more intricately rhymed poetic edifices. As a result of these differences in languages, even the fussiest of poetic translators must make choices about the best way to approximate the formal aspects of the original. It is small wonder if the verse translations presented below, which try to satisfy multiple objectives, do not always perfectly capture with full fidelity the literal meaning of the original. I offer this observation as a general statement now, and rely on specific notes later to remedy some of the more telling divergences from original meaning.

A word on our translators' respective interests in the troubadours and approaches to translation is in order—particularly since two of these translators, Pound and Snodgrass, are seminal poets in their own right. The troubadours were Pound's first love. As a precocious poet-scholar, Pound trained in Romance philology, taught and published essays on the troubadours, and haunted the Bibliothèque Nationale de France while transcribing the troubadour melodies. Then, in the summer of 1912, he set out, on foot and by train, to explore the ancient land of the troubadours. By foot alone, the sunburned young poet logged about five hundred kilometers while traversing the ruined courtyards and roads once frequented by Arnaut Daniel, Peire d'Alvernhe, and the rest. "I had set out . . . with numerous ideas, but the road had cured me of them," Pound later wrote. "There is this difference, I think between a townsman & a man doing something or going somewhere in the open, namely that the townsman has his head full of abstractions. The man in the open has his mind full of objects."[5] Images from this journey crop up throughout Pound's *Cantos,* his lifelong work, to the very last pages.

As a translator, Pound was drawn to the formalistic pyrotechnics of Arnaut Daniel, but he could also appreciate the rough-hewn truths of Bertran de Born. One can, in fact, trace something of an evolution in Pound's poetic technique between these two poles. With Arnaut Daniel, the young Pound attempted to precisely emulate the troubadour's complex formal schemes. Not even Pound could pull off this feat without strain. As he later disarmingly put it: "I have proved that the Provençal rhyme schemes are not *impossible* in English. They are probably *inadvisable.*"[6] By the time he got to Bertran de Born, however, Pound had loosened up: he trusted his own ear more and let the crutches of too-strict scansion and rhyme fall away, to greater effect. As he matured as a poet and translator, Pound also outgrew his early, fin-de-siècle love of archaisms—what he later called "the crust of dead English"—and found a more living voice.[7]

Pound's troubadour translations lie strewn across his published and unpublished works like the fragments of a meteorite come to rest across several states. At times his poetic instinct or the purpose at hand led Pound to translate only a portion of a particular song, or else to riff freely upon the original text. I have responded to such exercises of poetic prerogative via notes and, in a couple of instances, by offering alternative translations in an appendix. Also note that, at times, Pound translates only the first couple of stanzas of a given song in verse; then, as though other duties had called or inspiration had flagged, he lapses into a proselike translation presented in paragraph form.

Due in part to his formal musical training, W. D. Snodgrass has been drawn back time and again to the troubadours as composers of songs. "Years ago," he says, "I made a deep-sworn vow to stop translating anything except songs"—a vow that only occasionally he has felt compelled to break. In addition to being lured by the formal beauty of the troubadours' works, at times he also has enjoyed using translations to help overturn accepted notions. "Our vision of the Provencal Troubadour and his songs has almost completed changed," Snodgrass observes. "Gone is the wistful figure singing sweetly . . . to a far-off, idealized lady. . . . By now, we are almost ready to say that Troubadour songs have only two subjects: one, let's go crusading and kill lots of Moors; two, let's go get in the boss's wife" (*Six Troubadour Songs*). But Snodgrass also reveals a more personal motive for translating. No doubt he speaks for some of the best poet-translators everywhere when he writes: "I simply wanted to sing these songs myself" (*Selected Translations,* 13). Snodgrass's choices about which poets to translate reflect his admiration for the passionate lyricism of Bernart de Ventadorn, but he also finds a place in his heart for the earthy good humor of Guillem de Peiteus.

As one engrossed in poetry, I myself encountered the troubadours when I began to investigate how different poetic forms were first employed. I used the act of translation as a way to peer into the red-lit doorway of that smithy from which so much of Western poetic practice has emerged. I began by working with those troubadours who spoke to me the most—Marcabru, Peire d'Alvernhe, Guiraut de Bornelh, the incorrigible Monge de Montaudon. The idea for the anthology dawned on me when I realized that, co-incidentally, two of the poets writing in English who had most captured my attention—Ezra Pound and W. D. Snodgrass—both had translated a number of works by the troubadours. As I assembled their translations and the anthology started to take shape, I began to translate more purposefully, to fill in the remaining gaps. I hope that the reader finds the resulting work a pleasing and well-rounded whole.

I finally come to the happy moment to gratefully acknowledge help and support. First and foremost, thanks to W. D. Snodgrass, without whose encouragement this book would not have been possible, and whose comradeship and tequila shots in Mexico (with Kathy) helped to fortify my resolve. A special thanks to Randolph Petilos, acquisitions editor for poetry at University of Chicago Press, for believing in this project, and in me. Thanks also to the gracious and astute Margaret Mahan, manuscript editor, and Monica Holliday, production editor at the Press.

Drafts of this book benefited greatly from close readings by Stephen G. Nichols and Margaret Switten. Also thanks to William D. Paden, Barbara Keller, and Mark N. Taylor (the latter of the Société Guilhem IX) for research and editorial advice. Helpful reviews of draft sections also came from Jeffery Paine, David Hoof, and Dennis Myers.

Thanks to Don Gastwirth, my literary agent. Thanks to Christopher Whent, producer of WBAI's *Here of a Sunday Morning* in New York, for graciously agreeing to host supplemental musical materials on the program's Web site.

Thanks to numerous friends, family members, and teachers for support. For help with "troubadouring" in France, thanks to Sommie Atkinson. Finally, a special thanks to the proprietors and staff of the great coffeehouses, those havens for writers: Tryst in Washington DC, Trieste in San Francisco, La Luna in El Salvador, and the establishment of the late Robert Borsodi in New Orleans.

During the height of the Middle Ages, from out the narrow windows of the castles of southern France, a remarkable group of songs poured forth. With their pleasing melodies and intricate stanzaic patterns, these songs were different from much that had gone before. Even more striking than their form was their emotional content. The emotion that many of these songs expressed, while tinged with feudalism, is nonetheless clearly recognizable today as romantic love. Indeed, we owe a considerable debt to the long-vanished composers of these songs: before them, this sentiment had been little celebrated or even recognized in the West. The makers of this remarkable group of songs are known as the troubadours. For the exuberance of their song, the acrobatics of their versification, and the novelty of their expression at the dawn of the modern European era, collectively the troubadours truly were the "lark in the morning."

Who were these composers? The word *troubadour* has entered our vocabulary, and the late Victorians have furnished us with a romanticized image—the minstrel with the "trunk-hose and the light guitar" as Ezra Pound satirically put it. But who were the troubadours in fact?

Their collective name gives us our first clue. The word *troubadour* means finder or maker, and the troubadours were makers or composers of songs. They were active during the twelfth and thirteenth centuries. The troubadours wrote largely for the entertainment of the feudal nobles of southern France, and composed in the language of that region. That does not seem so remarkable today, yet "high" artistic expression in the vernacular was a breakthrough at the time: it represented no small development in a society where the language of the long-vanished Roman Empire still dominated elevated discourse.

The tongue in which the troubadours wrote was known as the *langue d'oc,* the "language of *oc,*" because the southerners' word for "yes" was *oc.* It

Opposite: **Musician and Juggler.** Codex of Latin hymns from the Church of St. Martial, Limoges, late tenth century (BN fonds latin 1118, f. 112). (Bibliothèque Nationale de France, Paris.)

was called this to distinguish it from the language of northern France, where "yes" was *oïl,* which has since evolved (and expanded out of its original territory) to become—*oui*—modern French. Back then, the *langue d'oc* was spoken in a somewhat broader region than the present-day French province of Languedoc that bears its name. Scholars refer to the language of the troubadours as Old Occitan and this broader linguistic territory as Occitania. Unlike the *pays d'oïl,* however, Occitania never coalesced into a stable political unit. As we shall see.

The troubadours were makers, but generally not singers, of songs. Sweet-voiced *joglars* performed their works. The makers of songs hailed from all classes. Guillem de Peiteus, the so-called First Troubadour, wrote with the devil-may-care assurance of one of the wealthiest and most powerful men of his day. Others were minor noblemen, while still others like Marcabru rose from humbler stock by dint of their poetic talent. Even more strikingly, while most of these composers were men, there were also a number of female troubadours or *trobairitz*—an anomalous development for the age.

The troubadours' compositions were in great demand: the noble classes not only of southern France but also of surrounding regions, particularly northern Spain and Italy, clamored for their works. We surmise that this thirst was nearly unquenchable because of the prodigious number of songs that the troubadours obligingly supplied. Even today the lyrics to some twenty-five hundred compositions survive—and no doubt many other Occitanian songs have been lost to the ravages of time. The ladies and lords of that era craved the poems that served as delivery devices for this compelling sentiment of love, much as they desired the exotic Eastern spices that were then beginning to add savor to their bland meals.

Let us examine more carefully this remarkable sentiment of which the troubadours sang, bearing in mind Henry Adams's warning that, in the eleven hundreds, "love was . . . complicated beyond modern conception" (*Mont-Saint-Michel and Chartres,* 219). The sentiment which inspired the troubadours was known as pure or refined love: *fin' amor.*

Fin' amor coincides with modern notions of romantic love only to a degree. At the root of both medieval and modern romantic sentiments lies sexual attraction between man and woman. The modern reader finds nothing hard to understand in Bernart de Ventadorn's hope that his lady might "Receive me in that place / She lies in, to embrace / And press against me, tight, / Her body, smooth and white." The Comtessa de Dia expresses much the same longing for her "naked knight." [1] While most troubadours sublimate love to some extent, Eros never completely loses his vitals. When love has been spiritualized to the degree of, say, Dante's feelings for Beatrice, who guided him toward heaven, we have transcended the limits of *fin' amor* and risen into the realm of a more purely religious emotion.

Past this common root of sexual attraction, however, medieval and modern notions of love between man and woman flourish in curiously divergent ways. *Fin' amor* has a distinctly feudal tinge. Cheyette flatly informs us that, in southern France in the Middle Ages, "love could be listed as part of a family's estate, like dues from peasants or lordship of castles" (*Ermengard of Narbonne*, 233–37). Cheyette further offers instances where the troubadours seem to "lift" lines directly from feudal oaths. We also see the protagonist in Bernart de Ventadorn's song "Pois preyatz me, senhor" ("You've Asked, My Lords, for Song") make the *immixtio manuum,* the feudal gesture of submission, to his loved one.[2]

Also firmly in the feudal spirit, the troubadours reserved their protestations of love for noblewomen. Their culture proscribed expressions of love for a lowborn wench. Marcabru's poem "L'autrier jost' una sebissa" ("The Peasant Lassie"), in which the knightly protagonist flatters a comely shepherdess in an effort to quickly seduce her, is the boundary-pushing exception that proves the rule. Such encounters with eye-catching *vilanas* are almost unknown in the troubadour corpus; rhapsodies about pure love felt for ladies of the court are the norm.

Yet despite this characteristic tone of courtly fealty, *fin' amor* sounds a subversive note. It was typically expressed toward a married woman, the wife of the troubadour's patron. It was thus an adulterous fantasy. (We cannot tell at this remove whether any of these expressions of longing were ever actually consummated.) To some degree these protestations of love were merely flattery of the powerful—and not only the lords but quite a few of the ladies of that time wielded great power in their own right. Yet at the same time one senses a longing for the tang of forbidden fruit. With such songs being sung to susceptible ladies while jealous husbands lurked nearby, it would seem that we have at last struck a vein of truth in the (generally unreliable) medieval biographies of the troubadours when they depict livid barons ordering chagrined composers to hit the road on short notice.

If *fin' amor* was fundamentally adulterous in nature, then by definition it could not flourish in a conjugal setting. C. S. Lewis pointed out that this was because the supplicating stance of the troubadour/lover toward the lady was at odds with the Roman Catholic Church's ideas about the proper relation between husband and wife. Indeed, the notion of *any* sort of romantic love blossoming within the confines of marriage was far from the minds of finger-wagging popes when, for example, they warned couples that although sex within marriage was permitted, the desire for it was wicked. During this era the nobles generally disposed of their children in matrimony on the basis of clearheaded assessments of interest and advancement, unclouded by considerations of romantic sentiment. These circumstances led Lewis to aver that "any idealization of sexual love, in a society where marriage is purely utilitarian, must begin by being an idealization of adultery" (*Allegory of Love*, 13–17, 36). It would take later generations, the great moralist concluded, to pour this sentiment of love between man and woman into a form of which morality could approve, that is, marriage.

Given this adulterous undercurrent, we are perhaps surprised that devotees believed that *fin' amor* exerted a positive and refining influence on the world. For them pure love prompted, as Denomy put it, "the lover's progress and growth in natural goodness, merit and worth" ("Courtly Love and Courtliness," 44). As Lanfranc Cigala expressed the sentiment in "Na Guilielma, maunt cavalier arratge" ("Which of the Two Behaved Most Fittingly?"): "there never will appear a chivalry that doesn't spring from love."

Fin' amor thus flourished, as Cheyette observes, "in the ambiguous realm between sentiment and power, politics and eroticism" (*Ermengard of Narbonne*, 235). Some scholars have found it useful to analyze the subtle social interactions set in motion by this sentiment as a "game." Conflicting objectives animate the players in the troubadour pastime. On the one hand the troubadour/lover desires, in Monson's words, "to advance as fast and as far as possible towards emotional and physical intimacy with [his lady] . . . but without offending her by his forwardness, which could cause him to lose ground." The lady, on the other hand, wary of vicious gossip, resists his blandishments. At the same time, however, "while minimizing the concessions, the lady must try to avoid completely discouraging the lover, unless she wishes to put an end to the game" ("Troubadours at Play," 200–201). And this she generally does not want to do. She may have in mind the overall improvement of the court via the salutary effects of *fin' amor*. Or her motive may be simply to hear her beauties and virtues sung throughout the land.

This "Simon Says" kind of set-up allows for an almost infinite number of intermediate steps. Living today in a more permissive society, we have to recalibrate our sense of proportion to best appreciate the gamesmanship of those social actors. Consider, for example, the finesse exhibited by the player who rewards her lover by allowing him to momentarily rest the back of his hand against her bare leg (see chapter on Raimbaut d'Aurenga); or the finely tuned concessions of the lady in Peire d'Alvernhe's "Rossinhol, el seu repaire" ("Nightingale for Me Take Flight"); or Bernart de Ventadorn's high-stakes ploy in "Be m'an perdut" ("Farewell to Ventadorn") when he threatens to quit the game of love altogether. Finally, the troubadour game also features a hovering ring of auxiliary players, all with their own agendas: the slanderer, the jealous husband, the gossip, and so on.

This social situation — and in particular this subservient attitude toward noblewomen — represented quite a divergence from business as usual. As Zink observes, "the originality of [the] courtliness [of the troubadours] lay in the essential role it gave to women and to love. It was original with respect to both the teachings of the Church and the customs of the day. The courtly lover's lady was his . . . feudal sovereign. He would do anything she wished" (*Medieval French Literature*, 35). To underscore this sense of fealty, the troubadours often addressed their lady as *midons*, a strange composite word containing the feminine version of "my" (*mia*) and the masculine noun for "lord" (*domnus*). Cheyette agrees that these poetic expressions of allegiance cannot be explained away as mere lip service, and emphasizes that this was by no means a world where men alone exercised political power (*Ermengard of Narbonne*, 237).

Not all found this new attitude toward women to be a refreshing step forward. Ordericus Vitalis, for one, would have none of it. Writing at the time, he took exception to "these effeminate men, these dirty libertines who deserve to burn in hell-fire, [who have] rejected their warrior customs. . . . They take pains to please the women with all kinds of lasciviousness. . . . Their external appearance is the sad reflection of their souls."[3] In more recent years, feminists and humanists have been divided over whether *fin' amor* and other forms of courtly love ultimately advanced or hindered the cause of women.[4]

Court society found the novel idea of *fin' amor* so intriguing, so absorbing, that it took it years and scores of its best poets to fully articulate it and explore its ramifications. Then, after the initial impulse had waned, it took society decades more, even centuries, to codify the sentiment, expose its contradictions, treat it satirically, and wear it threadbare.[5] Yet modern Western notions of love evolved out of *fin' amor*, and they still retain something of its early imprimatur.

Equally as remarkable as the troubadours' notions of love were their advances in poetic technique. As Jackson puts it, "it would be hard to find in European literature a period in which such tremendous strides were made in the mastery of imagery, meter, and the expression of beauty through poetic ornament" (*Literature of the Middle Ages*, 253). The troubadours crafted a whole suite of verse forms to meet their varied expressive needs—for, in addition to love, a host of other thoughts and emotions also clamored for poetic expression.

The predominant troubadour song type was, naturally enough, a form used to express sentiments of refined love, the *canso*.[6] Virtually all of the troubadours wrote *cansos:* within this vessel blossoms their finest flower. While the present anthology includes numerous *cansos,* Bernart de Ventadorn's "Can vei la lauzeta mover" ("The Skylark"), one of the most famous of the troubadour songs (and an inspiration for the title of the present book), is representative. As one can see in this poem, the first stanza (*cobla*) establishes a metric structure that the remaining stanzas strictly follow. This holds true until the end, when a shorter stanza (*tornada*) closes the work. As with the reference to "Tristan" in Bernart's poem, these closing lines typically dedicate the work to a patron, lady, or friend, sometimes one whose identity is cloaked in a pseudonym (*senhal*). While virtually all of the *cansos* follow this basic template, they vary greatly, one from another, in their stanzaic structure. In savoring the formal aspects of these lyrics, the reader should be aware that rhymes at the ends of lines typically are carried forward from one stanza to the next. We are not used to such effects. Because English is rhyme-starved compared to the Romance tongues, traditional poets writing in English rarely repeat rhyme sounds more than once or twice, and almost never from stanza to stanza.

Related in subject matter to the *canso* is the romance. While both song types are about love, the romance, as opposed to the *canso,* is a narrative poem. A classic example is Peire d'Alvernhe's "Rossinhol, el seu repaire" ("Nightingale for Me Take Flight").

The *alba,* or dawn song, is also a song of love. The masterpiece of the genre is Giraut de Bornelh's "Reis glorios" ("Day's Glorious Lord"). This poem treats of love's consummation, the attainment of the final stage in the troubadour "game." Rather than crudely depicting this moment head-on, however, Giraut approaches it obliquely. He does so by turning the spotlight on a minor player in the game: the Loyal Companion.

Whereas the above-mentioned song types deal with a love interest involving a highborn lady, the *pastorela* inverts this theme and narrates an encounter between two social unequals—a shepherdess and a knight. As suggested earlier, however, this latter individual is no "knight in shining armor": he is interested not so much in elevated love as in a quick roll in the hay. Marcabru's "L'autrier jost' una sebissa" ("The Peasant Lassie") is the earliest known example in the vernacular of this genre.

Those troubadours who wanted to sing about something other than love could try their hand at the *sirventes*, a satiric poem of social or political content. As opposed to *cansos* that featured original melodies, the *sirventes* often borrowed a tune from an existing song. Jensen (*Troubadour Lyrics*, 10–11) plausibly argues that this procedure allowed the poet to disseminate his topical message more quickly and to a broader audience.

Jensen also distinguishes between several different types of sirventes. The moral *sirventes* "fulminates against the moral decadence of the day," and Marcabru is its original exponent. The political *sirventes* takes an editorial stand on current events; a late-period example is Guillem Figueira's finger-pointing polemic against the Roman Catholic Church and its Albigensian Crusade in "D'un sirventes far en est son que m'agenssa" ("Rome, Where Goodness Declines"). The personal *sirventes*, on the other hand, slings mud at the enemies of the troubadour. A specialized version of this is the literary *sirventes*, which allows the composer to gleefully paint unflattering portraits of his fellow troubadours. Yet another subgenre related to the *sirventes* is the *gap*, in which the poet informs his audience about his prowess—in composing songs, on the battlefield, or in the bedroom. Guillem de Peiteus's bawdy "Faria un vers, pos mi somelh" ("Ladies with the Cat") contains *gap* elements.

One type of *sirventes* traditionally merits its own heading: the *canso de crozada* or crusade song. The popularity of this song type reflected the grip that the so-called holy wars held on the Western medieval imagination. These lyrics could be openly propagandistic, such as Marcabru's recruitment song "Pax in nomine Domini!" ("The Cleansing Place").

Related to the *sirventes* by its topicality is the *planh* or funeral lament. Thus Bertran de Born laments the death of the son of King Henry II of England, in "Si tuit li dol e·il plor e·il marrimen" ("Planh for the Young English King"). An example of the *planh* turned to a moralizing purpose is Sordel's "Planher vuelh En Blacatz en aquest leugier so" ("I Want to Mourn Blacatz").

Another major song type is the *tenso*. This form allows two speakers, generally in alternating stanzas, to exchange views. In the *tenso*'s popular variant, the *partimen*, two speakers rigorously debate a specific problem. The point of dispute in this troubadour version of the smackdown could concern love, literary style, or other topics. The female troubadours in particular embrace this form; see, for example, the debate poems between Maria de Ventadorn and Gui d'Ussel, and also between Guillelma de Rosers and Lanfranc Cigala.[7]

While all the song types mentioned above first appear early in the troubadour era, several forms were imported or appeared only later, during the troubadours' apogee. It was during this period that Arnaut Daniel apparently invented a complex new form, the sestina. In this form, only six words are used to end all the lines in the poem; these line endings are shuffled around throughout the work according to a rigid formula. Dante later seized on the sestina form, which is still revived occasionally today.

Several troubadour forms are associated with early French poetic practice and dance. In this group we find the *balada* with its two-line refrain (ancestor to the French rondel or rondeau), and the *dansa* (related to the French virelay). For an example of yet another dance form, the stamping-song or *estampida,* see Raimbaut de Vaqueiras's "Kalenda maia" ("May Day"). Finally there is the *descort,* a song of "discordant" structure. This discord may take the form of alterations in stanzaic structure from one cobla to another throughout the poem—a divergence from the "high" *canso* practice.

While the above list of forms serves as a useful pocket guide to the major troubadour flora, as we venture farther afield we should not be surprised to encounter a number of hybrids that elude clear-cut categories—*sirventes-cansos,* love-songs that morph into calls to arms, and so forth.

This discussion points up a remarkable fact about the troubadour phenomenon: the veritable Cambrian explosion of poetic forms that appeared at the dawn of their era. From whence, from what hidden springs, did these forms arise? For that matter, what propelled the troubadours to their high point? What led to their demise? To explore these questions, we need to look briefly at the history of the time, for like a rose wrapped around a cross— or a broadsword—the troubadours' blossoming is closely entwined with the era in which they lived.

The troubadours first appeared at a time when, after centuries of darkness, Western Christian Europe was enjoying a gleam of sunshine. By the end of the eleventh century the western Mediterranean had ceased to be a "Moslem lake."[8] Pisan and Genoese sailors were again plying the trade routes, and wealth was spreading up from the seaports of the south. The Vikings were no longer rapaciously driving their longboats upriver and into the heart of France. Likewise the beating hooves of the Magyars, once heard as far west as the Loire, had receded into distance and memory. Roads overgrown since late Roman times were again bearing traffic. As one contemporary described it, "the straggling vines are pruned once more and the waste land is tilled."[9]

At the same time local barons had forced the feudal system into being. Feudalism filled the vacuum left by the collapse of centralized authority; nobles still paid lip service but little else to the heirs to Charlemagne's throne in far-off Paris. With this newfound wealth and a degree of stability, for the first time in centuries society could afford to indulge itself in luxuries of taste and emotion—needs to which the troubadours were quick to cater.

Christian leaders also found ways to tap this accumulating wealth and social capital. In the mid-eleventh century, warriors backed by the Roman Catholic Church began the long, slow reconquest of Moorish Spain. Then, in 1095, in Clermont, France, Pope Urban II launched the First Crusade. He promised sinners that "whoever for devotion alone, not to gain honor or money, goes to Jerusalem to liberate the Church of God, can substitute this journey for all penance." [10] Guillem de Peiteus, the seventh count of Poitiers and the ninth duke of Aquitaine, was present on this occasion. He was unmoved by the rhetoric, however, and initially decided to sit out this so-called holy war. Instead, not content with ruling a territory a quarter the size of modern-day France, he took advantage of the absence of his more religiously fervent neighbor, Count Raimon, to invade Toulouse. When, however, rumors reached Poitiers of the capture of Jerusalem and of the Crusaders living in palaces encrusted with gold and jewels, wearing sables and gossamer robes and lolling on Damascene couches, Guillem suddenly got religion. In an abrupt volte-face, Guillem restored Toulouse to the son of Count Raimon in exchange for a considerable sum of money for his war chest, and rode east. When the Turks summarily crushed his army en route, Guillem retreated to the newly established Crusader state of Antioch to lick his wounds. [11]

These two great bellicose outreaches, the *Reconquista* of Spain and the First Crusade, figure as mechanisms in one of the most intriguing theories for the genesis of troubadour song: the importation of exotic materials from the Muslims and Moors into Christian France. For while recuperating in Antioch, Guillem may have found solace in Eastern music: these exotic strains influenced his songs, so the theory goes. Or the inspiration could have come earlier and by way of the orange-scented pleasure gardens of Moorish Spain. Guillem's father had fought in the early days of the *Reconquista*. After the capture of Barbastro in 1065, Guillem *père* had dragged captive singing girls back to the family palace at Poitiers. One cannot underestimate the impact that the mysterious songs echoing through those halls, sung by almond-eyed Moorish beauties, must have had upon our talented—and randy—First Troubadour when he was still an adolescent.

In support of the theory of Hispano-Arabic influence, a number of scholars find strong parallels between the writings of certain Moors and the troubadours. In 1027, for example, the Cordovan poet Ibn Hazm came out with *The Ring of the Dove,* a work in which he expounds his notions of love. When the Cordovan writes that "humiliation before the beloved is the natural character of a courteous man," or "For Love the proudest men abase / Themselves, and feel it no disgrace,"[12] certain aspects of *fin' amor* come to mind. Likewise there is more than an echo of Guillem de Peiteus's bawdier side in the poems of another Hispano-Arabic writer of the period, Ibn Quzman.[13] Another point of comparison between the Hispano-Arab poets and the troubadours is in the use of similar stock figures such as the watcher in the *alba,* gossips, slanderers, and the like. Further, the parallels exist not only in content but also in form. For example, Chambers and others consider it plausible that the Arabic *zejel* form served as the template for certain troubadour songs, including one early composition by Guillem de Peiteus.[14]

Other theories for the antecedents to troubadour songs, while more prosaic, are no less plausible. Crocker and others find antecedents to troubadour poetry in the liturgical music of the time.[15] Gradually during the eleventh century a new musical form, the *versus,* had won a place beside the older chants and hymns in church liturgy. These new songs were more rhythmic than the older pieces and often featured rhymed couplets. Musicians associated with the abbey of Saint Martial de Limoges (for whose holdings Guillem de Peiteus served as overlord) began to use the rhymed couplet as a building block with which to construct more and more intricate strophic edifices.

Other medieval Latin sources might also have inspired the troubadours. During this period the Goliards were composing their at-times irreverent tavern songs, some later compiled in the *Carmina Burana.* Contemporary Christian clerics likewise occasionally praised noble ladies in verse.

Yet another line of thought holds that poetry from the classical era influenced the troubadours. The works of certain troubadours from Guillem de Peiteus on suggest an acquaintance with the amatory advice of Ovid. On the whole, however, scholars conclude that classical Latin poets exercised at best a secondary influence on the Occitanian makers of song. As Bond sums it up, in contrast to troubadour conventions, "Ovid's lover is not a vassal, love service is absent, and there is no question of gradual refinement" ("Origins," 244).

Finally, Bond and others have argued that Guillem de Peiteus most likely was merely participating in a local oral tradition, all but lost to us, of vernacular song associated with the round dance. Into the warp of this home-spun material Guillem wove snips and scraps picked up from exotic sources. The end result was a new synthesis (ibid., 248–49). As this discussion shows, scholars have not yet reached consensus on a comprehensive theory of troubadour origins.

During Guillem de Peiteus's day and for most of the first half of the twelfth century, the troubadour phenomenon apparently remained confined to Poitiers and a handful of other courts in southern France and northern Spain. Cercamon and Marcabru both depended in part on the largesse of Guillem the eighth count of Poitiers, the son of the First Troubadour. Guillem VIII expired suddenly in 1137 while on pilgrimage to Santiago in northern Spain, where the bloody *Reconquista* continued to rage.[16] With the death of Guillem VIII, his headstrong young daughter became the wealthiest heiress in Europe. Contemporaries praised the young Eleanor of Aquitaine as *perpulchra,* more than beautiful. Louis VI, the king of France, lost no time in securing the fifteen-year-old for his son. The bride wore scarlet. When Louis VI (the Fat) died unexpectedly a week after their wedding, the stunned newlyweds suddenly found themselves crowned as king and queen of France.

Their marriage, however, was not a success. In 1147 Eleanor accompanied Louis VII on the Second Crusade.[17] Louis's monklike demeanor and inept leadership on this disastrous expedition did not awaken feelings of wifely devotion in her breast. Upon their return, Eleanor agitated for a marriage annulment on the grounds of a now conveniently recalled consanguinity. With court gossips also noting that she had not succeeded in providing Louis with any male heirs, Eleanor eventually wore down church and state. In 1152 the marriage was annulled. Eleanor swept out of Paris. Only two months later, without her overlord's consent or prior knowledge, the twenty-nine-year-old Eleanor married Henry of Anjou, eleven years her junior. Henry was a rising star in Europe. Two years later, Eleanor's energetic bridegroom became King Henry II of England; the royal couple and their Plantagenet descendents eventually would rule that sceptered isle for an incredible 331 years. Eleanor and Henry now surveyed a realm that stretched from the Pyrenees to the Scottish border—an expanse that dwarfed the French Royal Demesne.

The rise in the fortunes of Eleanor of Aquitaine coincides with the zenith of the troubadours. This is in part because, along with her daughter (by Louis) Marie de Champagne, Eleanor became one of the great patrons of all time. Between the two of them, mother and daughter patronized not only some of the greatest troubadours, most notably Bernart de Ventadorn, but also Chrétien de Troyes, who gave form to the Arthurian cycle; Thomas of England, who performed a similar service for Tristan and Isolde; and lesser lights such as Andreas Capellanus, who sought to codify the Rules of Love. (Andreas fancifully described "courts of love" at which Eleanor, Marie, and other noblewomen passed judgment upon cases involving infractions of the "laws" of *fin' amor.*) Likewise, one of Eleanor's sons by Henry, Richard the Lion-hearted, notably patronized troubadours such as Guiraut de Bornelh, Gaucelm Faidit, and Peire Vidal, in addition to penning his own quite competent verse (in the *langue d'oïl*).

But Eleanor's influence spread beyond her own court and immediate family circle. Partly in emulation of her brilliant court, every castle in southern France, not to mention many in Christian Spain, now had to ring with troubadour song.[18] Eleanor ushered in the era of the great patrons: Barral of Marseille, Raimon V of Toulouse, Ermengarde of Narbonne, Alfonso of Aragon, and William VIII of Montpellier were all active during the latter half of the twelfth century. It was the golden age of the troubadours.

With this rise in patronage, troubadour prosody reached exuberant new heights of sophistication. Some trace an arc from Bernart de Ventadorn and Peire d'Alvernhe at the dawn of this period, through Guiraut de Bornelh (who momentarily reigned as Master of the Troubadours), to Arnaut Daniel, who reached a summit of technical perfection rarely attained by poets anywhere.

Also during these years we perceive as a widening chasm what was still a fissure in the days of Marcabru: the division between the *trobar leu* and *trobar clus* schools of style. The former "easy" style of poetry, championed by Jaufre Rudel, Bernart de Ventadorn, Guiraut de Bornelh, and the Comtessa de Dia among others, favored simple, accessible songs. The latter school of "closed" poetry delighted in hermetic meaning and arcane word choice; its variant, *trobar ric,* promoted acrobatic versification. Marcabru was the patron saint and Raimbaut d'Aurenga the champion of the *trobar clus* coterie, while Arnaut Daniel was the darling of the *trobar ric* crowd. *Trobar clus* faded out in the late twelfth century, leaving the field to "easy" verse.

While the troubadours thus flourished during the golden days of Eleanor and Henry's reign, life was not all song and boar haunches for the king of England. During the latter half of the twelfth century, the kings of France, vexed by the perfidy of Henry and Eleanor as well as being motivated by more cold-blooded geopolitical reasons, sporadically battled the Plantagenets and their ilk, generally north of the Loire. With the attention of the great powers thus otherwise engaged, the minor barons of the atomized south enjoyed a spell of relative neglect and more localized squabbling, which allowed the troubadour phenomenon to luxuriate.

The wheel of fortune, however, began to turn for Eleanor and Henry, with far-reaching ramifications for the southern courts and their troubadour adherents. At first the royal couple's marriage seemed blessed. Eleanor dispelled any doubts about her ability to produce male heirs by giving birth, in quick succession, to eight children, including five boys. As they grew, however, these haughty youths chafed under Henry's controlling ways: on more than one occasion their resentment boiled over into an open rebellion that the king had to quell. The independent-minded barons of the south delighted in seeing Henry's prodigious energies thus squandered, and did what they could to aggravate such familial tensions. Troubadour and minor nobleman Bertran de Born raised the stinging nickname to the level of an art form in his dealings with the Plantagenet brood. Bertran taunted the king's son Henry, for example, as the "Lord of Little Land." [19]

Other factors also depleted the Plantagenet's resources and weakened their grip on their continental holdings. In 1192, on his way home from the Holy Land after leading a Crusade to confront the legendary Saladin, Richard the Lion-hearted, now king, was shipwrecked. Although he survived, he had to make his way sick and on foot through hostile Austrian territory. Despite an ingenious series of disguises, Coeur de Lion was apprehended in Vienna while pretending to be a servant turning chickens on a spit. From captivity in the hands of the Holy Roman emperor, King Richard sent home moving verses pleading for help. The emperor held Richard hostage until a frantic Eleanor, now on the far side of seventy, had milked Aquitaine and England dry. In 1194, in exchange for a staggering ransom of thirty-five tons of silver, Richard regained his freedom. But now, like a company in an overexposed position, his domains were ripe for a hostile takeover.

The downward-spinning wheel of fortune continued to disfavor the Plantagenets. In 1199 a long arrow-shot at dusk felled Richard. The barons of England held his successor, John, in such low regard that they nicknamed him Softsword.[20] Year by year, step by backward step, the miserable King John lost most of his continental possessions to the implacable King Philip Augustus of France—events that the southern barons no doubt viewed with trepidation.

But the real beginning of the end to the south's autonomy (and troubadour culture) came in 1208, with the murder of a papal legate on the banks of the Rhone River. As the pope's representative prepared to cross the river, a horseman rode up from behind and thrust his lance into the legate's back.

The assassin fled, but not before he was recognized as a servant of Count Raimon VI of Toulouse.

This murder represented an explosion at the end of a long-sputtering fuse in the southland. The root cause of this tension was a heresy known as Catharism, the apparent recrudescence of a belief system that had come together earlier in the East under the name of Manichaeism.[21] Cathars (the name derives from a word for "pure") believed that the material world was totally evil; only that which pertained to the spirit could be good. In its more extreme, dualist form, Catharism could be described not merely as a heretical deviation from Catholicism but rather as a full-blown religion in its own right. The dualists believed that there are not one but *two* gods, coequal and coeternal: one good and of the spirit, the other evil and of the material world. This more extreme faction gained momentum after 1167, when the head of the dualist church from Constantinople visited the French Cathars.[22] But even in its more moderate form, which held that the "sublime Father" had precedence over the "evil demiurge" of the material world, Catharism represented an attack upon the pillars of Roman Catholic belief. If the material world was completely evil, how could marriage be sanctified? How could a sacrament that involved the consumption of bread and wine be holy? Indeed, how could Christ have become flesh?

Just as California can give rise to both new-age cults and the John Birch Society, so the relatively tolerant climate of southern France permitted the flowery cult of *fin' amor* as well as thorny Catharism to take root and flourish. After the Catholic popes became aware of this spreading heresy, they began to send a series of persuasive preachers like Bernard and Dominic (both later canonized) to Occitania, to try to enlist the support of the nobles and voluntarily coax stray lambs back into the fold. (Dominic, however, griped that the southerners regarded his sermons as just "so many rotten apples.")[23] But as Catharism prospered, the popes grew increasingly impatient with the hand-wringing counts of Toulouse and their claims that they "neither could nor dared repress the evil."[24] (Despite occasional public condemnations of the Cathars addressed to Roman ears, these nobles privately numbered heretics among their closest friends and kin.) Upon assuming power, Raimon VI at first promised to confront heresy with force, but his deeds did not live up to his words. Fed up, Innocent III quenched a taper to signal Raimon's excommunication. No one was to serve him, "not even the farrier who shoes his horse."[25] It was at this combustible moment, the morning after an unsatisfactory meeting with the petulant count, that the pope's legate was assassinated.

News of the death of his emissary enraged Innocent III. He appealed to northern Frenchmen: "Forward, soldiers of Christ . . . ! Fill your souls with godly rage to avenge the insult done to the Lord!"[26] After some initial reluctance, King Philip Augustus agreed to let his vassals respond to this call to arms if they felt so moved. The Crusader's sword that the southern nobles had wielded with such fervor in the Holy Land was now to be turned and held tragically to their own throats.

While Raimon VI could not halt the swinging blow, he did manage to deflect it from his beloved Toulouse—but only by paying a heavy price with his pride. In June 1209, in front of the abbey at Saint-Gilles, the count stripped to the waist. He was then flogged and forced to run half-naked past the sarcophagus of the murdered legate. Later that month, the chastened Raimon himself took up the cross and joined the advancing northern troops.

For the next fifteen years the Albigensian Crusade (named for the town of Albi, a Cathar stronghold) ravaged the south. After the invaders ruthlessly massacred the inhabitants of Beziers for attempting resistance—one commander reportedly advised his knights to "kill them all; God will recognize his own"[27]—a number of towns hurriedly opened their gates to the Crusaders. As the war dragged on and its true rapacious nature became apparent, Raimon VI switched sides and began to fight the northerners. For the rest of his days, the Toulousain count would flip-flop between aiding and resisting the northern invaders.

Many of the troubadours of the day responded to this grim world by bearing witness to the horrors that they experienced. Choosing from the palette they had to work with, they were at their most convincing during this nightmarish period when they eschewed the springtime pastels of the *canso* and dipped their brushes into the more somber and even lurid hues of the *sirventes*. Thus we see Guillem Figueira vilifying Rome for the miseries of the Albigensian Crusade in "D'un sirventes far en est son que m'agenssa" ("Rome Where Goodness Declines"). But it was Peire Cardenal who was best able to rise above mere invective and create art. His parable "Un ciutatz fo . . ." ("There was a Town") anticipates Ionescu's *The Rhinoceros*, written amidst the horrors of a later century, as a universal statement about the perfidiousness of human nature.

The tide of war ebbed and flowed. In 1215 the Crusaders' reviled leader Simon de Montfort finally marched into Toulouse, where he was no doubt embraced by the troubadour-turned-bishop (and later chief inquisitor) Folquet de Marseilla. Three years later, however, a stone flung from a catapult felled Simon, dismaying the outnumbered invaders. By the time of his death in 1222, Raimon VI had retaken much of the land that had been lost; by 1224 his son Raimon VII appeared to have regained virtually all.

At this point, however, King Louis VIII of France waded into the blood-bath. For years, preoccupied with the English, he had watched with grim interest as the Crusaders and the southern defenders wore each other down. Now he stepped in, as Daniel-Rops puts it, to "chew the chestnuts that others had pulled out of the fire" (*Cathedral and Crusade*, 305). In 1226 Louis VIII occupied Languedoc. In 1229 he compelled the war-weary Raimon to sign the Treaty of Meaux, which provided for the count's lands to pass progressively into French hands. (This would in fact occur in 1271, at which time France assumed much of its present dimensions as a nation-state.) The Albigensian Crusade and, indeed, the whole era of the Crusades, had essentially ended. The remaining Cathars were driven underground; their final extirpation was left to what the Roman Catholic Church hoped would prove a much more surgical tool than the blunt instrument of the crusade for ridding humanity of heresy: the Inquisition.

With the decisive French victory, the troubadours and the whole culture of the south were on their way out.[28] The *langue d'oïl* was in the ascendant; the *langue d'oc* slowly declined into the obscurity of a regional patois. Stripped of their wealth and crushed in spirit, the southern barons found it increasingly beyond their means to patronize the makers of song. By the last decade of the thirteenth century, only a couple of superannuated troubadours were left. In 1292, near the end of his life, Guiraut Riquier, the so-called Last Troubadour, mourned the passing of an era that he had outlived. He lamented in "Be·m degra de chantar tener" ("It Would Be Best if I Refrained from Singing"):

> Now no art is less admired
> Than the worthy craft of song.
> These days the nobles' tastes have run
> To entertainments less inspired.
> Wailing mingles with disgrace:
> All that once engendered praise
> From the memory has died:
> Now the world is mostly lies.

So the troubadour light in Occitania slowly flickered out.

But the flame that the troubadours had ignited was not fully quenched. The makers of song had always ventured out beyond their linguistic region;

amator foeminarum—a lustful lover of women.[2] As a warrior and a philan-derer, Guillem was excommunicated or threatened with expulsion from the church more than once. (On one such occasion, when a shiny-pated bishop reproached him for his adulterous relations with a certain viscountess, Guillem retorted: "I will only repudiate her when your hair needs a comb.") By the time of his death in 1127, however, he had resolved his grievances with the church.

Critics have divided Guillem's eleven surviving songs into three groups. One subset addresses courtly themes; these poems show that the notion of *fin' amor* was already discussed and even parodied in Guillem's time. The first selection, "Ab la dolchor del temps novel" ("A New Song for New Days"), is from that group. This is undoubtedly one of Guillem's loveliest poems, with its comparison of love to a hawthorn bough—although the First Troubadour cannot resist a leer at the end.

Another set of poems consists of ribald songs written to amuse his *com-panhos* or drinking buddies. The remaining two selections are of that ilk. The bawdy tale of "Farai un vers, pos mi somelh" ("The Ladies with the Cat"), which features two ladies contending with the narrator for what Jew-ers terms "amorous mastery," seems appropriate for *Playboy*—where it has indeed appeared. Jewers points out that it is unusual to encounter a cat that is red such as the feline of this narrative. She speculates that Guillem may be alluding to "contemporary portrayals of the devil as a large red beast with devouring jaws," or else making a statement that "love is red in tooth and claw" ("Poetics of (S) Cat-Ology," 48–50).

A final subset of Guillem's poems, consisting of only one song (surely his last), repents a sinful life.

In the work of Guillem de Peiteus we find in nascent, rudimentary form many of the concepts that the later troubadours would elaborate. Bawdy tales, daydreams while one idles along on a horse, as well as refined expres-sions of love—on such foundations does modern European poetry rest.

Ab la dolchor del temps novel

Guillem de Peiteus

Ab la dolchor del temps novel
Foillo li bosc, e li aucel
Chanton, chascus en lor lati,
Segon lo vers del novel chan;
Adonc esta ben c'om s'aisi
D'acho don hom a plus talan.

De lai don plus m'es bon e bel
Non vei mesager ni sagel,
Per que mos cors non dorm ni ri,
Ni no m'aus traire adenan,
Tro que sacha ben de fi
S'el' es aissi com eu deman.

La nostr' amor vai enaissi
Com la branca de l'albespi
Qu'esta sobre l'arbre tremblan,
La nuoit, a la ploia ez al gel,
Tro l'endeman, que·l sols s'espan
Per la fueilla vert e·l ramel.

Enquer me membra d'un mati
Que nos fezem de guerra fi,
E que·m donet un don tan gran,
Sa drudari' e son anel:
Enquer me lais Dieus viure tan
C'aia mas manz soz so mantel.

Qu'eu non ai soing de lor lati
Que·m parta de mon Bon Vezi,
Qi'eu sai de paraulas com van,
Ab un breu sermon que s'espel,
Que tal se van d'amor gaban,
Nos n'avem la pessa e·l coutel.

A New Song for New Days

Guillem de Peiteus

Such sweetness spreads through these new days:
As woods leaf out, each bird must raise
In pure bird-latin of its kind
The melody of a new song.
It's only fair a man should find
His peace with what he's sought so long.

From her, where grace and beauty spring,
No word's come and no signet ring.
My heart won't rest and can't exult;
I don't dare move or take a stand
Until I know our strife's result
And if she'll yield to my demands.

As for our love, you must know how
Love goes—it's like the hawthorn bough
That on the living tree stands, shaking
All night beneath the freezing rain
Till next day when the warm sun, waking,
Spreads through green leaves and boughs again.

That morning comes to mind once more
We two made peace in our long war;
She, in good grace, was moved to give
Her ring to me with true love's oaths.
God grant me only that I live
To get my hands beneath her clothes!

I can't stand their vernacular
Who'd keep my love from me afar.[3]
By way of words, I guess I've found
A little saying that runs rife:
Let others mouth their loves around;
We've got the bread, we've got the knife.

W. D. Snodgrass

Farai un vers de dreyt nien

   Guillem de Peiteus

Farai un verse de dreyt nien:
Non er de mi ni d'autra gen,
Non er d'amor ni de joven,
   Ni de ren au,
Qu'enans fo trobatz en durmen
   Sobre chevau.

No sai en qual hora·m fuy natz:
No suy alegres ni iratz,
No suy estrayns ni sui privatz,
   Ni no·n puesc au,
Qu'enaissi fuy de nueitz fadatz,
   Sobr' un pueg au.

No sai quora·m suy endurmitz
Ni quora·m velh, s'om no m'o ditz.
Per pauc no m'es lo cor partitz
   D'un dol corau;
E no m'o pretz una soritz,
   Per Sanh Marsau!

Malautz suy e tremi murir,
E ren no·n sai mas quan n'aug dir;
Metge querrai al mieu albir,
   E no sai tau;
Bos metges es qui·m pot guerir,
   Mas non, si amau.

M'amigu' ai ieu, no sai qui s'es,
Qu'anc non la vi, si m'ajut fes;
Ni·m fes que·m plassa ni que·m pes,
   Ni no m'en cau,
Qu'anc non ac Norman ni Frances
   Dins mon ostau.

The Nothing Song

Guillem de Peiteus

Sheer nothing's what I'm singing of:
Not me and no one else, of course;
There's not one word of youth and love
    Nor anything;
I thought this up, once, on my horse
    While slumbering.

I don't know my own sign at birth;
I'm neither native here nor strange;
I don't feel either gloom or mirth.
    Don't blame me, though—
A fairy one night worked the change
    That's made me so.

I don't know if I sleep or wake
Unless somebody's told me that.
This heart of mine is like to break
    For grief and care;
Yet the whole thing's not worth one sprat
    To me, I swear.

I'm sick and shivering with death-fright
Though all I know is what I've heard.
I'll seek some doctor for my plight—
    Which one's best, though?
He's one fine doctor if I'm cured;
    If worse, not so.

My little friend (I don't know who,
Since she's the one girl I've not seen)
Gives me no grief or joy—that's true,
    Which suits me fine;
No French- or Norman's come between
    House-walls of mine.[4]

Anc non la vi et am la fort,
Anc no n'aic dreyt ni no·m fes tort;
Quan non la vey, be m'en deport,
   No·m pretz un jau
Qu'ie·n sai gensor et ballazor,
   E que mais vau.

No sai lo luec ves en s'esta,
Si es en pueg ho es en pla;
Non aus dire lo tort que m'a,
   Abans m'en cau;
E peza·m be quar sai rema,
   Ab aitan vau.

Fag ai lo vers, no say de cuy;
E trametrai lo a selhuy
Que lo·m trametra per autruy
   Lay vers Anjau,
Que·m tramezes del sieu estuy
   La contraclau.

Though I've not seen her, my love's strong;
Not seeing her, I'm scarce undone;
She never did me right or wrong
   And who cares, for
I know a nicer, fairer one
   Who's worth lots more.

As for her homeland, I don't know
Whether she's from the hill or plain;
I don't dare claim she's wronged me so
   I'll just pre-grieve;
Though staying here is such a pain
   I'm going to leave.

My song's all made—don't know what on—
I'll send it to someone, so he,
Through someone, sends it to someone
   In Anjou, there,
Who, from his box, will send the key
   To what stays here.[5]

   W. D. Snodgrass

Farai un vers, pos mi somelh

Guillem de Peiteus

Farei un vers, pos mi somelh
E·m vauc e m'estauc al solelh.
Domnas i a de mal conselh,
   E sai dir cals:
Cellas c'amor de cavalier
   Tornon a mals.

Domna fai gran pechat mortal
Qe no ama cavalier leal;
Mas si es monge o clergal,
   Non a raizo:
Per dreg la deuri'hom cremar
   Ab un tezo.

En Alvernhe, part Lemozi,
M'en aniey totz sols a tapi:
Trobei la moller d'en Guari
   E d'en Bernart;
Saluderon mi simplamentz
   Per sant Launart.

La una·m diz en son latin:
"E Dieus vos salf, don pelerin;
Mout mi semblatz de bel aizin,
   Mon escient;
Mas trop vezem anar pel mon
   De folla gent."

Ar auzires qu'ai respondut;
Anc no li diz ni bat ni but,
Ni fer ni fust no ai mentaugut,
   Mas sol aitan:
"Babariol, babariol,
   Babarian."

The Ladies with the Cat

Guillem de Peiteus

While sound asleep, I'll walk along
In sunshine, making up my song.
Some ladies get the rules all wrong;
    I'll tell you who:
The ones that turn a knight's love down
    And scorn it, too.

Grave mortal sins such ladies make
Who won't make love for a knight's sake;
And they're far worse, the ones who'll take
    A monk or priest—
They ought to get burned at the stake
    At very least.

Down in Auvergne, past Limousin,
Out wandering on the sly I ran
Into the wives of Sir Guarin
    And Sir Bernard;
They spoke a proper welcome then
    By St. Leonard.

One said in her dialect,
"Sir Pilgrim,[6] may the Lord protect
Men so sweet-mannered, so correct,
    With such fine ways;
This whole world's full of lunatics
    And rogues, these days."

For my reply—I'll swear to you
I didn't tell them Bah or Boo,
I answered nothing false or true;
    I just said, then,
"Babario, babariew,
    Babarian."

So diz n'Agnes a n'Ermessen:
"Trobat avem que anam queren.
Sor, per amor Deu, l'alberguem,
   Qe ben es mutz,
E ja per lui nostre conselh
   Non er saubutz."

La una·m pres sotz son mantel,
Menet m'en sa cambra, al fornel.
Sapchatz qu'a mi fo bon a bel,
   E·l focs fo bos,
Et eu calfei me volentiers
   Als gros carbos.

A manjar mi deron capos,
E sapchatz agui mais de dos,
E no·i ac cog ni cogastros,
   Mas sol nos tres,
E·l pans fo blancs e·l vins fo bos
   E·l pebr' espes.

"Sor, aquest hom es enginhos,
E laissa lo parlar per nos:
Nos aportem nostre gat ros
   De mantenent,
Qe·l fara parlar az estros,
   Si de re·nz ment."

N'Agnes anet per l'enujos,
E fo granz et ac loncz guinhos:
E eu, can lo vi entre nos,
   Aig n'espavent,
Q'a pauc non perdei la valor
   E l'ardiment.

So Agnes said to Ermaline,
"Let's take him home, quick; don't waste time.
He's just the thing we hoped to find:[7]
    Mute as a stone.
No matter what we've got in mind,
    It won't get known."

Under her cloak, one let me hide;
We slipped up to her room's fireside.
By now, I thought one could abide
    To play this role—
Right willingly I warmed myself
    At their live coals.

They served fat capons for our fare—
I didn't stop at just one pair;
We had no cook or cook's boy there,
    But just us three.
The bread was white, the pepper hot,
    The wine flowed free.

"Wait, sister, this could be a fake;
He might play dumb just for our sake.
See if our big red cat's awake
    And fetch him, quick.
Right here's one silence we should break
    If it's a trick."

So Agnes brought that wicked beast,
Mustachioed, huge, and full of yeast;
To see him sitting at our feast—
    Seemed less than good;
I very nearly lost my nerve
    And hardihood.

Qant aguem begut a manjat,
Eu mi despoillei a lor grat.
Detras m'aporteron lo gat
    Mal e felon:

La una·l tira del costat
    Tro al tallon.

Per la coa de mantenen
Tira·l gat et el escoissen:
Plajas mi feron mais de cen
    Aqella ves;
Mas eu no·m mogra ges enguers,
    Qui m'ausizes.

"Sor, diz n'Agnes a n'Ermessen,
Mutz es, qe ben es conoissen;
Sor, del banh nos apareillem
    E del sojorn."
Ueit jorns ez encar mais estei
    En aquel forn.

Tant las fotei com auzirets:
Cen e quatre vint et ueit vetz,
Q'a pauc no·i rompei mos coretz
    E mos arnes;
E no·us pues dir lo malaveg,
    Tan gran m'en pres.

Ges no·us sai dir lo malaveg,
    Tan gran m'en pres.

We'd had our fill of drink and food,
So I undressed, as they thought good.
They brought that vile cat where I stood—
    My back was turned;
And then they raked him down my side
    From stem to stern.

And all at once, they yanked his tail
To make him dig in, tooth and nail;
I got a hundred scars, wholesale,
    Right then and there.
They could have flayed me, though, before
    I'd budge one hair.

So Agnes said to Ermaline,
"He's mute for sure, sister; that's fine.
Let's take a nice warm bath, unwind,
    Then take things slow."
I stayed inside their oven there
    Eight days or so.

I screwed them, fairly to relate,
A full one hundred eighty eight.
My breech-strap near broke at that rate,
    Also my reins.
I can't recount all my distress
    Or half my pains.

No; I can't tell all my distress
    Or half my pains.

    W. D. Snodgrass

Cercamon

Cercamon was a jongleur. . . . And he wandered all over the world, wherever he could go, and that was why he was called Cercamon.[1]

We can surmise that Cercamon played an important role in carrying the troubadour culture out from its cradle in Poitiers to a broader audience. We know that he was associated with that court because he offered a *planh* on the death of Guillem the eighth count of Poitiers (the son of the First Troubadour) in 1137. Another topical reference in Cercamon's poetry, to the preaching of the Second Crusade, shows that he continued to compose in the 1140s, just prior to the time when a broader number of nobles were beginning to patronize the makers of song. Finally, his nom de plume, "Circle-the-World," hints at a peripatetic existence.

During his time under the eaves of the palace in Poitiers, Cercamon worked artistically with a much greater and more original troubadour, Marcabru. They both apparently hailed from Gascony. While one *vida* tell us that Marcabru learned the making of songs from Cercamon, it remains unclear who was the teacher and who the disciple, who the troubadour and who the *joglar,* in this professional relationship. Their roles may well have evolved over time.

The surviving works of Cercamon and Marcabru reveal more points of divergence than of similarity. Cercamon was not driven to express an original worldview as was Marcabru: his poems are more conventional. Regarding style, Cercamon himself claimed that "the *vers* is simple, and I am polishing it, without any vulgar, improper or false word, and it is entirely composed in such a way that I have used only elegant terms in it."[2] Here Cercamon may be taking a swipe at Marcabru, whose unique poetic voice does not shrink from occasionally salty or unconventional language. But literary criticism has moved away from a preoccupation with elegance, and now Marcabru's poetry is regarded as distinctly superior to that of "Circle-the-World."

Quant l'aura doussa s'amarzis

Cercamon

Quant l'aura doussa s'amarzis
E·l fuelha chai de sul verjan
E l'auzelh chanjan lor latis,
Et ieu de sai sospir e chan
D'amor que·m te lassat e pres,
Que eu anc non l'aic en poder.

Las! Qu'ieu d'Amor non ai conquis
Mas can lo trebalh e l'afan,
Ni res tan greu no·s covertis
Com fai so qu'ieu vauc deziran;
Ni tal enveja no·m fai res
Cum fai so qu'ieu non puosc aver.

Per una joia m'esbaudis
Fina, qu'anc re non amiey tan.
Quan suy ab lieys si m'esbahis
Qu'ieu no·ill sai dire mon talan,
E quan m'en vauc, vejaire m'es
Que tot perda·l sen e·l saber.

Tota la gensor qu'anc hom vis
Encontra lieys non pretz un guan;
Quan totz lo segles brunezis,
De lai on ylh es si resplan.
Dieus me respieyt tro qu'ieu l'ades
O qu'ieu la vej' anar jazer.

Totz trassalh e bran e fremis
Per s'amor, durmen o velhan.
Tal paor ai qu'ieu mesfalhis
No m'aus pessar cum la deman,
Mas servir l'ai dos ans o tres,
E pueys ben leu sabra·n lo ver.

When the Sweet Air Goes Bitter (Descant on a Theme by Cercamon)[3]

Cercamon

When the sweet air goes bitter,
And the cold birds twitter
Where the leaf falls from the twig,
I sough and sing

> that Love goes out
> Leaving me no power to hold him.

Of love I have naught
Save trouble and sad thought,
And nothing is grievous
> as I desirous,
Wanting only what
No man can get or has got.

With the noblest that stands in men's sight,
If all the world be in despite
> I care not a glove.
Where my love is, there is a glitter of sun;
God give me life, and let my course run

> 'Till I have her I love
> To lie with and prove.

I do not live, nor cure me,
Nor feel my ache—great as it is,
For love will give
> me no respite,
Nor do I know when I turn left or right
> nor when I go out.

> For in her is all my delight
> And all that can save me.

No muer ni viu ni no guaris,
Ni mal no·m sent, e si l'ai gran;
Quar de s'amor no suy devis,
Non sai si ja l'aurai ni quan,
Qu'en lieys es tota la merces
Que·m pot sorzer o decazer.

Bel m'es quant ilh m'enfolhetis
E·m fai badar e·n vauc muzan;
De leis m'es bel si m'escarnis
O·m torn dereires o enan,
C'aprop lo mal me venra bes
Ben tost, s'a lieys ven a plazer.

S'elha no·m vol, volgra moris
Lo dia que·m pres a coman;
Ai, dieus! tan suavet m'aucis
Quan de s'amor me fetz semblan,
Que tornat m'a en tal deves
Que nuill' autra no vuelh vezer.

Totz cossiros m'en esjauzis,
Car s'ieu la dopti e la blan,
Per lieys serai o fals o fis,
O drechuriers o ples d'enjan,
O totz vilas o totz cortes,
O trebalhos o de lezer.

Mas, cui que plass' o cui que pes,
Elha·m pot, si·s vol, retener.

Cercamons ditz: "greu er cortes
Hom qui d'amor se desesper."

I shake and burn and quiver
From love, awake and in swevyn,
Such fear I have she deliver
                              me not from pain,
          Who know not how to ask her;
          Who can not.
Two years, three years I seek
And though I fear to speak out,
                              Still she must know it.

If she won't have me now, Death is my portion,
          Would I had died that day
          I came into her sway.
God! How softly this kills!
When her love look steals on me.

Killed me she has, I know not how it was,
          For I would not look on a woman.

Joy I have none, if she make me not mad
          Or set me quiet, or bid me chatter.
Good is it to me if she flout
          Or turn me inside out, and about.
          My ill doth she turn sweet.

How swift it is.
          For I am traist and loose,
          I am true, or a liar,
          All vile, or all gentle,
          Or shaking between,
                              as she desire,
I, Cercamon, sorry and glad,
          The man whom love had
                              and has ever;
          Alas! who'er it please or pain,
          She can me retain.

I am gone from one joy,
From one I loved never so much,
    She by one touch
    Reft me away;

    So doth bewilder me
    I can not say my say
                nor my desire,
And when she looks on me
    It seems to me
             I lose all wit and sense.

The noblest girls men love
'Gainst her I prize not as a glove
Worn and old.
Though the whole world run rack
And go dark with cloud,
Light is
Where she stands,
And a clamor loud
        in my ears.

Ezra Pound

Marcabru

Marcabru was a foundling abandoned on the doorstep of a rich man, and thus no one ever knew from whom or from where he came. . . . Later he spent so much time with a troubadour named Cercamon that he himself began to write verse. . . . And he was famous throughout the world; people listened to him, and they feared him because of his tongue. And he said such evil things that finally he was killed by some chatelains of Guyenne of whom he had spoken ill.[1]

Marcabru most likely was born in Gascony around 1100, in modest circumstances. While the assertion that Marcabru was a foundling cannot be verified, his writings offer some clues that it was true. At the end of one poem, for example, where he likens the destructive power of carnal love to "the spark which makes the fire smoulder," the troubadour darkly hints that "Marcabru, son of Marcabruna, was sired under such auspices that he knows how Love casts its seed—Hear me!"[2]

As a young man Marcabru traveled as a *joglar,* one of the first, under the name of Panperdut ("Lost Bread"). He spent time at the palace in Poitiers whose then master, Guillem the eighth count of Poitiers, was the son of the First Troubadour. There he encountered Cercamon, and, as the *vida* suggests, Marcabru may well have graduated from *joglar* to maker of songs under the tutelage of the other troubadour. Marcabru also spent several years at the court of King Alfonso VII of Castile and León. It was apparently there, close to the front lines of the *Reconquista,* that Marcabru wrote the first extant Crusade song, "Pax in nomine Domini!" ("The Cleansing Place"), the third selection below. Marcabru was probably active from around 1130 to 1150.

Either because of a troubled upbringing, or for some other combination of reasons, Marcabru's poetry is arguably the most powerful and distinctive of any of the troubadours. Marcabru's urgent poetic project, which indelibly stamped troubadour thought thereafter, was to distinguish between true love and false love. On the one hand, he saw true love as, in Topsfield's words, "a force which can be used to give moral stability and happiness to the individual and society." Marcabru envisions this love as being "born in a noble dwelling . . . enclosed by an arbour of boughs." On the other hand, Marcabru paints a Boschian view of a world hagridden by false or venal love. In this hell, "the husband who scratches the wife of another man knows well that his own wife sins." Or again: the lustful woman is "covered by her desire as the greyhound bitch is covered by the cur."[3]

In Marcabru's dark view of the world, not only sinners reap the whirlwind. Particularly in the case of those who played prominent ethical and religious roles in society, moral decadence wreaked havoc in a broader sphere. Marcabru is thus concerned with the moral behavior of the nobility: "Long as the world's father was good Youth (Jovens) and fin' Amors its mother, Prowess stood tall in public and in private, but now he's brought low—and by dukes, kings, and emperors."[4]

To give vent to his moral outrage, Marcabru forged a unique poetic voice that melded peasant sayings and scathing obscenity with elevated expression, all within metric schemes that were relatively complex for their day. Because of his at-times gnarled and gnomic language, some consider Marcabru to be the spiritual father of the trobar clus or "closed" school of poetry. No records exist, however, of Marcabru defending the trobar clus approach. Only later, apparently, were the tenants of such a school formalized.

The following selections capture some of Marcabru's worldview and varied style. The first two poems are narratives: the one a romance, the other a pastorela—indeed, the earliest extant example of this form in the vernacular. Both tales contrast two figures: one, the woman, who reveals what constitutes correct behavior in a broader, societal context; the other, the man, who is venial and a seducer. Yet these men, and particularly these women, are not merely cardboard figures—and in this lies some irony. In his virulent denunciations of "deceitful women" and his boasts of never having fallen in love, Marcabru is not exempt from charges of misogyny. Yet both the distraught noble maiden with her existential cri de coeur of the first selection, and the spirited peasant girl of the second, offer examples of Marcabru's skill in feminine portraiture. Along with the Wife of Bath, these must surely rank among the most vivid portrayals of women to have come down to us from the Middle Ages.

A la fontana del vergier

Marcabru

A la fontana del vergier,
On l'erb' es vertz josta·l gravier,
A l'ombra d'un fust domesgier,
En aiziment de blancas flors
E de novelh chant costumier,
Trobey sola, ses companhier,
Selha que no vol mon solatz.

So fon donzelh' ab son cors belh,
Filha d'un senhor de castelh;
E quant ieu cugey que l'auzelh
Li fesson joy e la verdors,
E pel dous termini novelh,
E quez entendes mon favelh,
Tost li fon sos afars camjatz.

Dels huelhs ploret josta la fon
E del cor sospiret preon.
"Jhesus," dis elha, "reys del mon,
Per vos mi creys ma grans dolors,
Quar vostra anta mi cofon,
Quar li mellor de tot est mon
Vos van servir, mas a vos platz.

Ab vos s'en vai lo meus amicx,
Lo belhs e·l gens e·l pros e·l ricx;
Sai m'en reman lo grans destricx,
Lo deziriers soven e·l plors.
Ay mala fos reys Lozoicx,
Que fai los mans e los prezicx,
Per que·l dols m'es el cor intratz!"

By the Bank

Marcabru

By the bank where the green grass grows,
Where the orchard's fountain flows,
And the fruit tree's branch bestows
Shade on the flowers there arranged,
Listening to the year's new *chanson*
I found her, without companion,
Who my company disdains.

She was a girl of lovely figure,
Daughter of a castled *senhor*.
My hope was that the birds might bring her
Joy (and that their sweet refrains,
The greenness and the season's swelling
Might make my words the more compelling),
When suddenly her manner changed.

There by the welling spring she cried,
And from her breast escaped a sigh:
"Jesus, lord of earth and sky,
You have multiplied my pains—
I sorrow for the shame you suffer,[5]
But grieve that the best men we can offer
Leave to serve your higher aims.

"In your company goes my loved one,
Handsome, strong, of valor proven,
Gone; and in his place I'm given
Desire and weeping unrestrained.
Ah, a curse! upon King Louis,
He who calls men into service;[6]
Meanwhile my grieving heart lies slain."

Quant ieu l'auzi desconortar,
Ves lieys vengui josta·l riu clar.
"Belha," fi·m ieu, "per trop plorar
Afolha cara e colors;
E no vos qual dezesperar,
Que Selh qui fai lo bosc fulhar
Vos pot donar de joy assatz."

"Senher," dis elha, "ben o crey
Que Dieus aya de mi mercey
En l'autre segle per jassey,
Quon assatz d'autres peccadors;
Mas say mi tolh aquelha rey
Don joys mi crec: mas pauc mi tey,
Que trop s'es de mi alonhatz."

When I heard that maid thus sighing,
I drew close, the river idling.
"*Belha*," I said, "such copious crying
Makes all the lovely color drain
From your cheek. Don't spoil your fresh demeanor,
For he who makes the wood-ways greener
Can bring you joy, assuage the pain."

"Ah sir," she said, "I truly treasure
The hope that God will let me enter
The next world where there's bliss forever,
Along with other souls so stained.
But this world's different—he has taken
My love, who's left me here forsaken,
To go to lands distant and strange."

Robert Kehew

L'autrier jost' una sebissa

Marcabru

L'autrier jost' una sebissa
Trobei pastora mestissa,
De joi e de sen massissa,
Si cum filla de vilana,
Cap' e gonel' e pelissa
Vest e camiza treslissa,
Sotlars e caussas de lana.

Ves lieis vinc per la planissa:
"Toza, fi·m ieu, res faitissa,
Dol ai car lo freitz vos fissa."
"Seigner, so·m dis la vilana,
Merce Dieu e ma noirissa,
Pauc m'o pretz si·l vens m'erissa,
Qu'alegreta sui e sana."

"Toza, fi·m ieu, cauza pia,
Destors me sui de la via
Per far a vos compaignia;
Quar aitals toza vilana
No deu ses pareill paria
Pastorgar tanta bestia
En aital terra, soldana."

"Don, fetz ela, qui que·m sia,
Ben conosc sen e folia;
La vostra pareillaria,
Seigner, so·m dis la vilana,
Lai on se tang si s'estia,
Que tals la cuid' en bailia
Tener, no·n a mas l'ufana."

The Peasant Lassie

Marcabru

Near a hedgerow, sometime recent,
I met with a shepherd lassie
Full of mother wit and sassy,
Some good peasant woman's lassie,
Wearing shoes with woolen socks, too,
Blouse and skirt and linen smock, too,
All homespun, quite coarse but decent.

Toward her, through the fields I started;
"Lass," says I, "though you're so pretty,
Chill winds nip you, more's the pity."
"Master," said this peasant lassie,
"Thank the Lord and my good nurse, now,
Winds can blow—I'm none the worse, now,
Since I'm healthy and light-hearted."

"Lass," said I, "you're sweet and girlish;
I've turned off the highroad only
So you wouldn't be here, lonely;
Such an innocent young lassie
Shouldn't go out unbefriended
Keeping all these sheepflocks tended
In a land so rough and churlish."

"Sir," said she, "though you can take me
How you like, I know what's senseless.
Take your friendship for the friendless,
Master," said this peasant lassie,
"And please put it someplace fitting.
Girls like me can think they're getting
What they want, then find it's fakery."

"Toza de gentil afaire,
　Cavaliers fon vostre paire
　Que·us engenret en la maire,
　Con fon corteza vilana.
　Con plus vos gart, m'etz belaire,
　E per vostre foi m'esclaire,
　Si·m fossetz un pauc humana!"

"Don, tot mon ling e mon aire
　Vei revertir e retraire
　Al vezolig et a l'araire,
　Seigner, so·m dis la vilana;
　Mas tals se fai cavalgaire
　C'atrestal deuria faire
　Los seis jorns de la setmana."

"Toza, fi·m ieu, gentils fada,
　Vos adastret, quan fos nada,
　D'una beutat esmerada
　Sobre tot' autra vilana;
　E seria·us ben doblada,
　Si·m vezi' una vegada,
　Sobira e vos sotrana."

"Seigner, tan m'avetz lauzada,
　Que tota·n seri' enveiada;
　Pois en pretz m'avetz levada,
　Seigner, so·m dis la vilana,
　Per so n'auretz per soudada
　Al partir: bada, fols, bada,
　E la muz' a meliana."

"Toz', estraing cor e salvatge
　Adomesg' om per uzatge.
　Ben conosc al trespassatge
　Qu'ab aital toza vilana
　Pot hom far ric compaignatge
　Ab amistat de coratge,
　Si l'us l'autre non engana."

"Lass, but you're high-born, not common;
  Surely some knight was your father
  Or he couldn't give your mother
  Such a well-bred peasant lassie.
  Even now, you grow more lovely;
  Joy would get the better of me
  If you'd only be more human."

"Sir, I'll take an oath by heaven
  All my family's bloodlines trickle
  Straight back to the plow and sickle.
  Master," said this peasant lassie,
"Some folks play at being knightly
  Who should do such hard work rightly
  Six days out of every seven."

"Lass, some fairy queen must love you
  Since, at your birth, she bewitched you
  With a beauty that enriched you
  As the loveliest peasant lassie;
  Still, you'd seem just twice the wonder
  If, once, I could get you under
  While I was the one above you."

"Sir, plain folks will find it shocking
  To hear me so overrated;
  Why make my price so inflated,
  Master," said this peasant lassie.
"Here's the way you'll get rewarded:
  Clear out. Don't stand there, retarded,
  In the noonday sunshine, gawking."

"Lass, such wild hearts, fiercely beating,
  Gentle down with time and using.
  I can see, on slight perusing,
  Someone could provide a lassie
  With a valuable connection
  If his heart's filled with affection,
  And if they don't start in on cheating."

"Don, hom coitatz de follatge
 Jur' e pliu e promet gatge:
 Si·m fariatz homenatge,
 Seigner, so·m dis la vilana;
 Mas ieu, per un pauc d'intratge
 Non vuoil ges mon piucellatge,
 Camjar per nom de putana."

"Toza, tota creature
 Revertis a sa natura:
 Pariellar pareilladura
 Devem, ieu e vos, vilana,
 A l'abric lonc la pastura,
 Car plus n'estaretz segura
 Per far la cauza doussana."

"Don, oc; mas segon dreitura
 Cerca fols sa follatura,
 Cortes cortez' aventura,
 E·il vilans ab la vilana;
 En tal loc fai sens fraitura
 On hom non garda mezura,
 So ditz la gens anciana."

"Toza, de vostra figura
 Non vi autra plus tafura
 Ni de son cor plus trefana."

"Don, lo cavecs vos ahura,
 Que tals bad' en la peintura
 Qu'autre n'espera la mana."

"Sir, a man whose brain's gone balmy
 Swears great oaths, but he's still crazy;
 Why make vows and try to praise me?[7]
 Master," said this peasant lassie,
"At your price I feel no urging
 To sell my state as a virgin
 For the whore that folks would call me."

"Lass, each bird and beast, each dumb thing
 Always turns back to its nature:
 Side by side, creature to creature,
 Let us go down, little lassie,
 Through the meadowlands together;
 There in safety and deep heather
 We'll try out our own sweet something."

"Sir, you're right; it follows justly
 Madmen do make mad advances;
 Courtiers choose the court's romances;
 Peasants take a peasant lassie.
 Men who've got no good proportion
 Bring good sense straight to abortion;
 All the ancients warn us, thusly."

"Lass, I never met a lassie
 With a face so fair and sassy
 And a heart so cold and cruel."

"Sir, the owl gives you this saying:
 By an image, one man's praying
 While one gawks there like a fool."

W. D. Snodgrass

Pax in nomine Domini!

   Marcabru

Pax in nomine Domini!
Fetz Marcabrus los motz e·l so.
Aujatz que di:
Cum nos a fait, per sa doussor,
Lo seingnorius celestiaus
Probet de nos un lavador,
C'anc, fors outramar, no·n fo taus,
En de lai deves Josaphas;
E d'aquest de sai vos conort.

Lavar de ser e de maiti
Nos deuriam, segon razo:
Le·us o afi.
Chascus a del lavar legor:
Domentre qu'el es sans e saus,
Deuria anar al lavador,
Que·ns es verais medicinaus;
Que s'abans anam a la mort,
D'aut en sus aurem alberc bas.

Mas Escarsedatz e No-fes
Part Joven de son compaigno.
A! cals dols es
Que tuich volon lai li plusor,
Don lo gazains es enfernaus!
S'anz non correm al lavador
C'ajam la bocha ni·ls huoills claus,
Non i a un d'orguoill tant gras
C'a la mort non trob contrafort.

The Cleansing Place

Marcabru

Peace in the name of God I pray!
Marcabru wrote the words and song.
    Hear what he says:
By his sweetness, by his grace,
Our most high, celestial Lord
Made for us a Cleansing Place—
You won't find in all the world
Its like, save at Josaphat's side;
I call you to the one that's close.[8]

Wash yourself, I tell you rightly,
In the morning when you rise;
    Also nightly.
Every man has a chance to bathe:
While he's sound in mind and limb,
He should go to the Cleansing Place
Since it truly treats what ails him.
Die before you're purified,
It's not up but down you'll go.

But Avarice and Lack-Belief
Separate a Youth from friends.
    Ah! how I grieve,
Seeing how full and swift's the race,
Considering that Hell's the prize.
Get you to the Cleansing Place
Before death stops your mouth and eyes.
Even though you are flushed with pride,
When you die you'll face the foe.

Qe·l Seigner que sap tot qant es,
E sap tot cant er e c'anc fo,
Nos a promes
Honor e nom d'emperador.
E·il beutatz sera, sabetz caus,
De cels qu'iran al lavador?
Plus que l'estela gauzignaus;
Ab sol qe vengem Dieu del tort
Qe·ill fant sai, e lai vas Damas.

Probet del lignatge Caï,
Del primeiran home fello,
A tans aissi
C'us a Dieu non porta honor.
Veirem qui·ll er amics coraus;
C'ab la vertut del lavador
Nos sera Jhesus comunaus:
E tornem los garssos atras,
Q'en agur crezon et en sort!

E·il luxurios corna-vi,
Coita-disnar, bufa-tizo,
Crup-en-cami,
Remanran inz el folpidor.
Dieus vol los arditz e·ls suaus
Asajar a son lavador;
E cil gaitaran los ostaus,
E trobaran fort contrafort:
So per q'ieu a lor anta·ls chas.

En Espaigna sai lo marques,
E cill del temple Salamo,
Sofron lo pes
E·l fais de l'orguoill paganor,
Per que Jovens cuoill avol laus;
E·l critz per aqest lavador
Versa sobre·ls plus rics captaus
Fraitz, faillitz, de proeza las,
Que non amon joi ni deport.

The Lord who knows whatever was,
Whatever is and all to be,
    Has promised us
Honor through the Emperor's grace.[9]
Know you how God will be adorning
Those who go to the Cleansing Place?
Brighter than the star at morning
They'll shine, the avengers of His pride
Here and in Damascus's hold.

Of the lineage of Cain,
That initial treacherous fellow,
    I could name
Some who the name of God disgrace.
Let's see who is a loyal friend:
By the strength of the Cleansing Place
Jesus will dwell with us again.
Drive back the heathens who defy
God with all their mumbo-jumbo.

The libertines and drunken louts,
The flame-blowers and food-gorgers,
    The lie-abouts
Will stay mired in filth and waste.
God will take the meek and fearless
And test them in His Cleansing Place.
Those in homes that they hold dearest
Will find an enemy lurks inside;
So to their shame I bid them go.

Here in Spain, the good marquis
And the Templars of Solomon
    Know no relief
From that great weight the pagans place.[10]
Youth is put down and beleaguered;
Blame, because of this Cleansing Place,
Falls upon the strongest leaders.
They are broken, tired inside;
Neither joy nor sport is known.

Desnaturat son li Frances,
Si de l'afar Dieu dizon no,
Q'ie·us ai comes.
Antiocha, Pretz e Valor
Sai plora Guiana e Peitaus.
Dieus, seigner, al tieu lavador
L'arma del comte met en paus:
E sai gart Peitieus e Niort
Lo segner qui ressors del vas.

Degenerate are the Frenchmen all
If they reject the holy cause
    To which they're called.
Mourn the death of worth and grace,
Antioch, Guyenne, Poitou.
Dear God, at your Cleansing Place,
Bring peace to the good count's soul;
And may the Lord, who death defied,
Watch over Poitiers and Niort.[11]

  Robert Kehew

Jaufre Rudel

Jaufre Rudel . . . fell in love with the Countess of Tripoli without ever having seen her, simply because of the good things he had heard the pilgrims returning from Antioch tell of her, and for her he wrote many fine poems, rich in melody and poor in words. But wishing to see her, he took the Cross and went to sea. In the boat he became ill, and when he arrived in Tripoli, he was taken to an inn, for he was near death. The Countess was told about this and she came to him, to his bedside, and took him in her arms. He realized it was the Countess, and all at once recovered his sense of sight and smell, and praised God for having sustained his life until he had seen her. And then he died in her arms. And she had him buried with great ceremony in the house of the Knights Templars. And then, on that same day, she took the veil for the grief she felt at his death.[1]

This florid and fanciful tale overshadows the small nut of fact that we actually possess regarding Jaufre's life. The troubadour appears to have hailed from Blaye, a town on the Gironde River between Bordeaux and the sea. It is likely that Jaufre accompanied Eleanor of Aquitaine and Louis VII on the Second Crusade in the mid-eleven hundreds. We believe this because Marcabru sent a poem to "Jaufre Rudel, over the seas" around that time, while some of Jaufre's poems (including the two selections below) allude to a Crusade to the holy lands.

Jaufre Rudel is most famous for his longing for a "distant love." This reputation is commonly based on the tale, expressed in the *vida* above, of Jaufre pining for a woman whom he had never met, the countess of Tripoli. Here the troubadour's *amor* is portrayed as so pure that he does not even have to *meet* this lady in order to fall in love with her. This legend has inspired artists from Petrarch to Browning, and on down to the present day.

Critics, however, shrug at this myth and focus more closely on the poem that inspired it: "Lanquan li jorn" ("A Love Afar"), the first selection. Different readings of this work are possible. Topsfield (*Troubadours and Love*, 61–67) persuasively argues that the poem's controlling metaphor is the notion of the lover as crusader or pilgrim. A pilgrim, of course, endures great hardship on the road—it is no coincidence that the words *travel* and *travail* sound alike—in order to reach and worship the Holy. In Jaufre's poem, prior to the long sought meeting, neither the "sweet birds' song [nor] flowering briar" can cheer the pilgrim-poet. After this transfiguring encounter, however, the poet imagines that an ordinary chamber or garden will seem a "palace": not even being held "captive in a Moorish land" would be able to quell his joy. (The troubadours, like poets and thinkers of other times, were fascinated by the notion that there is a subjective aspect to our perceptions of reality.) In this reading, the lover entertains no thought of remaining permanently in his beloved's presence. Like a pilgrim who pauses at an altar with a throng of worshippers at his back, he realizes that his intersection with the holy will be moving but short-lived: he must then depart, go home, and pick up his (now transformed) ordinary life again. While Topsfield finds that the poem strongly implies this sequence of events, the versions of the song that have come down to us do not strictly follow this linear progression. This lack of linearity, of course, does not invalidate Topsfield's reading of the poem.

While considering possible readings of this evocative poem, the reader should also be attuned to the poetic delicacy of the original: the mysterious "auzels de lonh" or "far-off birds," for example.

The second selection, "Quan lo rossinhol el folhos" ("The Nightingale"), likewise reveals a complex medieval conception of love. Topsfield (ibid., 45–49 and 67) plausibly argues that, like the first selection, this poem takes the form of a spiritual journey, as the poet-narrator wends his way through progressively higher, more spiritual planes of existence. He begins his quest for joy in the first part of the poem, in the material world. Then, in the third and fourth stanzas, the poet pursues his fleeing love through a surreal, imaginative plane. Finally, in the concluding stanzas, he realizes that "the highest joy is to be found in the service of God"—on a more spiritual level of existence that yet is rooted in the world of action. This interpretation helps to clarify why the work morphs—surprisingly, to modern prejudices—from a *canso* about romantic love into a Crusade song. Unlike the spiritual traveler of "Lanquan li jorn," however, as Topsfield points out, the protagonist in "Quan lo rossinhol" ultimately must forgo *amor*.

Lanquan li jorn

Jaufre Rudel

Lanquan li jorn son lonc en may
M'es belhs dous chans d'auzelhs de lonh,
E quan mi suy partitz de lay
Remembra·m d'un' amor de lonh:
Vauc, de talan embroncs e clis
Si que chans ni flors d'albespis
No·m platz plus que l'yverns gelatz.

Be tenc lo senhor per veray
Per qu'ieu veirai l amor de lonh;
Mas per un ben que m'en eschay
N'ai dos mals, quar tan m'es de lonh.
Ai! car me fos lai pelegris,
Si que mos fustz e mos tapis
Fos pels sieus belhs huelhs remiratz!

Be·m parra joys quan li querray,
Per amor Dieu, l'amor de lonh:
E, s'a lieys platz, alberguarai
Pres de lieys, si be·m suy de lonh:
Adoncs parra·l parlamens fis
Quan drutz lonhdas er tan vezis
Qu'ab bels digz jauzirai solatz.

Iratz e gauzens m'en partray,
Quan veirai cest amor de lonh:
Mas non sai quoras la veyrai,
Car trop son nostras terras lonh:
Assatz hi a pas e camis,
E per aisso no·n suy devis...
Mas tot sia cum a Dieu platz!

A Love Afar

Jaufre Rudel

When days grow long and warm with May,
How sweet the birds' song sounds afar
Though, long exiled and far away,
They call to mind my love afar.
 Bent to eclipse by dark desire,
  No sweet birds' song, no flowering briar
  Content me more than winter's chill.

My lord keeps faith, so I believe
That I shall see my love afar;
Though for each pleasure I receive
I find two griefs when she's so far.
 Ay! If I visited that shrine
  My pilgrim's staff and cloak might shine
  Reflected in her eyes' clear rill.

By God's own love, what joys must lie
Within love's citadel, afar.
If she'd consent, I'd lodge nearby
Who now must lie alone afar.
 Never on earth shall speech seem dear
  As when this far-off love comes near
  To give joy and to take its fill.

Leaving her must seem sad and sweet
When once I've met my love afar,
Yet how we'll ever come to meet
I know not since her land's so far.
 Such tracks and trails, such land and sea,
  Lie still between my love and me
  That all must lie in God's good will.

Ja mais d'amor no·m jauziray
Si no·m jau d'est'amor de lonh,
Que gensor ni melhor no·n sai
Vas nulha part, ni pres ni lonh;
Tant es sos pretz verais e fis
Que lay el reng dels Sarrazis
Fos ieu per lieys chaitius clamatz!

Dieus que fetz tot quant ve ni vai
E formet sest'amor de lonh
Mi don poder, que·l cor ieu n'ai,
Qu'ieu veya sest'amor de lonh,
Verayamen, en luecs aizis,
Si que la cambra e·l jardis
Mi resembles tos temps palatz!

Ver ditz qui m'apella lechay
Ni deziran d'amor de lonh,
Car nulhs autres joys tan no·m play
Cum jauzimens d'amor de lonh.
Mas so qu'ieu vuoill m'es tant ahis,
Qu'enaissi·m fadet mos pairis
Qu'ieu ames e nos fos amatz.

Mas so q'ieu vuoill m'es tant ahis.
Totz sia mauditz lo pairis
Qe·m fadet q'ieu non fos amatz!

No joy in love shall e'er be mine
Until I see my love afar;
Above all worth her beauties shine,
Above all others, near and far.
    Gladly I'd lie, at her command,
    A captive in a Moorish land
    Her precious bidding to fulfill.

Dear Lord who formed this world entire
And shaped for me my love afar,
Pray grant the power I most desire:
To witness soon my love afar.
    Where I shall meet that glorious face,
    In chamber or in garden place,
    That spot shall be my palace still.

That man speaks true who'd say I burn
For naught else but my love afar;
Now for no other end I yearn—
Only to know my love afar.
    Yet as my fates lie still athwart,
    My curse fall on that godsire's heart
    Who's cursed me so my love runs ill.[2]

W. D. Snodgrass

Quan lo rossinhol el fulhos

Jaufre Rudel

Can lo rossinhol el fulhos
Dona d'amor e·n quier e·n pren
E mou son chan jauzen joyos
E remira sa par soven,
E·l rieu son clier e·l prat son gen
   Pel novel deport que renha,
Mi ven al cor gran joy çazer.

D'un' amistat soi enveios,
Car no sai joia plus valen,
C'or e dezir, que bona·m fos
Si·n fazia d'amar parven,
Que·l cors a gran, delgat e gen
   E sen ren que·l desconvenha:
Es s'amor bon' ab bon saber.

D'est' amor soi fort cossiros
Velhan, e pueys son ja dormen,
Car lay ay joy meravilhos
Per qu'ieu la jau ab joy jauzen;
Mas sas beutaz no·m val nïen,
   Quar nulhs amicx no m'esssenha
Cum ieu ja n'aya bon saber.

D'aquest' amor soi tan cochos
Que cant yeu vau vas luy corren,
Vejaire m'es que raïzos
Me·n torn e qu'ela m'an fugen,
E sos chivaus cor aitan len
   Que greu er mays qui l'atenha
S'amors no la·m fay remaner.

66

The Nightingale

Jaufre Rudel

Deep in the leaves, the nightingale
Knows love and pleads to seize love's prize
And while he tells his joyous tale
Still toward his mate he turns his eyes.
    Rivers run clear; green pastures rise.
      While this season's new pleasures start,
     Great joys go spreading through my heart.

Just to become her friend I yearn;
No gem's so precious anywhere
As that she'd grant me in return
Her love, a gift beyond compare—
    That shape so graceful, trim and spare,
      All her body's smooth, well-formed flesh,
     Her love so rare, her poise so fresh.

Such love as mine demands great care
Waking or in my dreams at night
For I find pleasure with her there
Taking and giving deep delight.
    Her beauty, though, inflames my sight.
      He would become this heart's best friend
     Who'd say I'll win her in the end.

Yet love brings great distress as well
For though I try to reach her side
Sometimes she seems to flee pell-mell
While I move backward, stride by stride.
    My mount's so tardy, we're denied
      Every hope to win our love's race
     Unless some fondness slowed her pace.

Amors alegre·m part de vos
Per tal car vau mo mielhs queren,
E soi de tan, aventuros
Qu'en breu n'auray mon cor jauzen
La merce de mon bel Guiren
    Que·m vol e m'apell' e·m denha,
E m'a tornat en bon esper.

E qui sai rema deleytos
E Dieu non siec en Belleen,
No sai cum ja mais sia pros
Ni cum ja venha guerimen,
Qu'ieu sai e cre mon escïen
    Que selh qui Jhesus ensenha
Segura escola pot tener.

Love, take no blame that I depart;
I go now at the Lord's behest;
New goals have risen in my heart
That send me forth upon this quest.
    Let my Protector's name be blest,[3]
       Who desires and calls, who binds too,
    Turning me toward a hope so true.

Who'd lounge in comforts like some knave,
Not seeking Bethlehem's true Lord—
I know not how to call him brave
Nor what hope waits for his reward
    Or what grace could our God afford;
       Yet the man our God leads His way
    Will surely never range astray.

W. D. Snodgrass

dia ella se ren
nao de la mort

Les tu
pr se
pr au
e eme
nasi
mar
ei flo

lu uex goles.
amas ven

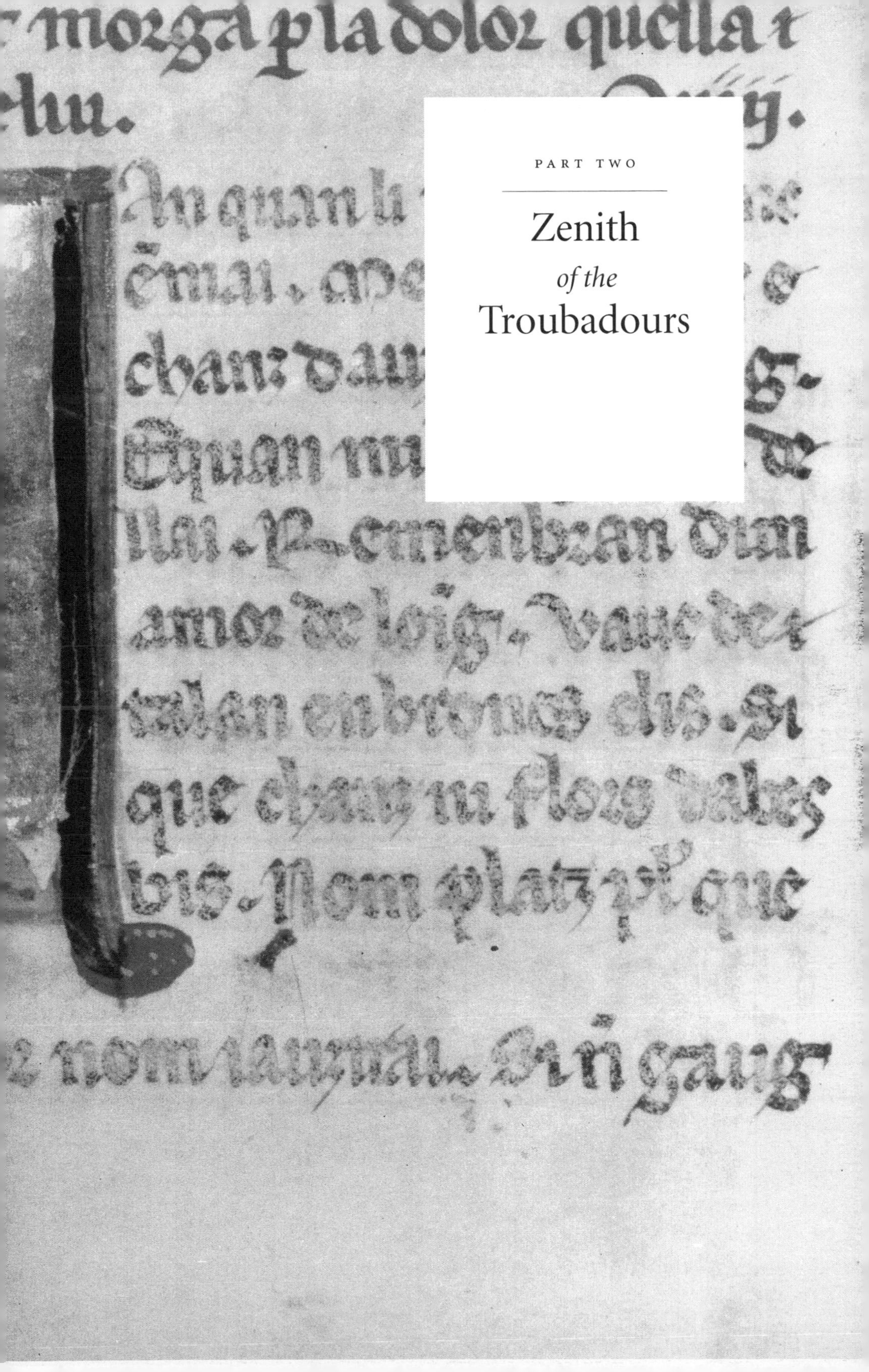

PART TWO

Zenith *of the* Troubadours

Bernart de Ventadorn

Bernart de Ventadorn was from the Limousin, from the castle of Ventadorn. He was of a poor family, the son of a servant who . . . heated the oven to bake the castle's bread. . . . And his lord, the Viscount of Ventadorn, took a great liking to him, to his poetry and to his singing, and he honored him greatly.

And the [wife of] the Viscount of Ventadorn . . . took a liking to En Bernart and his songs, and she fell in love with him, and he with her; he thus wrote his songs and verses for her, about the love he felt for her and about her merit. Their love lasted a long time before the Viscount or anyone else took notice of it. But when the Viscount did notice it, he . . . had his wife locked up and guarded. And he had her take leave of En Bernart and made him depart and go far from his lands.

And he left and went to the Duchess of Normandy [Eleanor of Aquitaine], who was young and of great merit, and who understood worth and honor and words of praise. And she was very pleased by En Bernart's songs, and she received him and gave him a warm welcome. He remained at her court for a long time, and fell in love with her and she with him, and he wrote many fine songs for her.[1]

Bernart de Ventadorn was born around 1120 or 1130, in the Limousin. Whether or not his parents were servants in the castle of Ventadorn as the *vida* states is not known. Scholars do accept that, after he became a maker

Preceding: **Zenith of the Troubadours.** Jaufre Rudel and the countess of Tripoli. Detail from medieval *Chansonnier I,* Italian, thirteenth century (BN fonds français 854). (Bibliothèque Nationale de France, Paris.)

of songs, Bernart wrote verse while attached to the court of Eleanor of Aquitaine and, later, to that of Raimon V of Toulouse. He appears to have been poetically active from around 1150 to around 1180.

Bernart de Ventadorn occupies a special niche in the troubadour pantheon as that maker of songs who appears to have been the most sincere about love. With him the sentiments expressed do not seem formulaic; see, for example, the second stanza of "Be m'an perdut" ("Farewell to Ventadorn"), the fifth selection below. En Bernart himself attributed his poetic success not so much to his technical virtuosity as to the sincerity of his emotions, as he states in the final selection:

> No marvel if my song's the best
> Of any sung by troubadour;
> My heart is drawn to love the more
> And I more shaped to love's behest.
> (trans. Snodgrass)

Was this true? Or were Bernart's protestations of sincerity merely a calculated rhetorical flourish? The reader may speculate.

At the start of the golden age of the troubadours, Bernart de Ventadorn brings to mind the "lark in the morning"—that rhapsodic bird immortalized in the first selection, "Can vei la lauzeta mover" ("The Skylark"). In this lyric, the lover-poet regrets that he cannot closely approach or fully attain his lady. Jackson points out that, here, "the figure of the lark is particularly apt, for [like the lover] it too is making for an unattainable source of light" (*Literature of the Middle Ages,* 250). The comparison of lover to lark, however, is vexed: the bird is content to fly toward the sun without ever reaching it, whereas the poet sulks. Unlike the bracing and tonic effect of unrequited love on, say, Jaufre Rudel, such unresolved aspirations exasperate and enervate Bertran.

Below is presented a short cycle of songs by Bernart de Ventadorn. After the springtime images of the first selections, the cycle progresses through summer to autumn. Within this seasonal movement, however, the composer's emotions do not fall into neat packages; rather, the songs reveal what Bonner calls the "strange mixture of joy and grief, [the varied] emotions that frequently exist side by side in [Bernart's] poems" (*Songs of the Troubadours,* 84).

The final selection has a valedictory ring. In the second stanza Bernart de Ventadorn peers down the generations at us with a quizzical eye. Do *our* lives measure up to his challenge?

Can vei la lauzeta mover

Bernart de Ventadorn

Can vei la lauzeta mover
De joi sas alas contral rai,
Que s'oblid' e·s laissa chazer
Per la doussor c'al cor li vai,
Ai! tan grans enveya m'en ve
De cui qu'eu veya jauzion,
Meravilhas ai, car desse
Lo cor de dezirer no·m fon.

Ai, las! Tan cuidava saber
D'amor, e tan petit en sai!
Car eu d'amar no·m posc tener
Celeis don ja pro non aurai.
Tout m'a mo cor, e tout m'a me,
E se mezeis e tot lo mon;
E can se·m tolc, no·m laisset re
Mas dezirer e cor volon.

Anc non agui de me poder
Ni no fui meus de l'or' en sai
Que·m laisset en sos olhs vezer
En un miralh que mout me plai.
Miralhs, pus me mirei en te,
M'an mort li sospir de preon,
C'aissi·m perdei com perdet se
Lo bels Narcisus en la fon.

De las domnas me dezesper;
Ja mais en lor no·m fiarai;
C'aissi com las solh chaptener,
Enaissi las deschaptenrai.
Pois vei c'una pro no m'en te
Vas leis que·m destrui e·m cofon,
Totas las dopt' e las mescre,
Car be sai c'atretals se son.

The Skylark

Bernart de Ventadorn

Now when I see the skylark lift
His wings for joy in dawn's first ray
Then let himself, oblivious, drift
For all his heart is glad and gay,
Ay! such great envies seize my thought
To see the rapture others find,
I marvel that desire does not
Consume away this heart of mine.

Alas, I thought I'd grown so wise;
In love I had so much to learn:
I can't control this heart that flies
To her who pays love no return.
Ay! now she steals, through love's sweet theft,
My heart, my self, my world entire;
She steals herself and I am left
Only this longing and desire.

Losing control, I've lost all right
To rule my life; my life's her prize
Since first she showed me true delight
In those bright mirrors, her two eyes.
Ay! once I'd caught myself inside
Her glances, I've been drowned in sighs,
Dying as fair Narcissus died
In streams that mirror captive skies.

Deep in despair, I'll place no trust
In women though I did before;
I've been their champion so it's just
That I renounce them evermore;
When none will lift me from my fall
When she has cast me down in shame,
Now I distrust them, one and all,
I've learned too well they're all the same.

D'aisso's fa be femna parer
Ma domna, per qu'e·lh o retrai,
Car no vol so c'om deu voler,
E so c'om li deveda, fai.
Chazutz sui en mala merce,
Et ai be faih co·l fols en pon;
E no sai per que m'esdeve,
Mas car trop puyei contra mon.

Merces es perduda, per ver,
Et eu non o saubi an mai,
Car cilh que plus en degr' aver,
No·n a ges; et on la querrai?
A! can mal sembla, qui la ve,
Qued aquest chaitiu deziron
Que ja ses leis non aura be,
Laisse morir, que no l·aon.

Pus ab midons no·m pot valer
Precs ni merces ni·l dreihz qu'eu ai,
Ni a leis no ven a plazer
Qu'eu l'am, ja mais no·lh o dirai.
Aissi·m part de leis e·m recre;
Mort m'a, e per mort li respon,
E vau m'en, pus ilh no·m rete,
Chaitius, en issilh, no sai on.

Tristans, ges no·n auretz de me,
Qu'eu m'en vau, chaitius, no sai on.
De chantar me gic e·m recre,
E de joi e d'amor m'escon.

She acts as any woman would—
No wonder I'm dissatisfied;
She'll never do the things she should;
She only wants all that's denied.
Ay! now I fall in deep disgrace,
A fool upon love's bridge am I;[2]
No one knows how that could take place
Unless I dared to climb too high.

All mercy's gone, all pity lost—
Though at the best I still knew none—
Since she who should yield mercy most
Shows me the least of anyone.
Wrongful it seems, now, in my view,
To see a creature love's betrayed
Who'd seek no other good but you,
Then let him die without your aid.

Since she, my Lady, shows no care
To earn my thanks, nor pays Love's rights
Since she'll not hear my constant prayer
And my love yields her no delights,
I say no more; I silent go;
She gives me death; let death reply.
My Lady won't embrace me so
I leave, exiled to pain for aye.

Tristan, you'll hear no more from me:
I leave to wander, none knows where;
Henceforth all joys in love I'll flee
And all my songs I now forswear.

W. D. Snodgrass

Can l'erba fresch'

Bernart de Ventadorn

Can l'erba fresch' e·lh folha par
A la flors boton' el verjan,
E·l rossinhols autet e clar
Leva sa votz e mou so chan,
Joi ai de lui, e joi ai de la flor
E joi de me e de midons major;
Daus totas partz sui de joi claus e sens,
Mas sel es jois que totz autres jois vens.

Ai las! com mor de cossirar!
Que manhtas vetz en cossir tan:
Lairo m'en poirian portar,
Que re no sabria que·s fan.
Per Deu, Amors! be·m trobas vensedor,
Ab paucs d'amics e ses autre senhor.
Car una vetz tan midons no destrens
Abans qu'eu fos del dezirer estens?

Meravilh me com posc durar
Que no·lh demostre mo talan.
Can eu vei midons ni l'esgar,
Li seu bel olh tan be l'estan:
Per pauc me tenh car eu vas leis no cor.
Si feira eu, si no fos per paor,
C'anc no vi cors melhs talhatz ni depens
Ad ops d'amar sia tan greus ni lens.

Tan am midons e la tenh car,
E tan la dopt' e la reblan
C'anc de me no·lh auzei parlar,
Ni re no·lh quer ni re no·lh man.
Pero ilh sap mo mal e ma dolor,
E can li plai, mi fai ben et onor,
E can li plai, eu m'en sofert ab mens,
Per so c'a leis no·n avenha blastens.

When Tender Grass and Leaves Appear

Bernart de Ventadorn

When tender grass and leaves appear
While buds along the branches throng,
The nightingale so high and clear
Uplifts his voice to spill his song;
Joy in the bird and full joy in the flower,
Joy in myself and my Lady much more.
Joy quite surrounds me; I live joy-possessed
Yet here's one joy that outjoys all the rest.

Alas, half dead with love's dismay,
Sometimes my sad thoughts fret me so
That thieves could carry me away
And I would be the last to know.
Love, in God's name, I have no least defense,
No other lord and but very few friends;
You should go torment my Lady this way;
Otherwise love's pain might waste me away.

I marvel how I still endure
To never let my longing show;
At any time I look at her
Her lovely eyes adorn her so,
All my keen urges run straight toward her there,
Where I'd have turned first, if not for this fear.
None that I've seen is so trim and well made,
Formed for love's role though hard to persuade.

I fear and cherish her so well
And passionately love her so,
Yet of this love I dare not tell
Nor ask the gifts she might bestow.
She, knowing all of my sorrow and pains,
Treats me with honor and grace when she deigns;
Yet when she deigns it, I make do with less
Lest blame should fall on her chaste guiltlessness.

S'eu saubes la gen enchantar,
Mei enemic foran efan,
Que ja us no saubra triar
Ni dir re que·ns tornes a dan.
Adoncs sai eu que vira la gensor
E sos bels olhs e sa frescha color,
E baizera·lh la bocha en totz sens
Si que d'un mes i paregra lo sens.

Be la volgra sola trobar,
Que dormis, o·n fezes semblan,
Per qu'e·lh embles un doutz baizar,
Pus no valh tan qu'eu lo·lh deman.
Per Deu, domna, pauc esplecham d'amor;
Vai s'en lo tems, e perdem lo melhor!
Parlar degram ab cubertz entresens,
E, pus no·ns val arditz, valgues no gens!

Be deuri'om domna blasmar,
Can trop vai son amic tarzan,
Que lonja paraula d'amar
Es grans enois e par d'enjan,
C'amar pot om e far semblan alhor,
E gen mentir lai on non a autor.
Bona domna, ab sol c'amar mi dens,
Ja per mentir eu no serai atens.[3]

Messatger, vai e no m'en prezes mens
S'eu del anar vas midons sui temens.

I wish that I could cast a spell;
I'd turn each foe into a child
So none of them could hear or tell
The tales by which our love's defiled.
Then I could see her, most lovely and dear,
Those beauteous eyes and that color so clear,
Swiftly I'd kiss her sweet mouth, left and right;
We'd leave the marks a whole month in plain sight.

If I could find her all alone,
Sleeping or playing so for fun,
I'd steal the sweetest kiss I've known—
I lack the worth to ask for one.
Lady, by God, our love's getting nowhere;
Time flies away while we lose the best share
We must speak only with signs or by sleight;
Boldness won't help us, but slyness just might.

Messenger, go seek my Lady so fair,
Scorning me not that I dare not go there.

W. D. Snodgrass

Pois preyatz me, senhor

Bernart de Ventadorn

Pois preyatz me, senhor,
Qu'eu chan, eu chantarai;
E can cuit chantar, plor
A l'ora c'o essai.
Greu veiretz chantador,
Be chan si mal li vai.
Vai me doncs mal d'amor?
Ans melhs que no fetz mai!
E doncs, per que m'esmai?

Gran ben e gran onor
Conosc que Deus me fai,
Qu'eu am la belazor
Et ilh me (qu'eu o sai).
Mas eu sui si, alhor,
E no sai com l'estai!
So m'auci de dolor,
Car ochaizo non ai
De soven venir lai.

Empero tan me plai
Can de leis me sove,
Que qui·m crida ni·m brai,
Eu no·n au nula re.
Tan dousamen me trai
La bela·l cor de se,
Que tals ditz qu'eu sui sai,
Et o cuid, et o cre,
Que de sos olhs no·m ve.

You've Asked, My Lords, for Song

Bernart de Ventadorn

You've asked, my lords, for song:
I sing for my reply
Yet never sing for long—
I've lost the heart to try.
How should a troubadour
Sing when his luck's run dry?
Has love, then, gone awry?
No; better than before.
Then why feel so heartsore?

With gifts beyond compare
The Lord has honored me;
I love a lady, fair,
Who loves me faithfully.
Yet while I languish here
I can't so much as tell
If she fares ill or well
Which fills my thoughts with care
Since I dare not go there.

Through her, such joys I find
That if men shout or call
While she invests my mind,
I'd never hear at all.
So subtly does she snare
The heart out of my breast
That men swear and attest
That they all see me here
Though my best part's still there.

Amors, e que·m farai?
Si guerrai ja ab te?
Ara cuit qu'e·n morrai
Del dezirer que·m ve,
Si·lh bela lai on jai
No m'aizis pres de se,
Qu'eu la manei e bai
Et estrenha vas me
So cors blanc, gras e le.

Ges d'amar no·m recre
Per mal ni per afan;
E can Deus m'i fai be,
No·l refut ni·l soan;
E can bes no m'ave,
Sai be sofrir lo dan,
C'a las oras cove
C'om s'an entrelonhan
Per melhs salhir enan.

Bona domna, merce
Del vostre fin aman!
Qu'e·us pliu per bona fe
C'anc re non amei tan.
Mas jonchas, ab col cle,
Vos m'autrei e·m coman;
E si locs s'esdeve,
Vos me fatz bel semblan,
Que molt n'ai gran talan!

Mon Escuder e me
Don Deus cor e talan
C'amdui n'anem truan;

Et el en men ab se
So don a plus talan
Et eu Mon Aziman!

Oh Love, what shall I do?
Shall we two live in strife?
The griefs that must ensue
Would surely end my life.
Unless my Lady might
Receive me in that place
She lies in, to embrace
And press against me, tight,
Her body, smooth and white.

I'll not renounce my love
For troubles or love's pains.
When God who reigns above
Gave much, I took my gains;
Now when his gifts abate,
I'll suffer that as much,
Seeing the times are such
Those far apart must wait
To overcome their fate.

Good Lady, thank you for
Your love so true and fine;
I swear I love you more
Than all past loves of mine.
I bow and join my hands
Yielding myself to you;
The one thing you might do
Is give me one sweet glance
If sometime you've the chance.

May God give heart and mind
To Escudor and me
Wandering endlessly.

He'll bring what he can find
To keep him company;
My Magnet goes with me.

W. D. Snodgrass

Lancan vei la folha

Bernart de Ventadorn

Lancan vei la folha
Jos dels albres chazer,
   Cui que pes ni dolha,
A me deu bo saber.
   No crezatz qu'eu volha
Flor ni folha vezer,
   Car vas me s'orgolha
So qu'eu plus volh aver.
   Cor ai que m'en tolha
Mas no·n ai ges poder,
   C'ades cuit m'acolha,
On plus m'en dezesper.

Estranha novela
Podetz de me auzir,
   Que can vei la bela
Que·m soli' acolhir,
   Ara no m'apela
Ni·m fai vas se venir.
   Lo cor sotz l'aissela
M'en vol de dol partir.
   Deus, que·l mon chapdela,
Si·lh platz, m'en lais jauzir,
   Que s'aissi·m revela,
No·i a mas del morir.

Now the Birds Are Leaving

Bernart de Ventadorn

Now the birds are leaving
    And leaves forsake the tree;
Others may go grieving,
    You'll see no grief in me.
How could leaves or flowers
    Be worth my while to see
When my lady lours
    And treats me scornfully.
I've a heart to leave her
    But never find the power;
Mine, I still believe her
    Through each despairing hour.

Strange new tidings of me
    May soon come to your ear;
When I see her, lovely,
    Who held me, once, so dear,
Yet who never calls me
    Nor wishes I were near
Till my sad heart galls me
    And soon must break, I fear.
Lord, this world's great ruler,
    Bring her to yield or I,
Seeing her grow crueller,
    Have no choice but to die.

Non ai mais fiansa
En agur ni en sort,
   Que bon' esperansa
M'a cofundut e mort,
   Que tan lonh me lansa
La bela cui am fort,
   Can li quer s'amansa,
Com s'eu l'agues gran tort.
   Tan n'ai de pezansa
Que totz m'en desconort;
   Mas no·n fatz semblansa
C'ades chant e deport.

   Als non sai que dire
Mas: mout fatz gran folor
   Car am ni dezire
Del mon la belazor.
   Be deuri' aucire
Qui anc fetz mirador!
   Can be m'o cossire,
No·n ai guerrer peyor.
   Ja·l jorn qu'ela·s mire
Ni pens de sa valor,
   No serai jauzire
De leis ni de s'amor.

   Ja per drudaria
No m'am, que no·s cove;
   Pero si·lh plazia
Que·m fezes cal que be,
   Eu li juraria
Per leis e per ma fe,
   Que·l bes que·m faria,
No fos saubutz per me.
   En son plazer sia,
Qu'eu sui en sa merce.
   Si·lh platz, que m'aucia,
Qu'eu no m'en clam de re!

I'll put no more faith, now,
    In lots or prophecy:
Ruin and my death, now,
    Such schemes have brought to me
For my lady, lovely,
    Whom I have loved so long
Takes no notice of me
    As if I'd done her wrong;
This despair's so fearful,
    All hope has fled away,
Though some think me cheerful
    Because I sing or play.

All this life's worth nothing
    But mockery and scorn
Longing so and loving
    The loveliest lady born.
Who first made a mirror
    Deserves his death from me;
Telling truth the nearer,
    I've no worse enemy.
Seeing herself clearer
    And learning all her worth,
Daily she'll grow dearer
    While I live on in dearth.

She'd not lustfully want me,
    For lust is far from right;
Still, suppose she'd grant me
    Some trifling small delight,
I would freely swear it
    By all that men hold true
None should ever hear it
    Whatever she might do.
Still, whate'er she will me,
    I'll take what she ordain;
If she desired to kill me
    I still would not complain.

Ben es dreihz qu'eu planha,
S'eu pert per mon orgolh
La bona companha
E·l solatz c'aver solh.
Petit me gazanha
Lo fols arditz qu'eu colh,
Car vas me s'estranha
So qu'eu plus am e volh.
Orgolhs, Deus vos franha,
C'ara·n ploron mei olh.
Dreihz es que·m sofranha
Totz jois, qu'eu eis lo·m tolh.

Encontra·l damnatge
E la pena qu'eu trai,
Ai mo bon usatge:
C'ades consir de lai.
Orgolh e folatge
E vilania fai
Qui·n mou mo coratge
Ni d'alre·m met en plai,
Car melhor messatge
En tot lo mon no·n ai,
E man lo·lh ostatge
Entro qu'eu torn de sai.

Domna, mo coratge,
·l melhor amic qu'eu ai,
Vos man en ostatge
Entro qu'eu torn de sai.

Yet complaints, resentments
    And tears are justified:
All my old contentment
    Is lost through foolish pride;
All my foolish boldness
    Brings me a sad return:
Merely scorn and coldness
    From her for whom I yearn.
Lord, this pride that grieves me,
    Destroy it if you deign;
Pleasure's right to leaves me
    Since I've caused my own pain.

Countering love's damnation
    And all the pains I bear,
I've this mitigation:
    My thoughts dwell with her there.
Who'd attempt such madness
    As to distract my heart,
Villainous pride and badness
    Are truly that man's part.
Through this world, my spirit's
    My truest messenger;
While I linger here, it's
    A hostage held by her.

Lady, this loyal spirit's
    The one friend I hold dear.
Keep it close; I fear it's
    Your hostage while I'm here.

W. D. Snodgrass

Be m'an perdut lai enves Ventadorn

Bernart de Ventadorn

Be m'an perdut lai enves Ventadorn
Tuih mei amic, pois ma domna no m'ama;
Et es be dreihz que ja mais lai no torn,
C'ades estai vas me salvatj' e grama.
Ve·us per que·m fai semblan irat e morn:
Car en s'amor me deleih e·m sojorn!
Ni de ren als no·s rancura ni·s clama.

Aissi co·l peis qui s'eslaiss' el cadorn
E no·n sap mot tro que s'es pres en l'ama,
M'eslaissei eu vas trop amar un jorn,
C'anc no·m gardei, tro fui en mei la flama,
Que m'art plus fort, no·m feira focs de forn;
E ges per so no·m posc partir un dorn,
Aissi·m te pres s'amors e m'aliama.

No·m meravilh si s'amors me te pres,
Que genser cors no crei qu'el mon se mire:
Bels e blancs es, e frescs e gais e les
E totz aitals com eu volh e dezire.
No posc dir mal de leis, que non i es;
Qu'e·l n'agra dih de joi, s'eu li saubes;
Mas no li sai, per so m'en lais de dire.

Totz tems volrai sa onor e sos bes
E·lh serai om et amics e servire,
E l'amarai, be li plass' o be·lh pes,
C'om no pot cor destrenher ses aucire.
No sai domna, volgues o no volgues,
Si·m volia, c'amar no la pogues.
Mas totas res pot om en mal escrire.

Farewell to Ventadorn

Bernart de Ventadorn

Now all my friends who live near Ventadorn
Have lost me, for my Lady does not love me;
It's right that I should nevermore return
When she grows heartless, glowering above me.
She turns her eyes to me with wrath and scorn
Because for her sweet love's delight I yearn;
She can attest no other evil of me.

Like some great trout that dashes to the bait
Until he feels love's hook, all hot and blindly
I rushed toward too much love, too rash to wait,
Careless, till ringed in by love's flames I find me
Seared as by furnace fires upon a grate
Yet not one hand's breadth can I move, so strait
And narrow does this love enchain and bind me.

Small wonder that her love can bind so tight;
No shape in all the world is lovelier,
Standing so graceful, fresh and smooth and white;
Just as she is, I yearn and long for her.
I've found no faults and cannot speak in spite;
If fault there were, I'd tell of it outright;
I know of none and speak no evil of her.

In luck and honor, let her still be blest,
And I her lover, liege and servant ever
Whether that makes her joyful or distressed.
Constrain the heart and it could die forever.
I could love anyone if that seemed best
Whether the lady like me or detest.
Yet some find harm in anything whatever.

A las autras sui aissi eschazutz;
La cals se vol me pot vas se atraire,
Per tal cove que no·m sia vendutz
L'onors ni·l bes que m'a en cor a faire;
Qu'enoyos es preyars, pos er perdutz;
Per me·us o dic, que mals m'en es vengutz,
Car traït m'a la bela de mal aire.

En Proensa tramet jois e salutz
E mais de bes c'om no lor sap retraire;
E fatz esfortz, miracles e vertutz,
Car eu lor man de so don non ai gaire,
Qu'eu non ai joi, mas tan can m'en adutz
Mos Bels Vezers e'n Fachura, mos drutz,
E'n Alvernhatz, lo senher de Belcaire.

Mos Bels Vezers, per vos fai Deus vertutz
Tals c'om no·us ve que no si' ereubutz
Dels bels plazers que sabetz dir e faire.

To other women, now, I've fall'n away;
I can be drawn to anyone who wants me.
I shall accept what pleasures they'd purvey
So long as they've not sold the gifts they grant me.
Rage fills a man who always prays in vain,
And I say all this evil comes my way
Because ill will from her bereaves and taunts me.

All health and joy to Provence I bequeath
And pleasures more than any man can number.
What prodigies and wonders I achieve
In granting others joys from which I'm sundered.
I have no joy else, save what I receive
From Fachura and Alvern, Belcaire's chief, [4]
And my own Eyes' Delight from whom I wander.

My Eyes' Delight, the Lord God must achieve
Great miracles through you since I perceive
Each heart that looks on you is rapt with wonder.

W. D. Snodgrass

Non es meravelha s'eu chan

Bernart de Ventadorn

Non es meravelha s'eu chan
Melhs de nul autre chantador,
Que plus me tra·l cors vas amor
E melhs sui faihz a so coman.
Cor e cors e saber e sen
E fors' e poder i ai mes.
Si·m tira vas amor lo fres
Que vas autra part no·m aten.

Ben es mortz qui d'amor no sen
Al cor cal que dousa sabor;
E que val viure ses valor
Mas per enoi far a la gen?
Ja Domnedeus no·m azir tan
Qu'eu ja pois viva jorn ni mes
Pois que d'enoi serai mespres
Ni d'amor non aurai talan.

Per bona fe e ses enjan
Am la plus bel' e la melhor.
Del cor sospir e dels olhs plor,
Car tan l'am eu, per que i ai dan.
Eu que·n posc mais, s'Amors me pren,
E les charcers en que m'a mes
No pot claus obrir mas merces,
E de merce no·i trop nien?

Aquest' amors me fer tan gen
Al cor d'una dousa sabor:
Cen vetz mor lo jorn de dolor
E reviu de joi autras cen.
Ben es mos mals de bel semblan,
Que mais val mos mals qu'autre bes;
E pois mos mals aitan bos m'es,
Bos er lo bes apres l'afan.

No Marvel If My Song's the Best

Bernart de Ventadorn

No marvel if my song's the best
Of any sung by troubadour;
My heart is drawn to love the more
And I more shaped to love's behest.
Toward love I've bent my self and soul,
My mind and body, heart and brain;
So tightly drawn upon love's rein,
My thoughts can seek no other goal.

That man's well dead who lacks the sense
Within his heart for love's sweet taste
And, lacking prowess, life lies waste,
Useless, and only breeds offense.
May Heav'n's Lord never hate me so
To let me live my life one day
When men, disgusted, turn away
And my desire for love shall go.

Without deceit, but true and plain,
I love the loveliest and best;
Tears fill my eyes and sighs my breast
Since love has brought me so much pain.
What hope have I whom love has bound
Where only pity holds the key
To loose love's cell and set me free,
Yet pity's nowhere to be found.

My heart by love is gently torn
Though love's wound has a savor sweet.
Each day, a hundred deaths I meet—
Each day, a hundred times reborn.
My evils wear a face so fair,
No good is sweeter than love's ill;
Since evil's sweet, then I may still
Hope joy requites love's pain and care.

Ai Deus, car se fosson trian
D'entrels faus li fin amador,
E·lh lauzenger e·lh trichador
Portesson corns el fron denan!
Tot l'aur del mon e tot l'argen
I volgr'aver dat, s'eu l'agues,
Sol que ma domna conogues
Aissi com eu l'am finamen.

Cant eu la vei, be m'es parven
Als olhs, al vis, a la color,
Car aissi tremble de paor
Com fa la folha contra·l ven.
Non ai de sen per un efan,
Aissi sui d'amor entrepres;
E d'ome qu'es aissi conques,
Pot domn' aver almorna gran.

Bona domna, re no·us deman
Mas que·m prendatz per servidor,
Qu'e·us servirai com bo senhor,
Cossi que del gazardo m'an.
Ve·us m'al vostre comandamen,
Francs cors umils, gais e cortes!
Ors ni leos non etz vos ges,
Que·m aucizatz, s'a vos me ren.

A Mo Cortes, lai on ilh es,
Tramet lo vers, e ja no·lh pes
Car n'ai estat tan lonjamen.

Dear Lord, if only loves forsworn
Might be discerned from love that's true;
Then jealous liars might get their due
In brows decked out with branching horns.
How gladly I'd give all the gold
And all the silver in this earth
If she could know my true love's worth
And the firm faith this heart might hold.

When seeing her my love shines clear
In face, in color, in my eyes;
As leaves that wind shakes in the skies,
I tremble just so in my fear.
I grow more senseless than a child
When love so wholly seizes me;
Toward someone vanquished utterly
A lady might show mercy mild.

Good Lady, I make no request
And never shall for more reward
Than serving you as your true lord
Who acts only at your behest.
Behold me here at your command,
You noble creature, frank and gay;
Never, like bear or lion, slay
Someone who's yielded to your hand.

To my Cortez, I sing this lay
That though I linger far away
No grief be hers in any land.

W. D. Snodgrass

Peire d'Alvernhe

Peire d'Alvernhe was from the bishopric of Clairmon. He was intelligent and well-read, and he was the son of a burgher. As a person he was handsome and of pleasant disposition. And he wrote good poetry and sang well, and he was the first good troubadour to go beyond the mountains. And he composed the finest melodies ever written . . . and he was considered the finest troubadour in the world until the appearance of Giraut de Bornelh.[1]

With Peire d'Alvernhe and Bernart de Ventadorn, we enter into the golden age of troubadour poetry. To Peire, in fact, we owe the term *cortez' amor,* "courtly love," which, along with the closely related phrase *fin' amor,* is used to describe the main emotional preoccupation of the troubadours.[2]

Peire d'Alvernhe became active sometime in the mid-to-late 1150s. He may have been a canon before leaving the church to become a *joglar.* After he became a composer, Peire was fêted by some of the greatest patrons of the day: Sancho III of Castile, Raimon Berenguer IV of Barcelona, Raimon V of Toulouse. Peire was active until around 1180. His *vida* suggests that he "did penance," perhaps by entering a religious order, before dying.

Not one for false modesty, Peire d'Alvernhe boasts that, "before me, no perfect poem was written. . . . I was the first to use perfect diction." We may take this to mean more than surface polish. Rather, in his best poems Peire achieves, in Bonner's words, "a flawless joining of sound, rhythm, meaning and association; and with this a nobility and purity of style that few other troubadours achieved. It was in this technical mastery, coupled with a kind of artistic self-consciousness, that lay his innovating role" (*Songs of the Troubadours*, 69).

The first selection, the beguiling "Rossinhol, el seu repaire" ("Nightingale, for Me Take Flight"), well displays these qualities. In this superb work, Peire seems to strike the proper balance (*mezura*) between warmth and courtly refinement that is a hallmark of *fin' amor*. The work is actually presented in the *chansonniers* as a set of two poems. In this diptych, the first poem (stanzas 1–6) portrays the hopeful male lover and the journey of his nightingale-messenger, while the second (stanzas 7–11) is given to the distant *domna*. By embracing this dual structure, Peire may have drawn inspiration from Marcabru, who also left a set of two poems (not included in the present volume), the only other such pairing in the troubadour corpus. As a further point of similarity, both sets of poems feature two lovers and a bird. Peire's mellifluent "nightingale," however, produces a much different effect than Marcabru's raucous "starling." [3]

Critics generally regard Peire as a disciple of the *trobar clus* school of poetry. The troubadour himself pokes fun at his sometimes obscure lyrics. He says of himself: "Peire d'Alvernhe's . . . melodies are sweet and pleasant, for he is master of them all, but it's a pity his meaning isn't clearer, for almost no one understands him." [4] The present selections do not appear very obscure because the twentieth century furnished us with new touchstones of difficulty, and also because editors of anthologies generally showcase poets at their most accessible; yet the second selection, "Dejosta·ls breus e·ls loncs sers" ("When Days Grow Short and Night Advances"), does display some typical *trobar clus* markings. This poem inverts a typical troubadour convention by setting a love poem on a dismal winter day rather than a balmy spring morning. Then the poem presents its complex central idea: the contrast between the external cold and the inner warmth that the poet derives from contemplating his loved one. Finally we encounter a *trobar clus* marker in the following paradox: "The service of love flourishes and grows . . . both green and white as snow." There is something of the English metaphysical poets here in the way that Peire d'Alvernhe and the other *trobar clus* poets seize on unlikely or difficult metaphors in an attempt to exactly express some complex concept, or else to startle listeners into fresh thought.

Rossinhol, el seu repaire

Peire d'Alvernhe

"Rossinhol, el seu repaire
M'iras ma domna vezer,
E digas li·l mieu afaire
Et ilh diga·t del sieu ver,
E man sai
Com l'estai,
Mas de mi·ll sovenha,
Que ges lai
Per nuill plai
Ab si no·t retenha,

Que tost no·m tornes retraire
Son star e son captener,
Qu'ieu non ai amic ni fraire
Don tant o vueilla saber."
Ar s'en vai
L'auzels gai
Dreit vas on ilh renha,
Ab essai
Ses esglai,
Tro qu'en trob l'ensenha.

Quan l'auzelet[z] de bon aire
Vi sa beutat aparer,
Dous cant comenset a braire,
Si com sol far contra·l ser;
Pueis se tai,
Que non brai,
Mas de liei s'engenha,
Co·l retrai
Ses pantai
So qu·ilh auzir denha.

Nightingale, for Me Take Flight

Peire d'Alvernhe

"Nightingale, for me take flight
And to my lady's home repair;
Tell her about my lonely plight
And find the truth of how she fares.
  Send word to me
  What you see;
 Remember me to her.
  Then don't wait
  But leave straight—
Do not linger there;

"For how she looks, how she behaves
I long to hear direct from you:
Of no close kinsman do I crave
So much to learn the latest news."
  Now straightaway
  This bird gay
 Wings it through the skies;
  It draws near
  With no fear
To where her banner flies.

Now when that bird of noble mien
Saw her beauteous form appear,
Liltingly it began to sing—
As birds will do when dusk draws near.
  But then it held
  Its song, compelled
 As it sought a way
  To express
  With gentleness
What it longed to say.

"Cel que·us es verais amaire
Volc qu'eu en vostre poder
Vengues sai esser cantaire,
Per so que·us fos a plazer;
E sabrai,
Quan veirai,
Per qu'er l'entresenha;
Que·il dirai,
Si ren sai,
Per qu'el lai s'en fenha.

E si·l port per que·s n'esclaire,
Gran gaug en devetz aver,
Qu'anc om no nasquet de maire,
Tan de be·us puesca voler.
Ie·m n'irai
E·m mourai
Ab gaug, on que·m venha...
No farai,
Quar non ai
Dig qual plag en prenha.

D'aisso·m farai plaidejaire:
Qui·n amor ha son esper,
No·s deuria tardar gaire,
Tan com l'amors n'a lezer;
Que tost chai
Blancs en bai,
Com flors sobre lenha;
E val mai
Qui·ls fagz fai,
Ans qu'als la·n destrenha."

Ben ha tengut dreg viatge
L'auzel[s] lai on e·l tramis,
Et ill envia·m messatge
Segon que de mi formis:
"Molt mi platz,
So sapchatz,
Vostra parladura;

"He who is your lover true
 Sent me here, that I might obey
 Your will: he bids me sing to you;
 That it might bring you joy he prays.
        Seeing how
        You live will show
    Me if there is some word,
        Some sign
        I can find
    To take back to my lord.

"And if I'm able to return
 With happy news, thank God above,
 For never was man of woman born
 Able to give you so much love.
        Now I'll leave
        Joyfully
    I'll be on my way . . .
        No I won't—
        I still don't
    Know what I should say!"

To this truth I will hold fast:
He who loves should ever aspire;
He shouldn't wait as long as he has
A chance to win his heart's desire.
        As easily
        As bud from tree
    Falls, can white turn blond?
        Don't hold back –
        Make sure you act
    Before you're acted on!

Straight now flew my messenger
Until it rested by her side,
And spoke; then she in sweet concord,
Forthwith offered this reply:
        "Little bird,
        Rest assured
    You have greatly pleased me.

Et aujatz,
Que·ill digatz
So don mi pren cura.

Fort mi pot esser salvatge
Quar s'es lonhatz mos amics,
Qu'anc joi de negun linhatge
No vi que tan m'abelis;
Trop viatz
Fo·l comjatz,
Mas s'ieu fos segura,
Mais bontatz
N'agr' assatz,
Per qu'ieu n'ai rancura.

Que tan l'am de bon coratge,
Qu'ades soi entredormis,
Ab lui ai en guidonatge
Joc e joi e gaug e ris;
E·l solatz
Qu'ai em patz
No sap creatura,
Tan quan jatz
E mos bratz,
Tro que·s trasfigura.

Tostemps mi fo d'agradatge,
Pos lo vi et ans que·l vis,
E ges de plus ric linhatge
No vuelh autr' aver conquis;
Mos cuidatz
Es bos fatz;
No·m pot far tortura
Vens ni glatz
Ni estatz
Ni cautz ni freidura.

Listen well—
You must tell
Him why I feel uneasy.

"I found it cruel, surpassingly,
That I was left here by my friend.
Never before nor since have I
Known the joy I felt with him.
        Too quickly he
        Took his leave—
I should have been more giving,
        And dared
        To share;
Now I'm left here grieving.

"I bear such love for him inside
That, when I've started my descent
To sleep, always he is my guide—
To joy, delight and merriment.
        At ease;
        The deep peace
I draw from his caresses
        Not a soul
        Can know—
Until he vanishes.

"Since first I lay my eyes on him,
I've been attracted to his ways;
I don't care to conquer any man
Who springs from higher lineage.
        I'm content
        No regrets
Nothing is displeasing:
        Wind nor sleet;
        Neither heat
Of sun nor weather freezing.

Bon' amors ha un uzatge
Co·l bos aurs, quan ben es fis,
Que s'esmera de bontatge,
Qui ab bontat li servis;
E crezatz
Qu'amistatz
Cascun jorn meillura,
Meilluratz
Et amatz
Es cui jois s'aura.

Dous auzels, vas son estatge
M'iretz, quan venra·l matis,
E digatz l'en dreg lengatge
De qual guiza l'obedis."
Abrivatz
N'es tornatz,
Trop per gran mesura
Doctrinatz
Emparlatz
De bon' aventura.

"Truest love I would compare
To gold that's pure and genuine:
If it's been embellished with care;
When with care it's been refined.
 Have faith
 That each day
Our bond can be improving;
 He is improved
 Who knows love
And feels its joy suffusing.

"Sweet nightingale, now to his dwelling
Fly, so that by break of day
Tomorrow, you are plainly telling
Him how well I do obey."
 Thus released,
 Swiftly on its
Way this bird was wending,
 With much to tell—
 Pleased how well
This gay adventure's ending.

 Robert Kehew

Deiosta·ls breus iorns e·ls loncs sers

    Peire d'Alvernhe

    Deiosta·ls breus iorns e·ls loncs sers,
    Quan la blanc'aura brunezis,
    Vuelh que branc e bruelh mos sabers
    D'un nou ioy que·m fruich'e·m floris,
Car del doutz fuelh vey clarzir los guarricx,
Per que·s retrai entre·ls enois e·ls freys
Lo rossinhols e·l tortz e·l guays e·l picx.

    Contr'aisso m'agrada·l parers
    D'amor lonhdana e de vezis,
    Quar pauc val levars ni iazers
    A lui ses lieys cuy es aclis,
Qu'amors vol gaug e grupis los enicx,
E qui s'esiau alhora qu'es destreys,
Be·m par qu'a dreit li vol esser amics.

    Qu'ieu vey e crey e sai qu'es vers
    Qu'amors engraissa e magrezis,
    L'un ab trichar l'autr'ab plazers
    E l'un ab plor e l'autr'ab ris;
Lo quals que·s vol n'es manens o mendicx,
Per qu'ieu n'am mais so que n'ay qu'esser reys
(Assatz nonre!) d'Escotz ni de Galics.

    Mas ieu no sai los capteners;
    Mas suefre q'una ma' conquis
    Don reviu ioys e nays valers,
    Tals que denant li·m trassalis;
Quar no m'enquier de dir, m'en ven destricx,
Tan tem que·l mielhs lays e prenda·l sordeys:
On plus n'ai cor, mi pens: "Car no t'en gicx?"

When Days Grow Short and Night Advances

Peire d'Alvernhe

When days grow short and night advances
And the air grows clear and darkens,
Would that my thoughts put forth fresh branches
To bear with joy new fruit and blossom,
For I see the oaks reft of their leaves,
While nightingale, thrush, woodpecker and jay
Shiver with cold, and from the chill retreat.

The vision that sustains me through
These times is of my distant love:
Sleeping, waking, what matters to
Him who from his love is removed?
Love wants joy: in times when strife is looming
He who can banish care (it's safe to say)
With his love is inwardly communing.

I've seen, believe, and know it's true
That love can make men lean or fatter
Through treachery or pleasure; through
Falling tears or peals of laughter.
One becomes rich or poor at love's command;
But still my paltry share of love I'd take
Over the sovereign crown of Wales or Scotland.

I don't know what to say or do . . .
I'll bide my time, for through my lady
Valor revives and joy's renewed—
Being in her presence makes me
Tremble. I dare not speak, hence my distress.
I hearten, but think: what if this good gave way
To ill fortune?—give up hope of success.

Ha! quar si fos dels mieus volers
Lo sieus rics coratges devis
Desque ma dompna·m tol poders
De so de q'ieu plus l'ai requis,
Mas no·l sai dir lauzenguas ni prezicx,
Mas meillor cor l'ai trop que non pareys!
S'ella no·l sap, morrai m'en totz anticx.

Tant m'es dous e fis sos vezers,
Pel ioy que·m n'es al cor assis,
E sobre tot lo bons espers
Qu'ieu n'ai, per que m'en enriquis,
C'anc tan non fuj mais coartz ni mendicx,
Ab qu'ieu la vis alques, aqui mezeys
No·m saubes far de gran paubretat ricx.

So es gaugz e ioys e plazers,
Que a manhtas gens abelhis,
E sos pretz mont'a grans poders
E sos ioys sobresenhoris,
Qu'ensenhamens e beutatz l'es abricx:
Dompneis, d'amor qu'en lieis s'espan e creys,
Plens de doussor, vertz e blancx cum es nix.

Per qu'ieu mi pens: "Ia non t'en desrazicx!"
Quan me conquis en loc on ylh mi seys
Plus que si·m des Fransa lo reis Loicx.

En aquest vers sapcha Vilans Audricx
Que d'Alvernhe manda qu'om ses dompneis
Non val ren plus que bels malvatz espicx.[5]

Oh if only her heart noble
Had been as ready to infer
My desires as she proved able
To take from me what I sought from her!
Alas I don't know how to praise or flatter . . .
Doesn't she know? I'll die with hair turned gray
If my longings for her remain unuttered.

Just to see her is sweet delight—
Both from the joy that she engenders
As from the hope that she excites
That knowing her will make me richer!
For never was I so mean-hearted or vicious
That glimpsing her wouldn't be enough to raise
Me instantly from poverty to riches.

This happiness is a joy and sweet
Pleasure that many wish to claim:
Its merit raises men to great
Power; its joy to high domain.
The service of love flourishes and grows,
Sheltered by beauty and safely hid away,
Spreading sweetness, both green and white as snow.

I tell myself, never leave these lands
Where she first conquered you then made you rei,
Even if Louis were to give you France.

Robert Kehew

Raimbaut d'Aurenga

[Raimbaut d'Aurenga] was lord of [Aurenga] and . . . a great many
other castles. . . . He wrote good *vers* and *cansos;* but he preferred to
write in difficult, subtle rhymes. . . . And then he fell in love with the
good Countess of Urgell. . . . And he then wrote his songs for her, and
he sent them to her by means of a jongleur called Nightingale. . . . For
a long time he courted the countess, without ever having the oppor-
tunity of going to see her. But I heard her say, after she had become a
nun, that if he had come she would have granted him his pleasure and
permitted him to touch her bare leg with the back of his hand.[1]

Raimbaut d'Aurenga, the first major troubadour to hail from Provence
proper, was born around 1144. As befitted a southern nobleman he partici-
pated in the local wars, allying himself with his cousin Guillem VII of Mont-
pellier and the counts of Barcelona against Raimon V of Toulouse. Raim-
baut did, however, find time to compose: during his short period of activity
he penned some forty songs. Raimbaut died young, at the age of twenty-
nine, in 1173. His friend and sometime collaborator Guiraut de Bornelh
lamented his death in verse.

   Although Raimbaut d'Aurenga pledges in "Escotatz, mas no say . . ."
("Beg Pardon, Lords") to "speak my feelings clear and plain," this he does
not do. Many of his poems are in the *trobar clus* style, where meaning is in-
tentionally occluded. Raimbaut, in fact, explicitly champions the obscure
style, which by now has become a recognized school. In a *tenso,* Raimbaut
defends the tenants of *trobar clus* writing against Guiraut de Bornelh, who

argues for more accessible poetry (although the latter troubadour could play both sides of the fence on this matter). The first selection, "Er resplan la flors enversa" ("Splendid Are the Flowers Reversed"), displays a hallmark of the *trobar clus* style in its abstruse central conceit of the "reversed flowers." Note also this poem's unconventional imagery: "Your lovely eyes flay me like sticks."

While a champion of poetry that was difficult in content, Raimbaut could also tinker with the formal aspects of verse in a way that anticipates Arnaut Daniel and the *trobar ric* school of poetry. The first selection features an unusual metrical pattern, whereby the end-words to lines are not rhymed from one stanza to another but, rather, repeated.

The second poem, "Escotatz, mas no say . . . ," furnishes an even more striking example of experimentation in prosody. The translator of this selection, W. D. Snodgrass, engagingly characterizes the piece as "the earliest example of what we might call a 'talking blues,' [where] the end of each stanza breaks down into a spoken prose complaint" (*Selected Translations*, 150). The work parodies many troubadour mannerisms, reaching all the way back to Guillem de Peiteus and his "Farai un verse de dreyt nien" ("The Nothing Song").

Bearing in mind Raimbaut's innovations in both content and form, Bonner acknowledges his "considerable historic importance" as a transitional figure between Marcabru and Arnaut Daniel. Bonner, however, finds that, "with Raimbaut, the effort to make poetry fit the mold of extremely complex technical devices never really succeeded; it was his fate merely to break the ground which Arnaut Daniel was later to cultivate so masterfully. . . . [Raimbaut] gives the impression of [being] a gifted dilettante" (*Songs of the Troubadours*, 101). "Gifted" Raimbaut d'Aurenga surely was; to what extent he was a dilettante the reader can form some opinion.

Er resplan la flors enversa

Raimbaut d'Aurenga

Er resplan la flors enversa
Pels trencans rancx e pels tertres.
Quals flors? Neus, gels e conglapis,
Que cotz e destrenh e trenca,
Don vey morz quils, critz, brays, siscles
Pels fuels, pels rams e pels giscles;
Mas mi te vert e jauzen joys,
Er quan vey secx los dolens croys.

Quar enaissi o enverse
Que·l bel plan mi semblon tertre,
E tenc per flor lo conglapi,
E·l cautz m'es vis que·l freit trenque,
E·l tro mi semblo chant e siscle,
E paro·m fulhat li giscle;
Aissi·m suy ferms lassatz en joy
Qeu re no vey que·m sia croy,

Mas una gen fada enversa,
Cum s'eron noirit en tertres,
Que·m fan pro pieigz que conglapis
Qu'us quecx ab sa lengua trenca
E·n parla bas et ab siscles;
E no y val bastos ni giscles
Ni menassas, ans lur es joys,
Quan fan so don hom los clam croys.

Qu'ar en baizan no·us enverse,
No m'o tolon plan ni tertre,
Dona, ni gel ni conglapi;
Mas non-poder trop m'en trenque.
Dona, per cuy chant e siscle,
Vostre belh huelh mi son giscle
Que·m castion si·l cor ab joy
Qu'ieu non aus aver talan croy.

Splendid Are the Flowers Reversed

Raimbaut d'Aurenga

Splendid are the flowers reversed
Among sharp crags, among the hills.
Flowers? Snow and ice and hoarfrost
That sting, destroy, and make their cuts.
So I perceive calls, chirps, and chips
Dead among leaves, branches, and sticks:
Joy's what keeps me green and glad;
Shriveled is all that I find bad.

So I perceive all things reversed:
Beautiful plains instead of hills;
I take for flower the pale hoarfrost,
Perceive some warmth that the chill has cut.
Thunder sounds like warbles and chips;
Leaves embellish the barren sticks:
So firmly am I bound to glad-
ness, no one seems to me that bad . . .

. . . Save for those foolish folk reversed
Who act like they were raised in hills.
They do more harm than any hoarfrost
When with their sharp tongues they cut:
Murmuring words, sibilant chips—
Against these neither rod nor stick
Avail—nor threat—it makes them glad
To do what men consider bad.

To kiss you, holding you reversed,
What now can stop me? Neither hill
Nor plain, lady, nor ice, nor frost.
Only one thing my will can cut:
Lady for whom I sing and chip,
Your lovely eyes flay me like sticks.
So mortified am I by glad-
ness my heart can harbor nothing bad.

Anat ai cum cauz' enversa
Sercan rancx e vals e tertres,
Marritz cum selh que conglapis
Cocha e mazelh' e trenca,
Qu'anc no·m conquis chans ni siscles
Plus que fols clercx conquer giscles.
Mas ar, Dieu lau, m'alberga joys
Mal grat dels fals lauzengiers croys.

Mos vers an, qu'aissi l'enverse
Que no·l tenhon bosc ni tertre,
Lai on hom non sen conglapi
Ni a freitz poder que y trenque:
A midons lo chant e·l siscle
Clar, qu'el cor l'en intro·l giscle,
Selh que sap gen chantar ab joy,
Que no·s tanh a chantador croy.

Doussa dona, amors e joys
Nos ten ensems mal grat dels croys.

Jocglar, granre ai menhs de joy,
Quar no·us vey e·n fas semblan croy.

I've wandered like some thing reversed,
Searching through crags, valleys, and hills,
Distracted like a man whom the frost
Bites while it torments and cuts.
Never before did songs or chips
Flay me, no more than a priest by sticks:
But now, praise God, I'm saved by glad-
ness, even from slanderers false and bad.

Go my song—you're so reversed
You shouldn't be stopped by woods or hill—
Travel to where man's free from hoarfrost,
Where the chill's lost power to cut.
Sing to my lady—chant and chip
So clearly that her heart by sticks
Is pierced: sing it full out and glad;
This is no song for one who's bad.

Sweetest lady, love and glad-
ness preserve us from those who are bad.

Singer, I find I'm not so glad—
You don't return; I appear sad.

Robert Kehew

Escotatz, mas no say que s'es

Raimbaut d'Aurenga

Escotatz, mas no say que s'es
Senhor, so que vuelh comensar.
Vers, estribot, ni sirventes
Non es, ni nom no·l sai trobar;
Ni ges no say co·l mi fezes
S'aytal no·l podi' acabar,
Que ia hom mays non vis fag aytal ad home ni a femna en
    est segle ni en l'autre qu'es passatz.

Sitot m'o tenetz a foles
Per tan no·m poiria layssar
Que ieu mon talan non disses:
No m'en cujes hom castiar;
Tot cant es non pres un pojes
Vas so c'ades vey et esgar,
E dir vos ay per que. Car si ieu vos o avia mogut, e no·us
    o trazia a cap, tenriatz m'en per fol. Car mais
    amaria seis deniers en mon punh que mil sols
    el cel.

Ja no·m tema ren far que·m pes
Mos amicx, aisso·l vuelh prejar;
S'als obs no·m vol valer manes
Pus m'o profer' ab lonc tarzar;
Pus leu que selh que m'a conques
No·m pot nulh autre galiar.
Tot ayso dic per una domna que·m fay languir ab belas
    paraulas et ab lonc respieg, no say per que.
        Pot me bon' esser, senhors?

Beg Pardon, Lords

Raimbaut d'Aurenga

Beg pardon, Lords, but who knows what
Kind of a song this is I'll sing?
Ballad, or blues or protest song?[2]
What do you call this sort of thing?
How can you say what's right, what's wrong?
How can I end it warranting
    that nobody ever saw one like it, made by man or by woman,
    in this whole century or the one just past?

You'll try to tell me I'm insane
But that won't make me break my vow
To speak my feelings clear and plain.
Don't blame me if I can't see how
This wide world could be worth one grain
Compared to things I see right now.
    I'll tell you why, too: if I started this thing and couldn't bring
    it off, you'd think I'm an idiot. I'd rather have six cents in hand
    than a thousand suns in the sky.

No friends of mine need ever fear
They'll anger me by things they've done;
If they can't help me now, this year,
They can relieve me later on—
Still, she defeats and cheats me here
More ardently than anyone—
    I say all this because of a lady who keeps me hanging on, with
    sweet talk and lots of waiting. My Lords, can she do me any good?

Que ben a passatz quatre mes,
(Oc! e mays de mil ans so·m par)
Que m'a autrejat e promes
Que·m dara so que m'es pus car.
Dona! Pus mon cor tenetz pres
Adossatz me ab dous l'amar.
Dieus, aiuda! In nomine patris et filii et spiritus sancti!
    Aiso, que sera, domna?

Qu'eiu soy per vos gays, d'ira ples;
Iratz-jauzens me faytz trobar;
E so m'en partitz de tals tres
Qu'el mon non a, mas vos, lur par;
E soy fols cantayre cortes
Tan c'om m'en apela ioglar.
Dona, far ne podetz a vostra guiza, co fes n'Ayma de
    l'espatla que la estujet lay on li plac.

Er fenisc mo no-say-que-s'es,
C'aisi l'ay volgut batejar;
Pus mays d'aital non auzi jes
Be·l dey enaysi apelar;
E diga·l, can l'aura apres,
Qui que s'en vuelha azautar.
E si hom li demanda qui l'a fag, pot dir que sel que
    sap be far totas fazendas can se vol.

It's been a full four months or more—
Yes, but a thousand years seem less—
Since she gave in to me and swore
She'd give what I long to possess.
My heart's your prisoner, therefore,
Lady, sweeten my bitterness.
    God help me! *In nomine patri et filii et spiritus sancti!* Lady,
    what's coming off?

You make me rage, make me cavort;
You make me write songs fierce with glee;
I've left three ladies of a sort
Who had no peer but you, Lady.
For these mad love songs through the court
Crooner's the name they're calling me.
    Lady, do just anything you please with me—like Lady Emma
    with the shoulder bone: she stuck it in just anyplace it pleased her.

Here's where I'll end my *What's its Name*
Since that's the label I've devised;
No other song sounds much the same;
That's how I'll have the thing baptized.
You'll like it best if you declaim
The whole thing once it's memorized.
    And if anybody ever asks you who made this thing, just say it's
    a man who knows how to do lots of things, and do them right
    just any time he wants to.

    W. D. Snodgrass

Guiraut de Bornelh

> [Guiraut de Bornelh] was from . . . Limoges. He was of low birth, but he was wise in matters of letters and had great natural intelligence. And he was the best troubadour of any of those who came before or after him. For this reason he was called Master of the Troubadours. . . . His life was such that he spent all winter in school learning letters, and all summer going from court to court, taking with him two jongleurs who sang his songs. But he never wanted to marry, and everything he earned he gave to poor relatives and to the church in the town where he was born.[1]

Guiraut de Bornelh's period of activity, from about 1165 to 1199, spans much of the golden age of the troubadours. He visited many courts in southern France and also in Aragon and Castile in Spain. Richard the Lion-hearted patronized Guiraut, and the troubadour accompanied the viscount of Limoges on the Third Crusade, which was led by Richard.

Being called *maestre dels trobadors* has proved a mixed blessing for Guiraut de Bornelh. At his peak he was highly respected. The biographer of the slightly earlier Peire d'Alvernhe noted that Guiraut unseated Peire as "the finest troubadour in the world." But later, when Guiraut himself was surpassed by Arnaut Daniel, the title "Master of the Troubadours" came back to mock him. In his *Comedy,* Dante concluded that "only fools claim Limoges produced a better" troubadour than Arnaut Daniel.[2] In the first half of the twentieth century, the French critic Jeanroy was even harsher: "This so-called 'Master of the Troubadours' seems to us like an infatuated pedant, pompously spinning out his banalities. . . . He reminds one of a tenor as pleased with himself as he is displeased with a public whom he cannot forgive for not going into ecstasies over his vocal flourishes."[3] Should we leave this once highly regarded troubadour in eclipse?

Guiraut de Bornelh writes with an effortless lyricism, where form admirably serves his meaning. This fusion of form and content produces what Bonner describes as the "immutable, hard, almost rock-like quality" of Guiraut's verse (*Songs of the Troubadours,* 115–16). In the second selection below ("Can lo freitz e·l glatz e la neus" or "When the Ice and Cold and Snow Retreat") note, for example, the way in which an extended conceit fills the fourth stanza to the brim but does not spill over. Van Vleck characterizes such writing as "more impressive [than the verse of earlier troubadours] for the sustained development of a single argument within a slightly longer stanza." She also offers an insightful interpretation of this work, pointing out how the sudden appearance of a ring half-way through the poem marks a turning point in the protagonist's attitude toward his lady: from elation to powerlessness ("The Lyric Texts," 32, 45–48).

Guiraut de Bornelh is, in a way, a victim of his own poetic success. His versatility and lack of mannerisms make him hard to pigeonhole. Unlike other troubadours, Guiraut does not specialize in any particular form: he seems equally at ease in turning out *cansos* (around 40), *sirventeses* (around 30), *tensos* (3), crusade songs (2), *planhs* (2), an *alba,* and so on. This *alba* or dawn song, incidentally, the first selection below ("Reis glorios" or "Day's Glorious Lord"), remains his best-known poem: it is still magnificent when sung. Guiraut also is hard to categorize in other ways. While he defended the "easy" *trobar leu* school of poetry (in a *tenso* with Raimbaut d'Aurenga), his natural proclivity toward spit-polish verse would seem to place him in the *trobar ric* camp.

But versatility is not a failing; on the contrary. Given his considerable strengths as a poet, today it doesn't seem to do any harm to restore to Guiraut de Bornelh the title of Master of the Troubadours. Perhaps we can only whisper parenthetically: "until Arnaut Daniel."

Reis glorios

Guiraut de Bornelh

Reis glorios, verais lums e clartatz,
Deus poderos, Senher, si a vos platz,
Al meu companh sïatz fizels ajuda,
Qu'eu non lo vi pos la nochs fo venguda,
    E ades sera l'alba.

Bel companho, si dormetz o veillatz?
Non dormatz plus, suau vos ressidatz,
Qu'en orïent vei l'estela creguda
Qu'amen·l jorn, qu'eu lai ben coneguda,
    E ades sera l'alba.

Bel companho, en chantan vos apel:
Non dormatz plus, qu'eu aug chantar l'auzel
Que vai queren lo jorn per lo boscatge,
Et ai paor que·l gilos vos assatge,
    E ades sera l'alba.

Bel companho, eissetz al fenestrel,
Et esgardatz las ensenhas del cel;
Conoisseretz si·us sui fizels messatge:
Si non o faitz, vostres n'er lo damnatge,
    E ades sera l'alba.

Bel companho, pos mi parti de vos,
Eu no·m dormi ni·m moc de ginolhos,
Ans preguei Deu, lo filh Santa Maria,
Que·us me rendes per lejal companhia,
    E ades sera l'alba.

Bel companho, la foras als peiros
Me prejavatz qu'eu no fos dormilhos,
Enans velhes tota noch tro al dia;
Aras no·us platz mos chans ni ma paria,
    E ades sera l'alba.[4]

Day's Glorious Lord

Guiraut de Bornelh

Day's glorious Lord, true clarity and light,
Earth's Emperor, in majesty and might,
Protect my friend who vanished from these eyes' sight
Leaving me here on guard in fading twilight;
    Now soon outshines all dawn's light.

My faithful friend, there where you sleep or rise,
Sleep you no more; in safety lift your eyes.
Far Orient, the morning star stands gleaming
Leading the day that drives us all from dreaming
    And soon outshines all dawn's light.

My faithful friend, I sing what you must hear
So sleep no more. The skylark's cries ring clear;
He seeks the light, beneath the branches flying.
Some jealous soul might find you where you're lying;
    And soon outshines all dawn's light.

My faithful friend, sit by your window high;
Come recognize day's banners through the sky;
Learn how your friend has kept his night-watch loyal;
Open your eyes or see your swift betrayal;
    For soon outshines all dawn's light.

My faithful friend, since last you left me here
I paced on guard or bent my knee in prayer
That our dear Lord, the spotless son of Mary,
Return you safe; then wake, no longer tarry;
    Now soon outshines all dawn's light.

My faithful friend, while parting on the stair
Last night you pled and made your heart-felt prayer
I'd wake all night to keep my watch untiring;
But care and song seem far from your desiring
    Though soon outshines all dawn's light.

W. D. Snodgrass

Can lo freitz e·l glatz e la neus

Guiraut de Bornelh

Can lo freitz e·l glatz e la neus
S'en fuich e torna la calors
E reverdis lo gens pascors
Et auch las voutas dels auzeus,
M'es aitant beus
Lo dotz tems a l'issen de martz,
Que plus sui salhens que leupartz
E vils non es cabrols ni sers.
Si la bela cui sui profers
Mi vol onrar
De tant qe·m denhe sofertar
Q'ieu sia sos fis entendens,
Sobre totz sui rics e manens.

Tant es sos cors gais et isneus
E complitz de belas colors
C'anc de rosier no nasquet flors
Plus fresca ni de nuils brondeus,
Ni anc Bordeus
Non ac senhor fos plus galhartz
De me, si ja m'acuoill ni partz
Tan que fos sos dominis sers,
E fos apelatz de Bezers,
Can ja parlar
M'auziri' om de nulh celar
Qu'ela·m disses, privadamens,
Don s'azires lo seus cors gens!

Bona domna, lo vostr' aneus
Qe·m detz, mi fai tan de socors
Qu'en lui refranhi mas dolors;
Can lo remir, e·n torn plus leus
C'us estorneus,
Puois sui per lui aissi auzartz
Que no·us cuidetz, lansa ni dartz
M'espaven ni acers ni fers

When the Ice and Cold and Snow Retreat

Guiraut de Bornelh

When the ice and cold and snow retreat
And warmth creeps back into the land,
When spring revives the greenness, and
The birds their melodies repeat,
    Then the sweet
Time at end of March is so pleasing
That like a leopard I am leaping;
Neither stag nor goat was ever
So swift. If she to whom I offer
    Myself as gift
Chose to accept, that honor would lift
Me over all men in wealth and power...
To the degree that she'd *let* me love her.

Lithe and quick her body flows,
With lovely colors it is completed;
Never was such fresh bloom exceeded
By rose or any other bough.
    Nor has Bordeaux
Possessed a lord so lively ever
As I would be if, apart or together,
She were mine and I were hers.
Call me a madman from Beziers[5]
    If I were heard
Repeating something that she'd shared
With me in confidence; thus betrayed,
That gentle heart would fill with rage!

Gracious lady, the precious ring
That you conferred upon me greatly
Helps, it makes my woes less heavy.
Gazing on it, suddenly I'm
    Light as a starling.
Because of you I take new heart:
I know neither arrow nor dart
Can harm me; no, nor steel can touch,

E d'autra part sui plus despers
Per sobramar
Que naus, qan vai torban per mar
Destrecha d'ondas e de vens,
Aissi·m destrenh lo pensamens.

Domna, aissi co·l frevols chasteus
Q'es assetjatz per fortz senhors,
Can la peiriera fraing las tors
E·l calabres e·l manganeus
Et es tant greus
La guerra devas totas partz
Que no lor ten pro genhs ni artz
E·l dols e·l critz es grans e fers
De cels dedins qe ant grans gers,
Sembla·us ni·us par
Quez aia·n merce a cridar
Aissi·us clam merce umilmens,
Bona domna, et avinens.

Domna, aissi com us paucs anheus
Non a forsa contra un ors,
Sui ieu, si la vostra valors
No·m val, plus febles c'us rauzeus,
Et er plus breus
Ma vida de las catre partz,
S'uoimais mi pren negus destartz,
Que no·m fassatz drech de l'envers.
E tu, fin' Amors, que·m sofers,
Que deus gardar
Los fis amans e chapdellar,
Sias me chabdeus e guirens
A ma domna, pos aissi·m vens!

Joglars, ab aquestz sos noveus
T'en vai, e·ls portaras de cors
A la bela, cui nais ricors,
E digas li qu'eu sui plus seus
Que sos manteus.[6]

Nor iron. Then, through overmuch
    Loving I'm lost—
Like a ship spun round and tossed
By wind and wave on sundering seas,
So my thoughts do pummel me.

Lady, as when lords with power
Besiege a castle, bringing to bear
Their catapult, perrier
And mangonel to topple tower;
    And war harder
Hits, gathering from all quarters, and
No amount of cunning can
Save the besieged: wrenching the cries
Then, the anguished shrieks of those inside—
    They are, you see,
Reduced to clamoring for mercy—
So I beg that you might save me,
Good and kind and gentle lady.

A lamb, my lady, is indeed
Powerless against a bear;
So I, who cannot claim one share
Of your strength, am weaker than a reed.
    My life would be
Over in a second's fraction,
If any harm my way should happen;
Yet what is mine you still deny me.
I pray, True Love, you'll fortify me;
    May God remove
From ways of folly those who love
Truly. As guide and witness aid me:
See how I'm conquered by my lady.

    Robert Kehew

Peire Bremon lo Tort

> Peire Bremon lo Tort was a poor knight from Viennois, and he was a good inventor of poetry and was honored by all the notable men.[1]

Peire Bremon lo Tort was not a major troubadour. Neither during his lifetime nor since has he excited much attention. His medieval biographer could not even bestir himself to speculate on the origin of his nickname, "lo Tort" or "the twisted one"—probably a blunt reference to some physical deformity. Peire's reputation, in fact, was so slight that Ezra Pound feared he would be totally forgotten and his surviving work erroneously lumped in with the songs of another, more illustrious troubadour, Guiraut de Bornelh (see Pound, *Collected Early Poems*, 93).

One of Peire's few claims to fame is the fact that he was the first troubadour known to have found patronage in Italy. We surmise that he spent some time in Casale, the site where the marquises of Monferrat held court, because in 1176 or 1177 he addressed the poem below, "En abril, quan vey verdeyar" ("From Syria"), to William Longsword. That gentleman was the eldest son of William, third marquis of Monferrat, who was then in Palestine. In the following decades, Casale won renown from traveling troubadours and *joglars* as a haven of culture and patronage. It served as a beachhead for further troubadour inroads into Italy.[2]

Despite—or, perhaps, because of—Peire's relative obscurity, Ezra Pound championed him. Much as later he would promote the works of up-and-coming poets such as Robert Frost and T. S. Eliot, a precocious Pound urged for Peire's obscure "En abril" to be remembered alongside such recognized troubadour masterpieces as Bernart de Ventadorn's "Can vei la lauzeta mover" and Peire Vidal's "Ab l'alen tir vas me l'aire" (*Spirit of Romance*, 48).

Peire apparently wrote the present selection "from Syria" (as Pound would have it). The Syria referred to was most likely the Christian county of Tripoli, a vital link for the Crusaders between the principality of Antioch to the north and the kingdom of Jerusalem to the south. This would have been an uneasy time in Tripoli—from his base in Damascus to the east, an upstart teenager named Saladin was then consolidating his grip on Moslem Syria. A decade later, Saladin would be prepared to wrest Jerusalem from the Crusaders.[3] Did Peire don the white-hooded mantle of the Templars? This and other facts about Peire's time in Syria remain unknown.

No doubt a part of the appeal of Peire's poem, for Pound as well as for the modern reader, lies in its fresh handling of the subject of "distant love." We can read this poem in light of the earlier work by Jaufre Rudel or else, because of the universality of the theme, on its own merits, without any need for the echoing chords of literary allusion.

En abril, quan vey verdeyar

Peire Bremon lo Tort

En abril, quan vey verdeyar
Los pratz vertz e·ls vergiers florir
E vey las aiguas esclarzir
Et aug los auselletz chantar,
 L'odors de l'erba floria
  E·l dous chanz que l'auzels cria
Mi fay mon ioy renovellar.

En cest temps soli' yeu pensar
Cossi·m pogues d'amor iauzir:
Ab cavalgar et ab garnir
Et ab servir et ab onrar;
 Qui aquestz mestiers auria,
  Per els es amors iauzia
E deu la·n hom mielhs conquistar.

Yeu chant, qui deuria plorar,
Qu'ira d'amor me fai languir;
Ab chantar mi cug esbaudir;
Et anc mais no·n auzi parlar
 Qu' hom chant qui plorar deuria.
  Pero no·m desesper mia,
Qu'enquer auray luec de chantar.

No·m dey del tot desesperar
Qu'ieu enquer midons non remir,
Qu'aisselh qui la m'a fag gequir
A ben poder del recobrar;
 E s'ieu era en sa bailia,
  Si mai tornava en Suria,
Ia Dieus no m'en laisses tornar.

From Syria

Peire Bremon lo Tort

In April when I see all through
Mead and garden new flowers blow,
And streams with ice-bands broken flow,
Eke hear the birds their singing do;
When spring's grass-perfume floateth by
Then 'tis sweet song and birdlet's cry
Do make mine old joy come anew.

Such time was wont my thought of old
To wander in the ways of love.
Burnishing arms and clang thereof,
And honour-services manifold
Be now my need. Whoso combine
Such works, love is his bread and wine,
Wherefore should his fight the more be bold.

Song bear I, who tears should bring
Sith ire of love mak'th me annoy,
With song think I to make me joy.
Yet ne'er have I heard said this thing:
"He sings who sorrow's guise should wear."
Natheless I will not despair
That sometime I'll have cause to sing.

I should not to despair give way
That somewhile I'll my lady see.
I trust well He that lowered me
Hath power again to make me gay.
But if e'er I come to my Love's land
And turn again to Syrian strand,
God keep me there for a fool, alway!

Ben se dec Dieus meravillar
Car anc mi poc de lieys partir,
E dec m'o ben en grat tenir
Quan per luy la volgui laissar;
   Qu'el sap ben, s'ieu la perdia,
   Que ia mais ioy non auria,
Ni elh no la·m pogr'esmendar.

Mout me saup gent lo cor emblar,
Quan pris comiat de chai venir,
Que non es iorns qu'ieu non sospir
Per un bel semblan que·l vi far,
   Qu'ella·m dis tuta marria:
  "Que fara la vostr'amia,
Bels amics? per que·m vols laissar?"

Chanzos, tu·t n'iras outra mar,
E, per Deu, vai a midons dir
Qu'en gran dolor et en cossir
Me fai la nuoit e·l iorn estar.
   Di·m a'n Guillelm Longa-Espia,
   Bona chanzos, qu'el li·t dia
E que i an per lieys confortar.

God for a miracle well should
Hold my coming from her away,
And hold me in His grace always
That I left her, for holy-rood.
An I lose her, no joy for me,
Pardi,[4] hath the wide world in fee.
Nor could He mend it, if He would.

Well did she know sweet wiles to take
My heart, when thence I took my way.
'Thout sighing, pass I ne'er a day
For that sweet semblance she did make
To me, saying all in sorrow:
"Sweet friend, and what of me to-morrow?"
"Love mine, why wilt me so forsake?"

ENVOI
Beyond sea be thou sped, my song,
And, by God, to my Lady say
That in desirous, grief-filled way
My nights and my days are full long.
And command thou William the Long-Seer[5]
To tell thee to my Lady dear,
That comfort be her thoughts among.

Ezra Pound

Bertran de Born

En Bertran . . . was brought to King Henry's pavilion and there was received very badly. And King Henry said to him, "Bertran, Bertran, you once said you never needed more than half your wits, but now you may be sure that you will need them all." "My Lord," said En Bertran, "it is true that I said that, and I spoke the truth." And the king said, "But now it would seem you have lost your wits altogether." "My Lord," said En Bertran, "indeed I have." "And how is that?" asked the king. "My Lord," said En Bertran, "the day your son, the valiant Young King died, I lost my wits, judgment and mind."

And when the king saw En Bertran's tears and heard what he said of his son, a great grief entered his heart and eyes, and he could not keep from fainting. And when he had recovered, he called out and said in tears, "En Bertran, En Bertran, it was only right that you should lose your wits for my son, for he loved you more than any other man in the world. And I, for love of him, shall set you free—your person, your belongings and your castle—and I shall grant you my love and my favor, and I shall also give you five hundred marks of silver for the injury you have received." And En Bertran fell at his feet, giving him thanks and gratitude.[1]

That it was Richard the Lion-hearted who captured Bertran de Born and destroyed his castle, and not Henry II of England as this *razo* implies,[2] does not detract from the charm of the tale; nor do these inaccuracies lessen the fundamental insight that the story offers into the life and times of the wily troubadour. For Bertran was born (around 1140) into a complex and shift-ing "network of ambitions, alliances and conflicts" dominated by local barons.³ But, much as they quarreled with each other, the southern lords shared a greater common fear: that one day the mighty kings of France and England might join forces and move together upon the lands of the south. So, to the best of his ability, Bertran de Born tried to manipulate and dis-tract the northern powers. As his medieval biographer explained:

> Whenever he so wished, [Bertran de Born] could dominate King Henry and his sons, but he always wanted them to be at war with one another—father, son and brother. And he always wanted the kings of France and England to be at war with each other. And if there was a peace or truce, he would try by means of his sirventes to undo it and prove how each had been dishonored by this peace.⁴

No wonder Dante would find Bertran to be an archetypical stirrer-up of strife. Here the Tuscan poet encounters the troubadour in the lurid light of the *Inferno*:

> Surely I saw, and still before my eyes
> Goes on that headless trunk, that bears for light
> Its own head swinging, gripped by the dead hair,
> And like a swinging lamp that says, "Ah me!
> I severed men, my head and heart
> Ye see here severed, my life's counterpart."⁵

Thus En Bertran's poems, written during the last two decades of the twelfth century, often represent an outgrowth or statement of his bellicose policy and spirit. In the first selection, "Be·m platz lo gais temps de pascor" ("A War Song"), for example, Bertran amusingly counsels his fellow barons to pawn their castles, because if they triumph they can redeem their posses-sions, while if they lose the debt falls to the victors. In this unusual source of poetic inspiration, Bertran de Born finds his original voice as a poet—of war. He does not wring his hands about armed conflict; rather, as the first two selections reveal, he unashamedly revels in the primitive emotions that it brings up. At the same time this barbaric side of his nature incongruously coexists with a refined poetic discernment. In our first selection, for ex-ample, note how the troubadour orchestrates the poem's striking effect by first lulling the listener into anticipating a joyous *canso* about love, then veering abruptly into a *sirventes* that celebrates the battlefield.

While he delights in battle, Bertran de Born also finds time to take off his hauberk and write songs about other topics. In our third selection ("Domna pois de me no'us cal" or "Lady, Since You Care Nothing for Me"), Bertran, spurned in love, tries to console himself by imaginatively assembling his ideal beauty from attributes borrowed from the women of his acquaintance: a limb here, a lock of hair there. Yet even in this apparently innocuous (if distasteful) pastime, Ezra Pound, who translated this poem, suspected that Bertran once again was "playing the desperate chess." In his own poem about the conniving troubadour, "Near Perigord," Pound advanced the theory that, in this song, Bertran sought to convey tactical information to his confederates through coded references. Every lady stood for a castle. The *joglar* sings, and

> No one hears aught save the gracious sound of compliments.
> Sir Arrimon counts on his fingers, Montfort,
> Rochecouart, Chalais, the rest, the tactic,
> Malemort, guesses beneath, sends word to Coeur-de-Lion.

While this provocative thesis has attracted few, if any, adherents, it is, broadly speaking, by no means inconsistent with Bertran's character or the times in which he lived.[6]

The fourth selection ("Ieu m'escondisc" or "He Protests His Innocence to a Lady") is an example, rare in the troubadour corpus, of an *escondich,* a poetic defense against an accusation. The reference in the fifth stanza to siblings squabbling over property ownership is an autobiographical snippet. En Bertran begrudgingly shared the family castle at Hautefort with siblings—male primogeniture only gradually displaced other practices of inheritance in southern France in the Middle Ages—until the troubadour apparently gave his brother the boot.

In the fifth selection ("Belh m'es" or "The Secret to Staying Young"), En Bertran enters the lists on the courtly concern of what characterizes youth (*joven*). Beginning with Marcabru, the troubadours were fascinated by the notion that aging, as an *attitude,* progresses at a different speed from the strictly chronological process. (Lazar posits that Marcabru, in turn, may have picked up this theme from Arabic sources while visiting courts in Castile.)[7] At the same time that the poem celebrates youth, it also shows its author bowing his head to the succession of generations and the passage of time.

After years of fighting, Sir Bertran entered a monastery. The one-time stirrer-up of strife took last rites sometime early in the thirteenth century. God had mercy on En Bertran: he did not live long enough to witness an age when even his formidable skills at pitting power against power would not have been enough to stave off disaster—an age when the church militant and the forces of France finally succeeded in overrunning his beloved south.

Be·m platz lo gais temps de pascor

Bertran de Born

Be·m platz lo gais temps de pascor,
Que fai fuoillas e flors venir;
E platz mi, qand auch la baudor
Dels auzels, que fan retentir
Lor chan per lo boscatge;
E platz mi, qand vei per los pratz
Tendas e pavaillons fermatz;
Et ai gran alegratge,
Qand vei per campaignas rengatz
Cavalliers e cavals armatz.

E platz mi, qan li corredor
Fan las gens e l'aver fugir;
E platz mi, qand vei apres lor
Gran ren d'armatz ensems venir;
E platz m'en mon coratge,
Qand vei fortz chastels assetgatz
E·ls barris rotz et esfondratz
E vei l'ost el ribatge,
Q'es tot entorn claus de fossatz
Ab lissas de fortz pals serratz.

E atressi·m platz de seignor,
Qand es primiers a l'envazir
En caval, armatz, ses temor,
Q'aissi fai los sieus enardir
Ab valen vassalatge.
E pois que l'estorns es mesclatz,
Chascus deu esser acesmatz
E segre·l d'agradatge,
Que nuills om non es ren prezatz,
Tro q'a maintz colps pres e donatz.

A War Song

Bertran de Born

Well pleaseth me the sweet time of Easter
That maketh the leaf and the flower come out.
And it pleaseth me when I hear the clamor
Of the birds, their song through the wood;
And it pleaseth me when I see through the meadows
The tents and pavilions set up, and great joy have I
When I see o'er the campagna knights armed and horses arrayed.

And it pleaseth me when the scouts set in flight the folk with their
    goods;
And it pleaseth me when I see coming together after
    them an host of armed men.
And it pleaseth me to the heart when I see strong
    castles besieged,
And barriers broken and riven, and I see the host on
    the shore all about shut in with ditches,
And closed in with lisses of strong piles.

Thus that lord pleaseth me when he is first to attack, fearless, on his armed
charger; and thus he emboldens his folk with valiant vassalage, and then
when stour is mingled, each wight should be yare, and follow him
exulting; for no man is worth a damn till he has taken and given many a
blow.

Massas e brans, elms de color,
Escutz traucar e desgarnir
Veirem a l'intrar de l'estor
E maintz vassals ensems ferir,
Don anaran arratge
Caval dels mortz e dels nafratz.
E qand er en l'estorn intratz,
Chascus om de paratge
Non pens mas d'asclar caps e bratz,
Que mais val mortz que vius sobratz.

E·us dic que tant no m'a sabor
Manjar ni beure ni dormir
Cum a, qand auch cridar: "A lor!"
D'ambas las partz et auch bruïr
Cavals voitz per l'ombratge,
Et auch cridar: "Aidatz!, aidatz!"
E vei cazer per los fossatz
Paucs e grans per l'erbatge,
E vei los mortz que pels costatz
An los tronzos ab los cendatz.

Baron, metetz en gatge
Castels e vilas e ciutatz
Enans qu'usqecs no·us guerreiatz!

Papiol, d'agradatge
Ad Oc-e-No t'en vai viatz
E digas li que trop estai en patz.

We shall see battle axes and swords, a-battering colored haumes and a-hacking through shields at entering melee; and many vassals smiting together, whence there run free the horses of the dead and wrecked. And when each man of prowess shall be come into the fray he thinks no more of (merely) breaking heads and arms, for a dead man is worth more than one taken alive.

I tell you that I find no such savor in eating butter and sleeping, as when I hear cried "On them!" and from both sides hear horses neighing through their head-guards, and hear shouted "To aid! To aid!" and see the dead with lance truncheons, the pennants still on them, piercing their sides.

Barons! put in pawn castles, and towns, and cities before anyone makes war on us.

Papiol, be glad to go speedily to "Yea and Nay," and tell him there's too much peace about.[8]

Ezra Pound

Un sirventes on motz no falh

Bertran de Born

Un sirventes on motz no falh
Ai fach, qu'anc no·m costet un alh,
Et ai apres un'aital art
Que, s'ai fraire, germa ni quart,
　　Part li l'uou e la mezalha,
E s'el puois vol la mia part
　　Ieu l'en get de comunalha.

Tot mo sen tenh dintz mo serralh,
Si tot m'an donat gran trebalh
Entre n'Azemar e·n Richart.
Lonc temps m'an tengut en reguart;
　　Mas aras an tal baralha
Que lor enfan, si·l reis no·ls part,
　　N'auran pro en la coralha.

Tot iorn resoli e retalh
Los baros e·ls refon e·ls calh,
Que cuiava metre en eissart;
E sui be fols quar m'en reguart,
　　Qu'ilh son de peior obralha
Que non es lo fers Saint Launart,
　　Per qu'es fols qui s'en trebalha.

Talairans no trota ni salh
Ni no·s muou de son arenalh
Ni no dopta lanza ni dart;
Anz viu a guiza de Lombart.
　　Tant es farzitz de nualha
Que, quan l'autra gens si compart,
　　El s'estendilh'e badalha.

Quarrels Where Words Don't Miss Fire

Bertran de Born

Quarrels where words don't miss fire
Have I made: that cost me never a garlic,
And I have moreover learned such skill
That if I have brother, cousin, cousins, son,
I share egg and penny,
And if he then wish my part,
I throw it into the common lot.

So all must my brain have I in my custody.
Altho as they have given me great trouble
Between Sir Azemar and Sir Richard,[9]
Long time have they held me in fear.
But now have they such strife
That their children, if the king part them not,
Will not have worth in the brain.

Everyday I resole and resew together
The barons, re-fuse, melt, and stir 'em up together,
Whom I thought to put in carnage;
And I am well a fool because I was afraid to care about it,
For they are of the worst workhands (the iron St. Lunart),[10]
Whereby he is a fool who bothers about them.

Talairan[11] neither trots nor gallops,
Nor is moved from his sand heap,
Nor fear shakes, lays up lance nor dart;
Rather I see him like a Lombard,
So is he filled full of laziness
That when the other folk take sides,
He stretches himself and yawns.

Guilhelms de Gordo, fol batalh
Avetz mes a vostre sonalh,
Et ieu am vos, si Dieus mi guart!
Pero per fol e per musart
   Vos tenon de la fermalha
Li dui vescomte, et es lor tart
   Que siatz en lor batalha.

Tot iorn contendi e·m baralh,
M'escrim e·m defen e·m tartalh,
E·m fon hom ma terra e la m'art
E·m fai de mos arbres eissart
   E mescla·l gra en la palha,
E non ai ardit ni coart
   Enemic qu'er no m'assalha.

A Peiregors, pres del muralh
Tan que i puosch'om gitar ab malh,
Venrai armatz sobre Baiart,
E se i trop Peitavi pifart,
   Veiran do mon bran com talha,
Que sus el chap li farai bart
   De cervel mesclat ab malha.

Baro, Dieus vos salf e vos guart
   E vos aiut e vos valha
E·us do que digatz a'n Richart
   So que·l paus dis a la gralha.

Guilhelms de Gordo, a fool bobbin and bone,
Have you put to your foil basket,
And I love you, so God grant me,
But for fool and for lazyman
They hold you of the contract,
The two viscounts, and it is late for their urge
That you be in their battle order.[12]

Everyday I contend and strive and cover myself
And defend and rush hither and thither,
And men tear down my land and burn me there
And make of my trees slaughter
And spill the corn in the stream,
And I have not bold nor coward enemy who doth
    Not now assail me.

At Perigord, near the wall,
So that their man could throw a mace,
I will come armed on Bayart,[13]
And if there I find the thick bellied Poitevin,[14]
They will see of my brand how it cuts,
That on his head I will make
Mush, mud, and brains mixed with the joints of his mail.

Baron, God save you and guard you
And aid you, and avail your strength,
And give you what you shall say to Sir Richard.
I know what the sow peacock said to the crow.[15]

    Ezra Pound

Domna, puois de me no·us chal

   Bertran de Born

Domna, puois de me no·us chal
E partit m'avetz de vos
Senes totas ochaisos,
No sai on m'enquieira;
Que ja mais
Non er per me tan rics jais
Cobratz; e, si del semblan
No trop domna a mon talan
Que valha vos qu'ai perduda,
Ja mais no vuolh aver druda.

Puois no·us puosc trobar engal,
Que fos tan bela ni pros,
Ni sos rics cors tan joios,
De tan bela tieira
Ni tan gais
Ni sos rics pretz tan verais,
Irai per tot achaptan
De chascuna un bel semblan
Per far domna soisseubuda,
Tro vos mi siatz renduda.

Frescha color natural
Pren, bels Cembelis, de vos
E·l doutz esgart amoros;
E fatz gran sobrieira
Quar re·i lais,
Qu'anc res de be no·us sofrais.
Midons n'Aelis deman
Son adrech parlar gaban,
Que·m don a midons aiuda;
Puois non er fada ni muda.

Lady, Since You Care Nothing for Me

Bertran de Born

Lady, since you care nothing for me,
And since you have shut me away from you
Causelessly,
I know not where to go seeking,
For certainly
I will never again gather
Joy so rich, and if I find not ever
A lady with look so speaking
To my desire, worth yours whom I have lost,
I'll have no other love at any cost.

And since I could not find a peer to you,
Neither one so fair, nor of such heart,
So eager and alert,
Nor with such art
In attire, nor so gay
Nor with gift so bountiful and so true,
I will go out a-searching,
Culling from each a fair trait
To make me a borrowed lady
Till I again find you ready.

Bels Cembelins, I take of you your colour,
For it's your own, and your glance
Where love is,
A proud thing I do here,
For, as to colour and eyes
I shall have missed nothing at all,
Having yours.
I ask of Midons Aelis (of Montfort)
Her straight speech free-running,
That my phantom lack not in cunning.

De Chales la vescomtal
Vuolh que·m done ad estros
La gola e·ls mas amdos.
Puois tenh ma charrieira,
No·m biais,
Ves Rochachoart m'eslais
Als pels n'Anhes que·m dara·n;
Qu' Iseutz, la domna Tristan,
Qu'en fo per totz mentauguda,
No·ls ac tan bels a saubuda.

N'Audiartz, si be·m vol mal,
Vuolh que·m do de sas faissos,
Que·lh estai gen liazos,
E quar es entieira,
Qu'anc no·s frais
S'amors ni·s vols en biais.
A mo Mielhs-de-be deman
Son adrech, nuou cors prezan,
De que par a la veguda,
La fassa bo tener nuda.

De na Faidid' autretal
Vuolh sas belas dens en dos,
L'acolhir e·l gen respos
Don es presentieira
Dintz son ais.
Mos Bels Miralhs vuolh que·m lais
Sa gaieza e son bel gran,
E quar sap son benestan
Far, don es reconoguda,
E no s'en chamja ni·s muda.

Bels Senher, ieu no·us quier al
Mas que fos tan cobeitos
D'aquesta com sui de vos;
Qu'una lechadieira
Amors nais,

At Chalais of the Viscountess, I would
That she give me outright
Her two hands and her throat,
So take I my road
To Rochechouart,
Swift-foot to my Lady Anhes,
Seeing that Tristan's lady Iseutz had never
Such grace of locks, I do ye to wit,
Though she'd the far fame for it.

Of Audiart at Malemort,
Though she with a full heart
Wish me ill,
I'd have her form that's laced
So cunningly,
Without blemish, for her love
Breaks not nor turns aside.
I of Miels-de-ben [16] demand
Her straight fresh body,
She is so supple and young,
Her robes can but do her wrong.

Her white teeth, of the Lady Faidita
I ask, and the fine courtesy
She hath to welcome one,
And such replies she lavishes
Within her nest;
Of Bels Mirals, [17] the rest,
Tall stature and gaiety,
To make these avail
She knoweth well, betide
No change nor turning aside.

Ah, Bels Senher, Maent, at last
I ask naught from you,
Save that I have such hunger for
This phantom
As I've for you, such flame-lap,

Don mos cors es tan lechais:
Mais vuolh de vos lo deman
Que autra tener baisan.
Doncs midons per que·m refuda,
Puois sap que tan l'ai volguda?

Papiols, mon Aziman
M'anaras dir en chantan
Qu'amors es desconoguda
Sai e d'aut bas chazeguda.[18]

And yet I'd rather
Ask of you than hold another,
Mayhap, right close and kissed.

Ah, lady, why have you cast
Me out, knowing you hold me so fast!

Ezra Pound

Ieu m'escondisc, domna, que mal no mier

Bertran de Born

Ieu m'escondisc, domna, que mal no mier
De so que·us an dich de mi lauzengier.
Per merce·us prec qu'om no puosca mesclar
Lo vostre cors fin, leial, vertadier,
Umil e franc, cortes e plazentier
Ab mi, domna, per messongas comtar.

Al primier get perda eu mon esparvier,
Que·l m'aucian el poing falcon lainier
E porton l'en, q'ieu·l lor veia plumar,
S'ieu non am mais de vos lo cossierier
Que de nuill' autra aver lo desirier
Qe·m don s'amor ni·m reteigna al colgar.

Autr' escondich vos farai plus sobrier,
E no mi puosc orar plus d'encombrier:
S'ieu anc failli vas vos neis del pensar,
Qan serem sol dinz cambra o en vergier,
Failla·m poders deves mon compaignier
De tal guisa que no·m posca aiudar.

S'ieu per jogar m'asset pres del taulier,
Ja no·i puosca baratar un denier
Ni ab "taula presa" no puosca entrar,
Anz get ades lo reir-azar derrier,
S'ieu autra domna deman ni enquier
Mas vos, cui am e desir e teing car.

Seigner sia eu de castel parsonier,
Et en la tor siam qatre parier,
E ja l'us l'autre no·ns poscam amar,
Anz m'aion ops totz temps arbalestier,
Metg' e sirven e gaitas e portier,
S'ieu anc aic cor d'autra domna amar.

He Protests His Innocence to a Lady

Bertran de Born

Pardon my lady, but I didn't do
What your flatterers have accused
Me of. Don't let a spat arise
Between your person—humble, true,
Loyal, generous, pleasant too—
And me, my lady, through their lies.

On its first flight, may falcons tear
My hawk from wrist and pluck it bare
Before my eyes and leave it dead,
If I do not prefer you over
Any other willing lover
Who'd like to keep me in her bed.

If ever I, in thought or action,
Failed you (and there's no stronger sanction
Than how I'll show I need no pardon),
When I'm in bed or where fruit trees flower,
Let every bit of my manly power
Fail me: let me lose my hard-on.

When I sit at a gaming table,
Make it so that I'm not able
To throw good dice or capture a square;
Rather, don't let me win a penny,
If I even think of wooing any-
One but you whom I hold dear.

May I live in a tower where
Four of us hold castle shares,
And we don't greatly love each other.
Let me be forever needing
Archers and guards and men to treat me
Medically, if I love another.

Ma domna·m lais per autre cavalier,
E pois, non sai a que, m'aia mestier;
E failla·m vens, quan serai sobre mar;
En cort de rei mi batan li portier;
Et en cocha fassa·l fugir primier,
Si no·us menti cel que·us anet comtar.[19]

Escut a col cavalc ieu ab tempier
E port sallat capairo traversier
E renhas breus qu'om no puesc' alongar
Et estreups loncs en caval bas, trotier;
Et a l'ostal truep irat l'ostalier,
Si no·us menti qui·us o anet comtar.

Fals, enveios, fe-mentit, lauzengier,
Pois ab midons m'avetz mes destorbier,
Be·us lauzera que·m laissassetz estar.

For some knight let my lady leave me,
Then let me be obscurely needy;
When I'm at sea let the wind be dying.
Let me bear the porters' blows,
And be the first to run from foes
If my accuser is not lying.

May I ride in a gale with my
Shield at neck, my hood awry,
My reins too short yet not adjustable;
Stirrups dangling on a short pony,
Innkeeper angry at me—*only*
If he who slanders me is trustable.

Envious liars, who have lately
Stirred up trouble with my lady,
I suggest you leave me straightly.

Robert Kehew

Belh m'es, quan vey camjar lo senhoratge

Bertran de Born

Belh m'es, quan vey camjar lo senhoratge,
Qe·lh vielh laixan als joves lur maisos,
E cascus pot giquir a son linhatge
Aitans d'efans que l'us puesc' esser pros.
Ladoncs m'es vis que·l segle renovelh
Mielhs que per flor ni per chantar d'auzelh.
E qui dona ni senhor pot camjar,
Vielh per jove, ben deu renovelar.

Per vielha tenc donna puois qu'a pelatge,
Et es vielha, quan cavalier non a.
Vielha la tenc, si de dos drutz s'apatge,
Et es vielha, si avols hom lo·il fa.
Vielha la tenc, si ama dins son chastelh,
Et es vielha, quan l'a ops de fachell.
Vielha la tenc, puois l'enuieion juglar,
Et es vielha, quan trop vuelha parlar.

Jov'es dona que sap onrar paratge,
Et es joves per bos fagz, quan los fa.
Joves se te, quan a adreg coratge
E vas bon pretz avol mestier non a.
Joves se te, quan garda son cors belh,
Et es joves dona, quan be·s chapdelh.
Joves se te, quan no·i cal devinar,
Qu'ab belh jovent si guart de mal estar.

Joves es om que lo sieu ben enguatge,
Et es joves, quan es ben sofraitos.
Joves se te quan pro·l costa ostatge,
Et es joves, quan fai estragatz dos.
Joves se te, quan art s'arqua e·l vaixelh,
E fai estorn e vouta e sembelh.
Joves se te quan li play domneyar,
Et es joves, quan ben l'aman juglar.

The Secret to Staying Young

Bertran de Born

It pleases me to see old men bequeathing
Their houses and to watch the power passing,
With every lord so many children leaving
That one at least is sure to be surpassing
In worth. That is how the world is renewed—
More than through singing bird or opening bud.
And whosoever, be it lady or lord,
Exchanges old for young will be restored.

A lady's old who has no hair to cover
Her head, who lacks a lusty knight to woo her.
She's old if she's content with a pair of lovers
Only, or if she'd let a vile man do her.
I call her old who limits her amorous sports
To the castle, or ladies who resort
To spells and such. You know she's old if she'd rather
Send away the singers and sit and blabber.

I call that lady young who knows to honor
Nobility; she's young when she performs
Good deeds. A lady keeps her youth when her manner's
Open-minded, when she refrains from scorning
Merit. A woman keeps her youth who saves
Her figure, who shows she knows how to behave
Becomingly. She's not a gossip-monger,
And with a handsome youth she guards her honor.

Young is the man who hazards his estate,
Who suffers to a remarkable degree;
He's young when playing the host results in great
Expense, when he makes gifts extravagantly.
He's young when he sets fire to coffer and chest,
And hunts and fights in battles and tournaments.
He's young if he still likes to woo the gals,
And singers are very fond of him as well.

Vielhs es rics om, quan re no met en gatge
E li sobra blatz e vis e bacos.
Per vielh lo tenc, quan liura huous e fromatge
A jorn carnal se e sos companhos.
Per vielh, quan viest chapa sobre mantelh,
Per vielh, si a caval qu'om sieu apelh.
Per vielh lo tenc quan no·l plai domneyar,
E vielh, si pot guandir ses baratar.

Mo sirventesc port de vielh e novelh
Arnautz juglars a Richart, que·l capdelh;
E ja thesaur vielh no vuelh' amassar,
Qu'ab thesaur jove pot pretz guazanhar!

That man is old who has become averse
To risk, who hoards his wheat and wine and bacon;
I esteem him old who, on meat days, serves
Eggs and cheese to himself and his companions.
He's old who throws a cape over his coat, and
Stables a horse that someone else has broken;
He's old who leaves the ladies unfêted,
And quits a game before he is indebted.

Arnaut, jongleur, carry my song of old
And young to Richard,[20] I'd have him forego
His search for old treasure—he would be wise
To know that youth is where the merit lies.

Robert Kehew

Si tuit li dol e·il plor e·il marrimen

Bertran de Born

Si tuit li dol e·il plor e·il marrimen
E las dolors e·il dan e·il chativier
Qu'om anc agues en est segle dolen
Fossen ensems, sembleran tuit leugier
Contra la mort del joven rei engles,
Don reman pretz e jovens doloros
E·l mons escurs e tenhs e tenebros,
Sems de tot joi, plens de tristor e d'ira.

Dolen e trist e plen de marrimen
Son remazut li cortes soudadier
E·il trobador e·il joglar avinen.
Trop an en Mort agut mortal guerrier!
Que tout lor a lo joven rei engles,
Vas cui eran li plus larc cobeitos.
Ja non er mais, ni no crezatz que fos,
Vas aqest dan el segle plors ni ira.

Estenta Mortz, plena de marrimen,
Vanar te potz qe·l meillor cavalier
As tout al mon qu'anc fos de nula gen
Qar non es res q'a pretz aia mestier,
Qe tot no fos el joven rei engles.
E fora mielhs, s'a Dieu plagues razos,
Qe visqes el que maint autre enoios
Q'anc no feiron als pros mas dol et ira.

D'aquest segle flac, plen de marrimen,
S'amors s'en vai, son joi teing menzongier,
Qe ren no·i a qe no torn en cozen.
Totz jorns veiretz qe val meinz oi que ier.
Chascuns se mir el joven rei engles
Q'era del mon lo plus valens dels pros!
Ar n'es anatz sos gens cors amoros,
Don es dolors e desconortz et ira.

Planh for the Young English King

Bertran de Born

If all the grief and woe and bitterness,
All dolour, ill and every evil chance
That ever came upon this grieving world
Were set together they would seem but light
Against the death of the young English King.
Worth lieth riven and Youth dolorous,
The world o'ershadowed, soiled and overcast,
Void of all joy and full of ire and sadness.

Grieving and sad and full of bitterness
Are left in teen the liegemen courteous,
The joglars supple and the troubadours.
O'er much hath ta'en Sir Death that deadly warrior[21]
In taking from them the young English King,
Who made the freest hand seem covetous.
'Las! Never was nor will be in this world
The balance for this loss in ire and sadness!

O skilful Death and full of bitterness,
Well mayst thou boast that thou the best chevalier
That any folk e'er had, hast from us taken;
Sith nothing is that unto worth pertaineth
But had its life in the young English King,
And better were it, should God grant his pleasure
That he should live than many a living dastard
That doth but wound the good with ire and sadness.

From this faint world, how full of bitterness
Love takes his way and holds his joy deceitful,
Sith no thing is but turneth unto anguish
And each to-day 'vails less than yestere'en,
Let each man visage this young English King
That was most valiant mid all worthiest men!
Gone is his body fine and amorous,
Whence have we grief, discord and deepest sadness.

Celui qe plac pel nostre marrimen
Venir el mon nos traire d'encombrier
E receup mort a nostre salvamen,
Com a seignor umil e drechurier
Clamem merce, q'al joven rei engles
Perdo, si·lh platz, si com es vers perdos,
E·l fassa estar ab onratz compaignos
Lai on anc dol non ac ne i aura ira!

Him, whom it pleased for our great bitterness
To come to earth to draw us from misventure,
Who drank of death for our salvacioun,
Him do we pray as to a Lord most righteous
And humble eke, that the young English King
He please to pardon, as true pardon is,
And bid go in with honouréd companions
There where there is no grief, nor shall be sadness.

Ezra Pound

Comtessa de Dia

> The Countess of Dia was the wife of Lord Guillem de Peitieu, a
> beautiful and good lady. And she fell in love with Lord Raimbaut
> d'Aurenga and composed many good songs about him.[1]

Even by the relaxed standards of medieval biography, the *vida* that exists for
the Comtessa de Dia is more than usually misleading. Even if this terse ac-
count of her relationships is based on fact, it is unspecific: by one reckoning
there are five different candidates for the Guillem cited.[2] Nor do other
sources shed any light on the Comtessa's shadowy figure. Jensen reports that
historical proof of the existence of a count of Dia is "totally lacking" (*Trou-
badour Lyrics*, 38). Still, the fact that any *vida* exists for the Comtessa at all,
when few of the other women troubadours were so distinguished, alerts us
that there must have been something remarkable about the woman behind
the legendary name.

Perhaps what makes the Comtessa de Dia stand out from the rest is her
startling directness. Not for her is the *tenso* form so favored by other
trobairitz, whereby the finer points of courtly love could be lightly debated
and any personal passion hidden behind a scrim of rhetoric. Instead, in the
four poems that can be positively attributed to the Comtessa,[3] she favors a
simple, even blunt *trobar leu* style of *canso*. This lets her get quickly to what
is on her mind, as here, from the first selection:

One night I'd like to take my swain
To bed and hug him, wearing no clothes—
I'd give him reason to suppose
He was in heaven, if I deigned
To be his pillow!

Unsublimated lust is only one of the emotions that course through her poems. As the two selections show, the Comtessa also expresses petulance, sarcasm, jealousy, and desire for control. She also likes to display her knowledge of the romances then sweeping Paris.

The Comtessa de Dia obviously was not a woman content to be made into a passive symbol of male desire. She haughtily refuses to accept *taciturnitas* (admirable silence) as the proper virtue toward which medieval women should aspire (Sankovitch, "Trobairitz," 115). No; rather, with the Comtessa de Dia, "we are miles from *midons*" (Bogin, *Women Troubadours*, 65).

Estat ai en greu cossirier

  Comtessa de Dia

Estat ai en greu cossirier A
Per un cavallier qu'ai agut, B
E voill sia totz temps saubut B
Cum eu l'ai amat a sobrier; A
Ara vei q'ieu sui trahida, C
Car eu non li donei m'amor, D
Don ai estat en gran error D - *alluding to mistake she made?*
En lieig e qand sui vestida. C

Ben volria mon cavallier A
Tener un ser en mos bratz nut, B
Q'el s'en tengra per ereubut B
Sol q'a lui fezes cosseillier; A
Car plus m'en sui abellida C
No fetz Floris de Blanchaflor: D
Eu l'autrei mon cor e m'amor, D
Mon sen, mos huoills e ma vida. C

Bels amics, avinens e bos,
Cora·us tenrai e mon poder?
E que jagues ab vos un ser
E qe·us des un bais amoros!
Sapchatz, gran talan n'auria
Qe·us tengues en luoc del marit,
Ab so que m'aguessetz plevit
De far tot so qu'eu volria.

Cruel Are the Pains I've Suffered

Comtessa de Dia

Cruel are the pains I've suffered   A
For a certain cavalier   B
Whom I have had. I declare   B
I love him—let it be known forever.   C
But now I see that I was deceived: D
When I'm dressed or when I languish   E
In bed, I suffer a great anguish—   E
I should have given him my love.   F

One night I'd like to take my swain   A
To bed and hug him, wearing no clothes—   B
I'd give him reason to suppose   B
He was in heaven, if I deigned   C
To be his pillow! For I've been more   D
In love with him than Floris was   \
With Blanchefluer: my mind, my eyes
I give to him; my life, *mon cor.*[4]   D

When will I have you in my power,
Dearest friend, charming and good?
Lying with you one night I would
Kiss you so you could feel my ardor.
I want to have you in my husband's
Place, of that you can rest assured—
Provided you give your solemn word
That you'll obey my every command.

Robert Kehew

A chantar m'er de so q'ieu no volria

Comtessa de Dia

A chantar m'er de so q'ieu no volria, A
Tant me rancur de lui cui sui amia, A
Car eu l'am mais que nuilla ren que sia; A
Vas lui no·m val merces ni cortesia, A
Ni ma beltatz, ni mos pretz, ni mos sens, B
C'atressi·m sui enganada e trahia A
Cum degr' esser, s'ieu fos desavinens. B

D'aisso·m conort car anc non fi faillenssa, C
Amics, vas vox per nuilla captenenssa, C
Anz vos am mais non fetz Seguis Valenssa, C
E platz mi mout qez eu d'amar vos venssa, C
Lo mieus amics, car etz lo plus valens; B
Mi faitz orguoill en digz et en parvenssa, C
E si etz francs vas totas autras gens. B

Be·m meravill cum vostre cors s'orguoilla, D
Amics, vas me, per q'ai razon qe·m duoilla; D
Non es ges dreitz c'autr' amors vos mi tuoilla D
Per nuilla ren qe·us diga ni·us acuoilla; D
E membre vos cals fo·l comensamens B
De nostr' amor. Ja Dompnideus non vuoilla D
Q'en ma colpa sia·l departimens! B

Proesa grand q'el vostre cors s'aizina
E lo rics pretz q'avetz m'en atayna,
C'una non sai loindana ni vezina
Si vol amar vas vos non si' aclina;
Mas vos, amics, etz ben tant conoisens
Que ben devetz conoisser la plus fina,
E membre vos de nostres covinens.

I'm Forced to Sing

Comtessa de Dia

I'm forced to sing of what I'd have preferred
Not to, so greatly has my friend distressed me;
For though I love him more than all the world,
I find that neither courtesy nor mercy
Avail; nor does beauty, merit, or wit:
If I behaved toward him disdainfully
I wouldn't expect such lies and vile treatment.

My behavior toward you has been above
Reproach, my friend, in this I find solace;
For I have loved you more than Seguin loved
Valensa,⁵ so I'm gratified to surpass
In ardor you, thought to be audacious.
The way you speak and act toward me suggests
Contempt, whereas toward others you're more gracious.

I truly marvel at the arrogance
You show toward me, my friend, I must reprove you;
For in spite of the liberties that this
Lady allows, for her to remove you
From me's simply not fair. Remember how
We loved at first. Lord God, may it not prove to
Be my fault, that we are distant now.

The great prowess, the noble worth that you
Possess prevents me from departing, for
I know no woman living near or far who
Wouldn't be drawn by you, provided she were
Open to love; but you, my friend, are so
Knowing that I'm sure you'll distinguish her
Who is most loyal; and recall our vows.

Valer mi deu mos pretz e mos paratges
E ma beutatz e plus mos fis coratges,
Per q'ieu vos mand lai on es vostr' estatges
Esta chansson que me sia messatges.
E voill saber, lo mieus bels amics gens,
Per que vos m'etz tant fers ni tant salvatges,
No sai si s'es orguoills o mals talens.

Mas aitan plus vuoill li digas, messatges,
Q'en trop d'orguoill ant gran dan maintas gens.

Of my beauty and worth I must avail
Myself, my line and even more so my
True heart; therefore I send to where you dwell
This song as messenger; and so my fine
And noble friend, what I'm longing to know
Is why you're mean and hostile toward me. Does pride
Or a malicious nature make you so?

But even more so, envoy, to him confide
That such haughtiness brings many to woe.

Robert Kehew

Maria de Ventadorn and Gui d'Ussel

You have surely heard of my lady Maria de Ventadorn, how she was the most esteemed lady who ever lived in Limousin. . . . And her reason always helped her, and folly never made her act foolishly. And God honored her with a beautifully pleasing body, without any artifice.

Lord Gui d'Ussel had lost his lady . . . so he lived in great pain and in great sadness. And he had not sung or invented poetry in a long time, and all the good ladies from that region were very grieved about it, and Lady Maria more than any other, for Lord Gui d'Ussel praised her in all his songs.

And the Count of La Marche . . . was [Maria's] knight, and she had granted him as much honor and as much love as a lady can bestow on a knight. And one day as he was courting her, they had an argument between them: the Count of La Marche said that every true lover, from the time his lady gives him her love and takes him as her knight and friend, must have . . . as much suzerainty and authority [over] her as she has [over] him. And Lady Maria forbade that the friend should have suzerainty or authority over her.

Lord Gui d'Ussel was in the court of Lady Maria and she, to make him return to his songs and his joy, composed a couplet in which she asked him if it was proper for the friend to have as much suzerainty over the lady as she had over him. And on this subject my lady Maria challenged him to a *tenson* exchange.[1]

If one indicator of a healthy, civilized society is that it allows mature friendship to flourish between men and women, then, on the evidence of this tale, noble Occitan society could at least intermittently rise to that standard. There is something appealing in Maria's ministrations toward her grieving friend, as well as in the good-natured badinage between the two in the debate poem that ensued, the selection below.

At the same time that she could be a kind friend, Maria had been sensitized to what we might refer to today as gender issues of power—a topic upon which, as the selection shows, Maria entertained firm opinions. She grew up as the daughter of Raimon II, viscount of Turenne, one of the four viscounties of the Limousin. As a young girl, Maria and her two sisters heard themselves praised in song by Bertran de Born. This idyllic tableau was shattered when the three sisters, for strategic reasons, were all married and packed off to the lords of neighboring viscounties. Maria's new home at Ventadorn, also in the Limousin, holds a venerated place in troubadour lore. It was here that the shadowy Ebles II, the great-grandfather of Maria's husband, apparently played a role (perhaps a large role) in launching the troubadour movement.

As she grew to maturity in her new home, Maria began to patronize various troubadours, including the Monge de Montaudon and Gaucelm Faidit, as well as the coauthor of the present selection, Gui d'Ussel. Gui's birthplace, Ussel, lies not far from the Ventadorn castle. He appears to have been one of those minor noblemen who became a wandering troubadour more or less of necessity, as an alternative to staying at home and squabbling with siblings over control of the family castle. If his medieval biographer is correct, Gui's comeback as a maker of songs at Maria's insistence was short-lived. According to his *vida*, a legate of Pope Innocent III eventually convinced Gui to renounce his devil music. This confrontation apparently took place before the start of the Albigensian Crusade; it reveals some of the more minor tensions that simmered between Occitania and Rome that later were to tragically explode.

Maria's collaboration with Gui is the only composition that has come down to us from this noblewoman. It demonstrates the aptness of the *tenso* form for debate over the fine points of courtly behavior.[2] Those interested in the power of artistic creativity to help heal the wounded soul, no less than those intrigued by the topics of friendship and gender dynamics, will find matter for reflection here.

Gui d'Ussel be·m pesa de vos

Maria de Ventadorn and Gui d'Ussel

Gui d'Ussel be·m pesa de vos
Car vos etz laissatz de chantar,
E car vos i volgra tornar
Per que sabetz d'aitals razos,
Vuoill que·m digatz si deu far egalmen
Dompna per drut, qan lo qier francamen,
Cum el per lieis, tot cant taing ad amor,
Segon los dreitz que tenon l'amador.

Dompna Na Maria, tenssos
E tot cant cuiava laissar,
Mas aoras non puosc estar
Q'ieu non chant als vostres somos.
E respond eu a la dompna breumen
Que per son drut deu far comunalmen
Cum el per lieis ses garda de ricor,
Q'en dos amics non deu aver maior.

Gui, tot so don es cobeitos
Deu drutz ab merce demandar,
E·il dompna pot o comandar,
[Mas ben deu esgardar sazos;]
E·l drutz deu far precs e comandamen
Cum per amiga e per dompna eissamen,
E·il dompna deu a son drut far honor
Cum ad amic, mas non cum a seignor.

Dompna, sai dizon demest nos
Que, pois que dompna vol amar,
Engalmen deu son drut onrar,
Pois engalmen son amoros.
E s'esdeven que l'am plus finamen,
E·l faich e·l dich en deu far aparen,
E si ell'a fals cor ni trichador,
Ab bel semblan deu cobrir sa follor.

When a Lady Loves

Maria de Ventadorn and Gui d'Ussel

Gui d'Ussel, I've been distraught
Since you gave up singing. In
Hopes that you'll make a new beginning
At this, and since you know about
Such things, I ask you: when a lady freely
Falls in love with a gentleman, should she
Do as much for him as he does for her,
According to the tenants of *amor*?

Lady Maria, I thought I'd given
Up debates and all those other
Forms of song, but when you order
It, how can I refuse your bidding?
Here is my opinion since you ask me:
A lady ought to treat her love exactly
As he treats her, with no regard to station—
In friendship rank is no consideration.

Gui, the lover should request
All that he desires, humbly;
And the lady should comply
Within the bounds of common sense:
And the lover should obey her commands,
Treating her as a lady and a friend
Equally; she, however, should regard
Him as a friend but never as her lord.

Lady, here the people say
That when a lady wants to love,
She owes the man an equal share of
Honor, since they are equally
Smitten: and if it happens that she loves
To excess, then her words and deeds should prove
It; but if her heart is treacherous or fickle,
With a smooth face she should disassemble.

Gui d'Uissel, ges d'aitals razos
Non son li drut al comenssar,
Anz ditz chascus, can vol preiar,
Mans iointas e de genolos:
"Dompna, voillatz qe·us serva franchamen
Cum lo vostr'om," et ella enaissi·l pren.
Eu vo·l iutge per dreich a trahitor
Si·s rend pariers ei·s det per servidor.

Dompna, so es plaitz vergoignos
Ad ops de dompna razonar
Que cellui non teigna per par
A cui a faich un cor de dos.
O vos diretz, e no·us estara gen,
Que·l drutz la deu amar plus finamen
O vos diretz q'il son par entre lor,
Que ren no·il deu drutz mas qant per amor.

Gui d'Ussel, when they begin,
Lovers do not behave like that;
They join their hands together and get
Down on their knees to try to win
A lady's favor: they say, "Grant that I
May be your man and freely serve you, lady,"
And she accepts; to say she should receive him
As a servant *and* an equal's treason!

It's truly a disgrace to argue
That a lady's greater than
The man who loves her, lady, when
She has fashioned one heart from two.
You must either say that the man exceeds
The lady in love (scant praise), or else concede
That with respect to honor they're the same:
The lover only owes what bears love's name

Robert Kehew

Monge de Montaudon

The Monk of Montaudon . . . was made a monk in the abbey of Or-
lac. And then the abbot gave him the priorate of Montaudon, and
there he did a great deal for the good of the house. While he was in the
monastery he wrote *coblas* and *sirventes* on subjects that were popular
in that region. And knights and barons brought him forth from
the monastery, did him great honor and gave him whatever he wanted
or requested; and he took everything back to Montaudon, to his
priorate. . . .

And he returned to Orlac, to his abbot . . . and he begged the abbot
to allow him to follow Alfonso of Aragon's advice, and the abbot con-
sented. For the king had commanded him to eat meat, court women,
sing and write poetry, and thus he did. And he was made lord of [the
festival of] Puoi Santa Maria and was chosen as the one to give the
sparrow hawk.[1]

Reading his song lyrics, we can readily conclude that this bon vivant (active
around 1180 to 1215) was not exactly cut out for the tonsure and the hair
shirt. This is just one of the conclusions that we feel qualified to draw about
the Monge de Montaudon after we have perused his verse, for he was one of
those rare writers blessed with the gift of manifesting his ample personality
through his every word. The two uncommon poetic forms used below, the
plazer (a poem cataloguing pleasant things) and its counterpart the *enueg* (a
poem listing unpleasant things), were ideal for such a character.

Another form that suited the ready wit of the Monge de Montaudon was the literary *sirventes*. Building on an earlier example by Peire d'Alvernhe, the good monk wrote a satire in this form around 1195, using the opportunity not so much to set forth his views on the literary merits of the various troubadours of his day as to poke fun at their personal foibles. We picture him trotting out this composition at some late-century troubadour jolly-up. Among the various composers whom he skewers are Arnaut Daniel (who has "never sung well except for some foolish words that no one understands"), Arnaut de Marueill ("with a bad disposition, as his lady has no compassion on him"), Gaucelm Faidit ("who from a lover became the husband of the one he used to follow around"), Peire Vidal (that "peasant who used to be a fur merchant"), and Peirol ("who has worn the same suit for thirty years"), all represented in the following chapters.[2]

In the end, this troubadour-monk succeeds in parting the mists of the Middle Ages: he stands before us, fully realized. We come to know an obscure monk from the late twelfth century better than we know the family that lives next door, better than the person who works in the next cubicle.

Mout me platz deportz e gaieza

Monge de Montaudon

Mout me platz deportz e gaieza,
Condugz e donars e proeza,
E dona franca e corteza
E de respondre ben apreza.
E platz m'a ric home franqueza
E vas son enemic maleza.

E platz me hom que gen me sona
E qui de bon talan me dona,
E ricx hom quan no mi tensona.
E·m platz qui·m ditz be ni·m razona,
E dormir quan venta ni trona,
E gras salmos ad ora nona.

E platz mi be, lai en estiu,
Que·m sojorn a font o a riu,
E·lh prat son vert e·l flors reviu,
E li auzelhet chanton piu,
E m'amigua ven a celiu,
E lo·y fauc una vetz de briu.

E platz mi be qui m'aculhia,
E quan gaire no truep fadia.
E platz mi solatz de m'amia,
Baizars, e mais si lo·y fazia.
E si mos enemicx perdia
Mi platz, e plus s'ieu lo·y tolhia.

E plazon mi ben companho,
Quant entre mos enemicx so
Et auze be dir ma razo
Et ill l'escouton a bando.

What I Like

Monge de Montaudon

I love amusements and gaiety,
Feasts and gifts and tests of endurance,
And when a well-bred, courteous lady
Expresses herself with self-assurance.
I love a lord who speaks with candor,
Who shows his enemies his anger.

I love the man who treats me right,
Who's open-handed in his lending;
He doesn't want to pick a fight,
But my good name is quick defending.
I love to sleep when there's wind and showers,
And eat a fat fish in the ninth hour.

I love it when, in the summer season,
I rest down where the water burbles—
The meadow's green, the flowers pleasing,
The sweet birds practicing their warbles—
And my *amigua,* in stealthy fashion,
Comes to make love, once, with passion.

I love a court where they heed my wishes,
Where seldom do I hear a "no."
I love her company, her kisses,
And . . . anything else she cares to bestow.
I love when my rival gets the short end of it—
Specially if I stand to benefit.

I love well my loyal friends
If I'm met with those who would mistreat me,
And someone rises to my defense
And they accept his words, completely.

Robert Kehew

Be m'enueia, s'o auzes dire

Monge de Montaudon

Be m'enueia, s'o auzes dire,
Hom parliers qu'es avols servire;
Et hom que trop vol autr' aucire
M'enueia, e cavals que tire;
Et enueia·m, si Dieus m'ajut,
Joves hom, quan trop port' escut
Que negun colp no·i a avut,
Capellan e monge barbut
E lausengier bec esmolut.

E tenc dona per enoiosa
Quant es paubra ni orgoillosa
E marit qu'ama trop sa sposa,
Neus s'era domna de Tolosa;
Et enueia·m de cavallier
Fors de son païs ufanier,
Quant en lo sieu non a mestier
Mas sol de pizar el mortier
Pebre o d'estar al foguier.

Et enueia·m de fort maneira
Hom volpilz que porta baneira,
Et avols austors en ribeira,
E pauca carns en gran caudeira;
Et enueia·m, per Saint Marti,
Trop d'aiga en petit de vi;
E quan trob escassier mati
M'enueia, e d'orp atressi,
Car no m'azaut de lor cami.

What I Don't Like

Monge de Montaudon

I don't care much, I do declare,
For servants who are jabbering bores,
For the blusterer who always swears
He'll kill someone, and the old cart horse.
And I dislike, God only knows,
The dandy who is fond of bearing
A shield that's never received a blow;
Monks and priests and the beards they're wearing;
Slanderers and the lies they're sharing.

I find that lady most annoying
Who's poor and yet holds haughty views;
Also the husband whose love is cloying,
Although his lady's from Toulouse.³
And I dislike Sir Cavalier
Who boasts and preens outside his border,
But home has no more work, I fear,
Than crushing peppercorns in the mortar;
Around the hearth he likes to loiter.

I cannot stand, I can't abide
The cowardly, flag-waving fop,
A mangy hawk by the riverside,
A scrap of meat in a large pot.
By Saint Martin, there's no delight
In too much water in too little wine;
Nor am I crazy at first light
To bump into someone crippled or blind;
Leading them's no fun, I find.

Enueia·m longa tempradura,
E carns quant es mal coita e dura,
E prestre qui men ni·s perjura,
E veilha puta que trop dura;
Et enueia·m, per Saint Dalmatz,
Avols hom en trop gran solatz,
E corre quant per via a glatz;
E fugir ab cavalh armatz
M'enueia, e maldir de datz.

Et enueia·m, per vita eterna,
Manjar ses fuec, quan fort iverna,
E jaser ab veill' a galerna,
Quan m'en ven flairors de taverna;
Et enueia·m e m'es trop fer,
Quan selh que lav' olla enquer;
Et enueia·m de marit fer,
Quan eu li vey belha molher,
E qui no·m dona ni·m profer.

Et enueia·m, per Saint Salvaire,
En bona cort avols violaire,
Et a pauca terra trop fraire,
Et a bon joc paubres prestaire;
Et enueia·m, per Saint Marsel,
Doas penas en un mantel,
E trop parier en un castel,
E rics hom ab pauc de revel,
Et en tornei dart e quairel.

Et enueia·m, se Dieus mi vailla,
Longa taula ab breu toailla,
Et hom qu'ap mas ronhazas tailla,
Et ausbercs, pesanz d'avol mailla;
Et enueia·m estar a port
Quan trop fa greu temps e plou fort;
Et entre amics dezacort
M'enueia, e·m fai piegz de mort,
Quan sai que tenson a lor tort.

I hate an excess of abstention,
And meat that's poorly cooked and stringy;
Priests who are given to invention,
And old whores who, when done, are clingy.
And I dislike, by Saint Dalmatius,
A loathsome man with heavy purses,
Running when there's ice in places,
Fleeing on well-armored horses,
And flinging down the dice, with curses.

I'll dislike till the heavens fail
To sup without a fire in winter;
To sleep with a hag when the north wind wails
And odors from the tavern enter.
Too many questions are offensive
From a wench scrubbing the pot;
I don't like a husband who's defensive
With the gorgeous wife he's got;
Of gifts for me he's never thought.

By Saint Salvador, I cannot bear
A good court with a bad viola,
A scrap of land with too many *frères,*
A good game when they won't bankroll you.
By Saint Marcel, I do deplore
Two fur linings in apparel,
A castle owned by too many lords,
A rich man who's not gay and social,
And tourneys with the dart and quarrel.[4]

So help me God, I think it's shabby
A short cloth thrown on a long table,
A man who carves whose hands are scabby,
A heavy hauberk made of poor metal.
Crossing the mountains, I don't care
For drenching rain in a nasty season
When tempers 'mongst my comrades flare:
I hate like death, it's no-ways pleasing
To know they're peevish with no reason.

E dirai vos que fort me tira:
Veilla gazals qu'a trops atira
E paubra soudadier' aira,
E donzels que sas cambas mira;
Et enueia·m, per Saint Aon,
Dompna grassa ab magre con,
E senhoratz que trop mal ton;
Qui no pot dormir, quant a son,
Major enueg no·m sai el mon.

Ancar i a mais que m'enueia:
Cavalcar ses capa, de ploia,
E quan trop ab mon caval troia
Qui sa manjadoira li voia;
Et enueia·m e no·m sab bo
De sella quan croll' a l'arço,
E fivella ses ardaillo,
E malvaitz hom dinz sa maiso
Que no fa ni ditz si mal no.

I'll say what else I can forego:
An old whore with too many buyers,
A wench who's always short of dough,
The rake who his own legs admires.
By Saint Abundas, it little pleases
A fat dame whose vagina's tight;
The scoundrel who closely fleeces
His serfs. On Earth there's no worse plight
Than being too tired to sleep at night.

There's even more I'll disavow:
In rain, sans cape, to go out slogging;
Finding my horse with a fat sow—
It's the whole manger she'll be hogging.
I detest, I can't take long
A saddle that's been poorly fastened,
A buckle that's without a prong,
And a blackguard with a mansion,
Who's evil in his thought and action.

Robert Kehew

Arnaut Daniel

Arnaut Daniel came from . . . a castle called Ribairac in . . . Perigord, and he was of gentle birth. He learned his letters well and took great delight in writing poetry. And then he abandoned his letters and became a jongleur, and began writing a kind of poetry with difficult rhymes, which is why his songs are not easy to understand or to learn.[1]

Arnaut Daniel has enjoyed praise from the highest sources. Dante called Arnaut *il miglior fabbro* ("the better craftsman"), while Petrarch considered him the *gran maestro d'amor*.[2] In more recent times, Ezra Pound concluded that "The Twelfth Century . . . has left us two perfect gifts: the church of San Zeno in Verona, and the canzoni of Arnaut Daniel" (*Spirit of Romance*, 22). These accolades stem largely from Arnaut's poetic virtuosity. Arnaut Daniel is a poet's poet.

Grasping Arnaut Daniel's accomplishment, however, does not require a lot of arcane knowledge of verse technique. We can do so at a glance. Compare any of the mostly eight- or ten-syllable-per-line poems that we have encountered up to now with, for example, the following lines from a poem by Arnaut Daniel (with Ezra Pound's translation):

L'aura amara	The bitter air
Fa·ls bruoills brancutz	Strips panoply
Clarzir	From trees
Qe·l doutz espeissa ab fuoills,	Where softer winds set leaves,
E·ls letz	The glad

Becs	Beaks
Dels auzels ramencs	Now in brakes are coy,
Ten balps e mutz,	Scarce peep the wee
Pars	Mates
E non pars.	And un-mates.

In "L'aura amara" ("The Bitter Air"), Arnaut has taken the longer lines of his predecessors and chopped them up into smaller lines of uneven length. This innovation provides a lightness and swing that is far removed from poems with a blocky stanza structure: compare a nocturne by Chopin, say, with a typical church hymn.

If we examine this poem more closely, however, we begin to notice other aspects of Arnaut Daniel's superlative craftsmanship. Note the easy, flowing use of internal rhyme and near rhyme. At the same time not every end word rhymes with other end words in the stanza. (Lines do rhyme, however, from one stanza to another, in the conventional practice known as *estramp* rhyme.) The effect of reducing the number of rhymes within a single stanza is like clearing off a crowded knickknack shelf: the choice specimens that remain can then stand out. Arnaut eventually pushed this innovation to the point that, in the poem "Sols sui" (not included in the present book), the stanza contains *no* rhyming end words. Ezra Pound admiringly joked that, in "Sols sui," Arnaut "made the first piece of 'blank verse'" ("Arnaut Daniel," 110).

In his single-minded pursuit of artistic perfection, Arnaut Daniel contorts language as necessary. As Jensen observes, Arnaut shows "little respect for the standard vocabulary. He favors the use of rare words and does not hesitate to coin new words or give new shape and meaning to already existing ones" (*Troubadour Lyrics,* 34). Ezra Pound, Arnaut's most assiduous translator, was not slow to mimic this predisposition in his translations. Pound plausibly attributes Arnaut's inventiveness to a deep understanding of language, coupled with a restless drive for new effects. At a time when language itself seemed to be falling into a rut, Arnaut Daniel "tried to make almost a new language, or at least to enlarge the Langue d'Oc, and make new things possible" ("Arnaut Daniel," 112).

As a result of his technical and linguistic innovations, as his medieval biographer points out Arnaut Daniel's poems are not always easy to understand. For this reason, some critics mistakenly have classified Arnaut with the *trobar clus* poets who favored arcane meaning. Unlike typical *trobar clus* poetry, however, the content in Arnaut's lyrics is fairly conventional. Difficulties in interpretation spring not from obscure tropes but rather from the poems' intricate strophic structures and verbal whimsies. For those reasons Arnaut's work is better described as *trobar ric,* rich or ornate poetry.

Pound offers sensitive commentary on the following selections, which are presented here as a song cycle, moving from spring to fall. Pound praises the musicality of the first selection, "Chansson do·il." He finds the second poem ("Autet e bas") beguiling because of "the way in which Arnaut breaks the flow of the poem to imitate the bird call in *Cadahus en son us,* and the repetitions of this sound in the succeeding strophes" (ibid., 112, 123).

Pound considers the third selection, "Doutz brais e critz," to be "perhaps the most beautiful of all [Arnaut's] surviving poems." (The poem's heavy-handed, *sirventes*-like conclusion, however, shatters the amorous mood of the earlier stanzas.) Pound rightly singles out this song's fourth stanza for praise, noting that its concluding lines "may be taken to differentiate Arnaut Daniel from all other poets of Provence . . . [in their] absolute sense of beauty." Pound further suggests that one of the poem's central images, that of the lady's "cloak of indigo," may have had a "visionary significance" for the author. Far from being merely a "light and pleasant phrase," this was the sort of mystical vision that the medieval "servants of Amor" might have been vouchsafed. Perhaps the emotions of *fin' amor* occasionally led the troubadours to "an interpretation of the cosmos by feeling" (*Spirit of Romance,* 33–34, 89–96). Does Pound miss the mark here? Or has he somehow managed to touch the hem of a vanished truth about the Middle Ages?

The fourth song, "Can chai la fueilla," Pound describes as "interesting for its rhythm, for the sea-chantey swing produced by the simple device of caesurae" ("Arnaut Daniel," 116). The fifth selection, "L'aura amara," which "the greatest of poets [Dante] has praised," beguilingly simulates "the angry chatter of the birds in autumn" (*Spirit of Romance,* 28, 30).

The final poem in this part, "En cest sonet coind'e leri" ("Of the Trades and Love"), occasions an extended gloss. Pound points out how, from stanza to stanza, using "metaphor that is scarce metaphor, by suggestive verbs," *il miglior fabbro* paints scenes from the workaday world. Thus, "in stanza I [Arnaut] makes his vignette in the shop of the joiner and finisher, in II the metal-worker's shop . . . , in III the church . . . ; in IV the low-lying fields, where the grain is fostered by the river-flush; in V Rome, of the church and empire; in VI the suggestion . . . may be of a farm hand working in a grey, barren stretch of field" (*Translations,* 423–24). The poem closes with the *tornada* that became Arnaut's signature line: "I, Arnaut who loves the wind, and chases the hare with the ox, and swims against the current" (*Spirit of Romance,* 36).

Arnaut's engagement with poetic form is even deeper than what we have been able to suggest here. Arnaut is generally credited with having invented the sestina, an elaborate form that is still revived occasionally today. The sestina consists of six stanzas of six lines each, with a concluding tercet. This form does not use any rhyming end words. Instead, like intricate knotwork, the end words of the first stanza reappear to end lines in succeeding stanzas according to a strictly prescribed pattern. Pound admired the sestina form per se, particularly as later used by Dante and others, likening it to "a thin sheet of flame folding and infolding upon itself." However he disparaged Arnaut's pioneering use of the form in the poem "Lo ferm voler qu'el cor m'intra." He mocked this poem's use of awkward end words such as "nail" and "uncle," and only deigned to translate a portion of it, including its opening stanza (ibid., 27, 36; and *Translations,* 425):

> Firm desire that doth enter
> My heart will not be hid by bolts nor nailing
> Not slanderers who loose their arms by lying
> And dare not fight with even twigs and switches.
> Yea, by some jest, there where no uncle enters
> I'll have my joy in garden or in chamber.

In surveying Arnaut Daniel's entire output, Pound reminds us that his achievement, like that of other troubadours, "is not literature but the art of fitting words well with music. . . . [His] triumph is . . . in an art between literature and music" ("Arnaut Daniel," 116). While the musical dimension of Arnaut Daniel's work is all but lost to us—only a couple of his melodies survive—we do well to bear in mind this missing aural component as we peruse his rich verse.

Chansson do·il mot son plan e prim

    Arnaut Daniel

Chansson do·il mot son plan e prim
Farai puois que botono·ill vim,
E l'aussor cim
Son de color
De mainta flor,
E verdeia la fuoilla,
E·il chan e·il braill
Son a l'ombraill
Dels auzels per la broilla.[3]

Pelz bruoills aug lo chan e·l refrim
E, per so que no·m fassa crim,
Obre e lim
Motz de valor
Ab art d'Amor,
Don non ai cor qe·m tuoilla;
Que si be·is faill,
La sec a traill,
On plus vas mi s'orguoilla.

Petit val orguoills d'amador
Que leu trabucha son seignor
Del luoc aussor
Jus el terraill
Per tal trebaill
Que de joi lo despuoilla;
Dreitz es lagrim
Et arda e rim
Qi'n contra Amor janguoilla.

I'll Make a Song

Arnaut Daniel

I'll make a song   with exquisite
Clear words, for buds are blowing sweet
Where the sprays meet,
And flowers don
Their bold blazon
Where leafage springeth greenly
O'ershadowing
The birds that sing
And cry in coppice seemly.

The bosques among   they're singing fleet.
In shame's avoid my staves compete,
Fine-filed and neat,
With love's glaives on
His ways they run;
From him no whim can turn me,
Although he bring
Great sorrowing,
Although he proudly spurn me.

For lovers strong   pride is ill won,
And throweth him who mounts thereon.
His lots are spun
So that they fling
Him staggering,
His gaudy joys move leanly,
He hath grief's meat
And tears to eat
Who useth Love unseemly.

Ges per janglor no·m vir aillor,
Bona dompna, ves cui ador;
Mas per paor
Del devinaill,
Don jois trassaill,
Fatz semblan qe no·us vuoilla;
C'anc no·ns gauzim
De lor noirim;
Mal m'es que lor acuoilla.

Si be·m vau per tot a est daill,
Mos pessamens lai vos assaill;
Q'ieu chant e vaill
Pel joi qe·ns fim
Lai on partim;
Mout sovens l'uoills mi muoilla
D'ira e de plor
E de doussor,
Car per joi ai qe·m duoilla.

Er ai fam d'amor, don badaill,
E non sec mesura ni taill:
Sols m'o egaill!
C'anc non auzim
Del temps Caym
Amador meins acuoilla
Cor trichador
Ni bauzador;
Per que mos jois capduoilla!

Bella, qui qe·is destuoilla,
Arnautz dreich cor
Lai o·us honor,
Car vostre pretz capduoilla!

Though tongues speak wrong   of wrangles none
Can turn me from thee. For but one
Fear I have gone
Dissembling;
Traitors can sting,
From their lies I would screen thee,
And as they'd treat
Us, with deceit,
Let fate use them uncleanly.

Though my swath long   's run wavering
My thoughts go forth to thee and cling,
Wherefore I sing
Of joys replete
Once, where our fcct
Parted, and mine eyes plainly
Show mists begun
And sweetly undone,
For joy's the pain doth burn me.

Save 'neath Love's thong   I move no thing,
And my way brooks no measuring,
For right hath spring
In that Love's heat
Was ne'er complete
As mine, since Adam. 'Tween me
And sly treason
No net is spun,
Wherefore my joy grows greenly.

CODA
Lady, whoe'er demean thee
My benison
Is set upon
Thy grace where it moves queenly.

Ezra Pound

Autet e bas entrels prims fuoills

Arnaut Daniel

Autet e bas entrels prims fuoills
Son nou de flors li ram eil renc
E noi ten mut bec ni gola
Nuills auzels, anz braia e chanta
Cadahus
En son us;
Per joi qu'ai d'els e del tems
Chant, mas amors mi asauta
Quils motz ab lo son acorda.

Dieu o grazisc e a mos huoills,
Que per lor conoissensam venc.
Jois, qu'adreich auci e fola
L'ira qu'ieu n'agui e l'anta,
Er va sus
Qui qu'en mus,
D'Amor don sui fis e frems;
C'ab lieis c'al cor m'azauta
Sui liatz ab ferma corda.

Merces, Amors, c'aras m'acuoills!
Tart mi fo, mas en grat m'o prenc,
Car si m'art dinz la meola
Lo fuocs non vuoill que s'escanta;
Mas pel us
Estauc clus
Que d'autrui joi fant greus gems
E pustell ai' en sa gauta
Cel c'ab lieis si desacorda.

Now High and Low, Where Leaves Renew

Arnaut Daniel

Now high and low, where leaves renew,
Come buds on bough and spalliard pleach
And no beak nor throat is muted;
Auzel each in tune contrasted
Letteth loose
Wriblis⁴ spruce.
Joy for them and spring would set
Song on me, but Love assaileth
Me and sets my words t' his dancing.

I thank my God and mine eyes too,
Since through them the perceptions reach,
Porters of joys that have refuted
Every ache and shame I've tasted;
They reduce
Pains, and noose
Me in Amor's corded net.
Her beauty in me prevaileth
Till bonds seem but joy's advancing.

My thanks, Amor, that I win through;
Thy long delays I naught impeach;
Though flame's in my marrow rooted
I'd not quench it, well 't hath lasted,
Burns profuse,
Held recluse
Lest knaves know our hearts are met,
Murrain on the mouth that aileth,
So he finds her not entrancing.

De bon' amor false l'escuoills,
E drutz es tornatz en fadenc,
Qui di qu'el parla noil cola
Nuilla res quel cor creanta
De pretz l'us;
Car enfrus
Es d'aco qu'eu mout ai crems;
E qui de parlar trassauta
Dreitz es qu'en la lengais morda.

Vers es qu'ieu l'am et es orguoills,
Mas ab jauzir cela loi tenc;
Qu'anc pos Sainz Pauls fetz pistola
Ni nuills hom dejus caranta,
Non poc plus,
Neis Jhesus,
Far de tals, car totz absems
Als bos aips don es plus auta
Cella c'om per pros recorda.

Pretz e Valors, vostre capduoills
Es la bella c'ab sim retenc,
Qui m'a sol et ieu liei sola,
C'autra el mon nom atalanta;
Anz sui brus
Et estrus
Als autras el cor teing prems,
Mas pel sieu joi trepa e sauta
No vuoill c'autra m'o comorda.

Arnautz ama e no di nems,
C'Amors l'afrena la gauta
Que fols gabs no laill comorda.

He doth in Love's book misconstrue,
And from that book none can him teach,
Who saith ne'er's in speech recruiting
Aught, whereby the heart is dasted,
Word's abuse
Doth traduce
Worth, but I run no such debt.
Right 'tis if man over-raileth
He tear tongue on tooth mischancing.[5]

That I love her, is pride, is true,
But my fast secret knows no breach.
Since Paul's writ was executed
Or the forty days first fasted,
Not Cristus
Could produce
Her similar, where one can get
Charms total, for no charm faileth
Her who's memory's enhancing.

Grace and valour, the keep of you
She is, who holds me, each to each,
She sole, I sole, so fast suited,
Other women's lures are wasted,
And no truce
But misuse
Have I for them, they're not let
To my heart, where she regaleth
Me with delights I'm not chancing.

Arnaut loves, and ne'er will fret
Love with o'er-speech, his throat quaileth,
Braggart voust's not to his fancying.

Ezra Pound

Doutz brais e critz

Arnaut Daniel

Doutz brais e critz,
Lais e cantars e voutas
Aug del auzels qu' en lor latins fant precs
Quecs ab so par, atressi cum nos fam
A las amigas en cui entendem;
E doncas ieu qu' en la genssor entendi
Dei far chansson sobre totz de bell' obra
Que noi aia mot fals ni rima estrampa.

Non fui marritz
Ni non presi destoutas
Al prim qu' intriei el chastel dinz lo decs,
Lai on estai midonz, don ai gran fam
C' anc non l' ac tal lo nebotz Sain Guillem;
Mil vetz lo jorn en badaill em n' estendi
Per la bella que totas autras sobra
Tant cant val mais fis gaugz qu' ira ni rampa.

Ben fui grazitz
E mas paraulas coutas,
Per so que jes al chausir no fui pecs,
Anz volgui mais prendre fin aur que ram,
Lo jorn quez ieu e midonz nos baizem
Em fetz escut de son bel mantel endi
Que lausengier fals, lenga de colobra,
Non o visson, don tan mals motz escampa.

Dieus lo chauzitz
Per cui foron assoutas
Las faillidas que fetz Longis lo cecs,
Voilla, sil platz, qu' ieu e midonz jassam
En la chambra on amdui nos mandem
Uns rics convens don tan gran joi atendi,
Quel seu bel cors baisan rizen descobra
E quel remir contral lum de la lampa.

Sweet Cries and Cracks

Arnaut Daniel

Sweet cries and cracks
    and lays and chants inflected
By auzels who, in their Latin belikes,
Chirm each to each, even as you and I
Pipe toward those girls on whom our thoughts attract;
Are but more cause that I, whose overweening
Search is toward the Noblest, set in cluster
Lines where no word pulls wry, no rhyme breaks gauges.

No cul de sacs
    nor false ways me deflected
When first I pierced her fort within its dykes,
Hers, for whom my hungry insistency
Passes the gnaw whereby was Vivien wracked; [6]
Day-long I stretch, all times, like a bird preening,
And yawn for her, who hath o'er others thrust her
As high as true joy is o'er ire and rages.

Welcome not lax,
    and my words were protected
Not blabbed to other, when I set my likes
On her. Not brass but gold was 'neath the die.
That day we kissed, and after it she flacked
O'er me her cloak of indigo, for screening
Me from all culvertz' eyes, whose blathered bluster
Can set such spites abroad; win jibes for wages.

God, who did tax
    not Longus' sin, [7] respected
That blind centurion beneath the spikes
And him forgave, grant that we two shall lie
Within one room, and seal therein our pact,
Yes, that she kiss me in the half-light, leaning
To me, and laugh and strip and stand forth in the lustre
Where lamp-light with light limb but half engages.

Ges rams floritz
De floretas envoutas
Cui fan tremblar auzelhon ab lurs becs
Non es plus frescs, per qu' ieu no volh Roam
Aver ses lieis ni tot Jherusalem;
Pero totz fis mas juntas a lim rendi,
Qu' en liei amar, agr' ondral reis de Dobra
O celh cui es l' Estel e Luna-pampa.

Bocca, que ditz?
Qu' eu crei quem auras toutas
Tals promessas don l'emperaire grecs
En for' onratz ol senher de Roam
Ol reis que ten Sur e Jherusalem;
Doncs ben sui fols que queir tan quem rependi
Ni eu d' Amor non ai poder quem cobra,
Ni saveis es nuls om que joi acampa.

Los deschausitz
Ab las lengas esmoutas
Non dupt' ieu jes, sil seignor dels Galecs
An fag faillir, perqu' es dreitz s' o blasmam,
Que son paren pres romieu, so sabem,
Raimon lo filh al comte, et aprendi
Que greu faral reis Ferrans de pretz cobra
Si mantenen nol solv e nol escampa.

Eu l' agra vist, mas estiei per tal obra,
C' al coronar fui del bon rei d' Estampa.

Mos sobrecors, si tot grans sens lo sobra,
Tenga que ten, si non gaire nois ampa.[8]

The flowers wax
     with buds but half perfected;
Tremble on twig that shakes where the bird strikes—
But not more fresh than she! No empery,
Though Rome and Palestine were one compact,
Would lure me from her; and with hands convening
I give me to her. But if kings could muster
In homage similar, you'd count them sages.[9]

Mouth, now what knacks!
     What folly hath infected
Thee? Gifts, that th' Emperor of the Salonikes
Or Lord of Rome were greatly honored by,[10]
Or Syria's lord, thou dost from me distract;
O fool I am! to hope for intervening
From Love that shields not love! Yea, it were juster
To call him mad, who 'gainst his joy engages.

Political Postcript
The slimy jacks
     with adders' tongues bisected,
I fear no whit, nor have; and if these tykes
Have led Galicia's king to villeiny[11]—
His cousin in pilgrimage hath he attacked—
We know—Raimon the Count's son—my meaning
Stands without screen. The royal filibuster
Redeems not honour till he unbar the cages.

CODA
I should have seen it, but I was on such affair.
Seeing the true king crown'd here in Estampa.[12]

Ezra Pound

Can chai la fueilla

Arnaut Daniel

Can chai la fueilla
   dels ausors entrecims,
El freitz s'ergueilla
   don sechal vais' el vims,
Dels dous refrims
   vei sordezir la brueilla;
Mas ieu soi prims
   d'amor, qui que s'en tueilla.

Tot quant es gela
   mas ieu non puesc frezir,
C'amors novela
   mi fal cor reverdir;
Non dei fremir
   c'Amors mi cuebr' em cela
Em fai tenir
   ma valor em cabdela.

Bona es vida
   pos joia la mante,
Que tals n'escrida
   cui ges no vai tan be;
No sai de re
   coreillar m'escarida,
Que per ma fe
   del miells ai ma partida.

De drudaria
   nom sai de re blasmar,
C'autrui paria
   torn ieu en reirazar; [13]
Ges ab sa par
   no sai doblar m'amia,
C'una non par
   que segonda noill sia.

When Sere Leaf Falleth

Arnaut Daniel

When sere leaf falleth
   from the high forkèd tips,
And cold appalleth
   dry osier, haws and hips,
Coppice he strips
   of bird, that now none calleth.
Fordel[14] my lips
   in love have, though he galleth.

Though all things freeze here,
   I can naught feel the cold,
For new love sees, here
   my heart's new leaf unfold;
So I am rolled
   and lapped against the breeze here:
Love who doth mould
   my force, force guarantees here.

Aye, life's a high thing,
   where joy's his maintenance,
Who cries 'tis wry thing
   hath danced never my dance,
I can advance
   no blame against fate's tithing
For lot and chance
   have deemed the best thing my thing.

Of love's wayfaring
   I know no part to blame,
All other pairing,
   compaired, is put to shame,
Man can acclaim
   no second for comparing
With her, no dame
   but hath the meaner bearing.

No vueill s'asemble
   mos cors ab autr' amor
Si qu'eu jail m'emble
   ni volva cap aillor;
Non ai paor
   que ja cel de Pontremble
N'aia gensor
   de lieis ni que la semble.

Ges non es croia
   cella cui soi amis;
De sai Savoia
   plus bella nos noiris;
Tals m'abelis
   don ieu plus ai de joia
Non ac Paris
   d'Elena, cel de Troia.

Tan pareis genta
   cella quem te joios
Las gensors trenta
   vens de belas faisos;
Ben es razos
   doncas que nos chans senta,
Quar es tan pros
   e de ric pretz manenta.

Vai t'en chansos
   denan lieis ti prezenta;
Que s'ill no fos
   noi meir [15] Arnautz s'ententa.

I'ld ne'er entangle
   my heart with other fere,
Although I mangle
   my joy by staying here
I have no fear
   that ever at Pontrangle
You'll find her peer
   or one that's worth a wrangle.

She'd never destroy
   her man with cruelty
'Twist here 'n' Savoy
   there feeds no fairer she,
Than pleaseth me
   till Paris had ne'er joy
In such degree
   from Helena in Troy.

She's so the rarest
   who holdeth me thus gay,
The thirty fairest
   can not contest her sway;
'Tis right, par fay,
   thou know, O song that wearest
Such bright array,
   whose quality thou sharest.

Chançon, nor stay
   till to her thou declarest:
'Arnaut would say
   me not, wert thou not fairest.'

   Ezra Pound

L' aura amara

Arnaut Daniel

L' aura amara
Fals bruoills brancutz
Clarzir
Quel doutz espeissa ab fuoills,
Els letz
Becs
Dels auzels ramencs
Ten balps e mutz,
Pars
E non-pars;
Per qu'eu m'esfortz
De far e dir
Plazers
A mains per liei
Que m'a virat bas d'aut,
Don tem morir
Sils afans no m' asoma.

Tant fo clara
Ma prima lutz
D'eslir
Lieis don crel cors los huoills,
Non pretz
Necs
Mans dos aigonencs; [16]
D'autra s'esdutz
Rars
Mos preiars,
Pero deportz
M'es adauzir
Volers,
Bos motz ses grei
De liei don tant m' azaut
Qu'al sieu servir
Sui del pe tro c'al coma.

The Bitter Air

Arnaut Daniel

The bitter air
Strips panoply
From trees
Where softer winds set leaves,
And glad
Beaks
Now in brakes are coy,
Scarce peep the wee
Mates
And un-mates.
  What gaud's the work?
  What good the glees?
What curse
I strive to shake!
Me hath she cast from high
In fell disease
I lie, and deathly fearing.

So clear the flare
That first lit me
To seize
Her whom my soul believes;
If cad
Sneaks,
Blabs, slanders, my joy
Counts little fee
Baits
And their hates.
  I scorn their perk
  And preen, at ease.
Disburse
Can she, and wake
Such firm delights, that I
Am hers, froth, lees
Bigod! from toe to earring.

Amors, gara,
Sui ben vengutz
C'auzir
Tem far sim desacuoills
Tals detz
Pecs
Que t'es miells quet trencs;
Qu'ieu soi fis drutz
Cars
E non vars,
Mal cors ferms fortz
Mi fai cobrir
Mains vers;
Cab tot lo nei
M'agr' ops us bais al chaut
Cor refrezir
Que noi val autra goma.

Si m' ampara
Cill cuim trahutz
D'aizir,
Si qu'es de pretz capduoills,
Dels quetz
Precs
C'ai dedinz a rencs,
L'er fort rendutz
Clars
Mos pensars;
Qu'eu fora mortz
Mas fam sofrir
L' espers
Queill prec quem brei,
C'aissom ten let e baut;
Que d'als jauzir
Nom val jois una poma.

Doussa car', a
Totz aips volgutz,
Sofrir
M'er per vos mainz orguoills,

Amor, look yare!
Know certainly
The keys:
How she thy suit receives;
Nor add
Piques,
'Twere folly to annoy.
I'm true, so dree
Fates;
No debates
   Shake me, nor jerk.
   My verities
Turn terse,
And yet I ache;
Her lips, not snows that fly
Have potencies
To slake, to cool my searing.

Behold my prayer,
(Or company
Of these)
Seeks whom such height achieves;
Well clad
Seeks
Her, and would not cloy.
Heart apertly
States
Thought. Hope waits
   'Gainst death to irk:
   False brevities
And worse!
To her I raik,[17]
Sole her; all others' dry
Felicities
I count not worth the leering.

Ah fair face, where
Each quality
But frees
One pride-shaft more, that cleaves

Car etz
Decs
De totz mos fadencs,
Don ai mains brutz
Pars
E gabars;
De vos nom tortz,
Nim fai partir
Avers,
C'anc non amei
Ren tan ab meins d'ufaut,
Anz vos desir
Plus que Dieus cill de Doma.

    Erat para
Chans e condutz,
Formir
Al rei qui t'er escuoills;
Car pretz
Secs
Sai, lai es doblencs,
E mantengutz
Dars
E manjars:
De joi lat portz,
Son anel mir,
Sil ders,
C'anc non estei
Jorn d'Aragon quel saut
Noi volgues ir,
Mas sai m'an clamat Roma.

CODA
    Faitz es l' acortz
Qu'el cor remir
Totz sers
Lieis cui domnei
Ses parsonier Arnaut;
Qu'en autr' albir
N'es fort m'ententa soma.

Me; mad
Frieks
(O' thy beck) destroy,
And mockery
Baits
Me, and rates.
   Yet I not shirk
   Thy velleities,
Averse
Me not, no slake
Desire. God draws not nigh
To Dome,[18] with please
Wherein's so little veering.

Now chant prepare,
And melody
To please
The king, who'll judge thy sheaves.
Worth, sad,
Sneaks
Here; double employ
Hath there. Get thee
Plates
Full, and cates,
   Gifts, go! Nor lurk
   Here till decrees
Reverse,
And ring thou take.
Straight t' Arago I'd ply
Cross the wide seas
But 'Rome' disturbs my hearing.

CODA
And midnight mirk,
In secrecies
I nurse
My served make[19]
In heart; nor try
My melodies
At other's door nor mearing.[20]

   Ezra Pound

En cest sonet coind'e leri

Arnaut Daniel

En cest sonet coind'e leri,
Fauc motz, e capuig e doli,
Que serant verai e cert
Qan n'aurai passat la lima,
Qu'Amors marves plan'e daura
Mon chantar, que de liei mou
Que Pretz manten e governa.

Tot jorn meillur et esmeri
Car la gensor serv e coli
Del mon—so·us dic en apert;
Sieus sui del pe tro c'en cima,
E si tot venta·ill freid'aura
L'Amors, q'inz el cor mi plou,
Mi ten chaut on plus iverna.

Mil messas n'aug e·n proferi,
E n'art lum de cera e d'oli,
Que Dieus m'en don bon issert
De lieis on no·m val escrima;
E qand remir sa crin saura
E·l cors q'a grailet e nou,
Mais l'am que qi·m des Luserna.

Tan l'am de cor e la queri
C'ab trop voler cuig la·m toli
(S'om ren per ben amar pert).
Lo sieus cors sobretracima
Lo mieu tot e non s'isaura;
Tan ai de ver fait renou
C'obrador n'ai e taverna.

Canzon: Of the Trades and Love

Arnaut Daniel

Though this measure quaint confine me,
And I chip out words and plane them,
   They shall yet be true and clear,
  When I finally have filed them.
Love glosses and gilds them knowing
  That my song has for its start
One who is worth's hold and warrant.

Each day finer I refine me
And my cult and service strain them
   Toward the world's best, as ye hear,
  "Hers" my root and tip have styled them.
And though bitter winds come blowing,
  The love that rains down in my heart
Warmeth me when frost's abhorrent.

To long masses I resign me,
  Give wax-lights and lamps, maintain them
   That God win me issue here.
  Tricks of fence? Her charm's beguiled them.
Rather see her, brown hair glowing;
  And her body fine, frail art,
Than to gain Lucerna for rent! [21]

Round her my desires twine me
'Till I fear lest she disdain them.
   Nay, need firm love ever fear?
  Craft and wine, I have exiled them.
Yet her high heart's overflowing
  Leaves my heart no parched part;
Lo, new verse sprouts in the current.

Non vuoill de Roma l'emperi
Ni c'om mi fassa apostoli,
Q'en lieis non aia revert,
Per cui m'art lo cors e·m rima;
E s'il maltraich no·m restaura
Ab un baissar anz d'annou,
Mi auci, e si enferna.

Ges pel maltraich q'ieu soferi
De ben amar no·m destoli
Liei (sitot me ten en desert);
Car si·m fatz los motz en rima,
Pieitz trac aman c'om que laura;
C'anc plus non amet un ou
Cel de Moncli N'Audierna.

Ieu sui Arnautz, q'amas l'aura,
E chatz la lebre ab lo bou,
E nadi contra suberna.

If they'd th' empire assign me
Or the Pope's chair, I'd not deign them
   If I could not have her near.
  My heart's flames have so high piled them,
If she'll not, ere th' old year's going
  Kiss away their deadly smart,
Dead am I and damned, I warrant.

  Though these great pains so malign me
I'd not have love's powers restrain them
    —Though she turn my whole life drear—
  See, my songs have beamed and tiled them.
Yes, love's work is worse than mowing,
  And ne'er pains like mine did dart
Through Moncli for Audierent.

I, Arnaut, love the wind, doing
  My hare-hunts on an ox-cart,
And I swim again the torrent.

  Ezra Pound

Arnaut de Marueill

Arnaut de Marueill was from . . . Périgueux, from a castle called
Marueill; he was of a poor family and became a clerk. But since he
could not live by his letters, he went out into the world. And he could
write good poetry, and he was a man of intelligence.

   The heavens and good fortune brought him to the court of the
Countess of Burlatz. . . . This Arnaut was handsome, and he sang well,
and read romances. And the Countess did much for him and honored
him greatly. And he fell in love with her and dedicated his songs to her,
but he did not dare tell her nor anyone else that it was he who had
written them, but instead he pretended somebody else had done so.[1]

Arnaut de Marueill became active poetically around 1170. We know that he
continued to compose at least through 1195, for the Monge de Montaudon
skewered Arnaut in the satiric gallery of troubadours that he composed
around that year. The good monk mockingly chided Arnaut's lady for not
showing more compassion toward him, even though "his eyes are always
calling out for mercy; the more he sings, the more his tears are flowing."[2]
And, indeed, our first selection (particularly in its final two stanzas) hints at
a troubadour who could become overwrought at times.

   Arnaut wrote at the high tide of the troubadours, and swam with that
tide. While he seldom strays far from convention, he composed when the
conventions themselves were still relatively fresh. And he handled them
adroitly, if not brilliantly. In our first selection, "Si·m destreignetz, dompna,
vos et Amors" ("Lady, By You and Love I Am So Swayed"), note the con-

ventional springtime opening, the linking of beauty with virtue, the *descriptio puellae* (description of beauty) of his ladylove. Arnaut's lyric is typical of much troubadour versifying in that, as Page put it, a "great show of decorum [is] achieved by an accumulation of potent courtly words" (*Voices and Instruments,* 15).

Despite his conventionality, Arnaut de Marueill had his admirers. While Petrarch found him the "less famous Arnaut" by comparison with Arnaut Daniel, the Italian still held the troubadour from Marueill in high esteem. Likewise Ezra Pound, never one to pull his punches, praised this troubadour: "For the simplicity of adequate speech Arnaut [de Marueill] is to be numbered among the best of the courtly 'makers'" (*Spirit of Romance,* 57). Pound found these admirable qualities in the second selection, "Belh m'es quan lo vens m'alena," which he translated as "Fair Is It to Me."

Si·m destreignetz, dompna, vos et Amors

Arnaut de Marueill

Si·m destreignetz, dompna, vos et Amors,
C'amar no·us aus ni no m'en puosc estraire:
L'us m'encaussa, l'autre·m fai remaner,
L'us m'enardis e l'autre·m fai temer,
Preiar no·us aus per enten de jauzir;
Mas, si cum cel qu'es nafratz per morir,
Sap que mortz es e pero si·s combat,
Vos clam merce ab cor desesperat.

Bona dompna, paratges e ricors,
On plus aut es e de maior afaire,
Deu mais en si d'umilitat aver,
Car ab orguoill non pot bos pretz caber,
Qui gen no·l sap ab chausimen cobrir.
E pois no·m puosc de vos amar sofrir,
Per merce·us prec e per humilitat,
C'ab vos trobes calacom pietat.

No mi nogues vostra rica valors,
C'anc no la puoc un jorn plus enan traire,
Pos qu'ieu vos vi aic lo sen e·l saber
E·l vostre pretz creisser a mon poder;
Qu'en mains bos luocs l'ai dich e faich auzir.
E si·us plagues c'o deignassetz grazir,
No·us quezira plus de vostr' amistat
E gauzira per guizerdon lo grat.

Totz los forfaitz e totas las clamors
Que·us mi podetz rancurar ni retraire,
Es car m'ausatz abellir ni plazer
Mas d'autra ren qu'ieu anc pogues vezer;
Autr' ochaison, dompna, no·m sabetz dir
Mas car vos sai conoisser e chausir
Per la meillor et ab mais de beutat:
Ve·us tot lo tort en que m'avetz trobat.

Lady, by You and Love I Am So Swayed

Arnaut de Marueill

Lady, by you and Love I am so swayed
That I dare not love, and yet I cannot refrain:
Part of me wants to flee, the other remain;
I am at once courageous and afraid.
I dare not plead with you to satisfy me,
But rather like a man wounded and dying
Who clings to life full knowing what's in store,
So, despairing, your mercy I implore.

Where lineage and true nobility
Reside and merit is surpassing, there
Humility should also dwell, for where
There's worth, we should not meet with vanity...
Unless it's veiled by a sweet clemency.
I pray the mercy and humility
That you possess will lead you to want to aid me,
For I can't leave off loving you, good lady.

Don't think that I'm unmoved by your high merit;
My praise of you will never have an ending.
Since the moment we met, I have been bending
My skills to sing your praises, to ensure that
Men acknowledge your worth both near and far.
Should you ever desire to thank me for
This, friendship is the most I'd hope to earn—
That to me would seem sufficient return.

All your accusations, that I complain
Unendingly, commit a series of wrongs,
Stem from the fact that you exude more charm
Than any other creature I have seen.
No, the only sin that I admit to
Is that of having recognized that you,
Lady, exceed the rest in grace and beauty:
That's the only wrong of which I'm guilty.

Vostre beill huoill, vostra fresca colors
E·il doutz semblan plazen que·m sabetz faire
Vos mi fan tant desirar e voler
Que mais vos am, on plus m'en desesper,
E fatz que fols car no m'en sai partir.
Mas quand ieu pens cals etz que·m faitz languir,
Cossir l'onor et oblit la foudat,
E fuich mon sen e sec ma voluntat.

Belhs Carboncles, no·us cal pus de ben dir,
Ni qui·l Marques mentau de Monferrat,
Ja plus no·l laus, qu'assatz l'aura lauzat.[3]

Your lovely eyes and your limpid complexion,
And the charming way that you behave
Toward me, have so kindled my needs and cravings
That both my love and my desperation
Increase. That I can't leave you seems like madness,
Yet when I consider for whom I languish
I do not think of folly but the honor:
I flee my sense and follow my desire.

Robert Kehew

Belh m'es quan lo vens m'alena

Arnaut de Marueill

Belh m'es quan lo vens m'alena
En abril ans qu'entre mais,
E tota la nueg serena
Chanta·l rossinhols e·l jais;
Quecx auzel en son lenguatge,
Per la frescor del mati,
Van menan joi d'agradatge,
Com quecx ab sa par s'aizi.

E pus tota res terrena
S'alegra quan fuelha nais,
No·m puesc mudar no·m sovena
D'un' amor per qu'ieu sui jais;
Per natur' e per uzatge
Me ve qu'ieu vas joi m'acli,
Lai quan fai lo dous auratge
Que·m reve lo cor aissi.

Pus blanca es que Elena,
Belhazors que flors que nais,
E de cortezia plena,
Blancas dens ab motz verais,
Ab cor franc ses vilanatge,
Color fresc' ab saura cri.
Dieus, que·l det lo senhoratge,
La sal, qu'anc gensor non vi!

Merce fara, si no·m mena
D'aisi enan per loncs plais,
E don m'en un bais d'estrena
E segon servizi·l mais!
E pueis farem breu viatge
Sovendet e breu cami,
Que·l sieus belhs cors d'alegratge
Me a mes en est trahi.[4]

Fair Is It to Me

Arnaut de Marueill

Fair is it to me when the wind "blows down my throat,"[5]
In April ere May come in,
And all the calm night the nightingale sings, and the jay,
Each bird in his own speech,
Through the freshness of the morning[6]
Goes bearing joy rejoicingly
As he lodges him by his mate.

And since every terrene thing
Rejoices when the leaf is born,
I cannot keep silent the memory
Of a love whence I am happy.
Through nature and usage it happeneth
That I lean toward joy,
There where I did the sweet folly
That thus comes back into my heart.

More white than Helen is my "fair-adorned,"
And than a flower that is born,
She is full of courtesy,
And her teeth are white with true words,
And heart frank, sans villeiny.
Fresh is her hue, and her hair brown golden.
May God save her, who hath given her this seignory,
For never have I seen a nobler lady.

Ezra Pound

Gaucelm Faidit

Gaucelm Faidit was from a town called Uzerche, which is in the bishopric of Limousin, and he was the son of a burgher. And he sang worse than anyone in the world, but he composed many good melodies and good rhymes. And he became a minstrel because he lost all his belongings in a game of dice. He was a man of great girth, and he exhibited great gluttony in eating and drinking. . . .

And he married a prostitute whom he took with him around the courts, and her name was Guillelma Monja ["nun"]. She was extremely beautiful and extremely learned, and she became as large and as fat as he was.[1]

Gaucelm Faidit was one of the most prolific troubadours. Some seventy of his compositions, penned between about 1172 and 1203, have survived. Various nobles patronized the troubadour, apparently attracted to his simplicity of style and sincerity of emotion. Gaucelm Faidit's patrons included Richard the Lion-hearted, upon whose death Gaucelm wrote a moving *planh*. Another dozen of Gaucelm's poems are dedicated to Maria de Ventadorn, not only a patroness but also a *trobairitz* in her own right, represented elsewhere in the present anthology.

Other sources corroborate certain aspects of Gaucelm's marriage as set forth in his *vida*. As noted elsewhere in this book the Monge de Montaudon, a man of his time, mocked Gaucelm as one who "from a lover became the husband of the one he used to follow around." And a poetic exchange between Elias d'Ussel and Gaucelm himself pokes fun at the corpulence of the married couple. But the medieval biographer's other remarks about Gaucelm's wife cannot be substantiated.

At the dawn of the thirteenth century, Gaucelm Faidit set out on pilgrimage to the Holy Land. He celebrated his safe return from that perilous adventure in 1203 with the poem that follows. Referring to this and other poems by Gaucelm Faidit, Jensen writes that he "ranks as the first poet in France to have expressed his longing for his home province" (*Troubadour Lyrics*, 37, 351). But is this poem even more of an anomaly in the troubadour corpus with its heartfelt celebration of conjugal love?

Del gran golfe de mar

Gaucelm Faidit

Del gran golfe de mar
E dels enois dels portz,
E dels perillos far,
Soi, merce Dieu, estortz!
Don posc dir e comdar
Qe mainta malanansa
I hai suffert, e maint turmen!
E pos a Dieu platz que torn m'en
En Lemozi, ab cor jauzen,
Don parti ab pesansa,
Lo tornar e l'onransa
Li grazisc, pos el m'o cossen.

Ben dei Dieu mercejar,
Pos vol que, sans e fortz,
Puesc' el païs tornar,
On val mais uns paucs ortz,
Qe d'autra terr' estar
Rics ab gran benanan. a!
Qar sol li bel acuillimen,
E·il onrat fag e·il dig plazen
De nostra domn' e·il prezen
D'amorosa coindansa,
E la doussa semblansa,
Val tot can autra terra ren.

From the Depths of the Sea

Gaucelm Faidit

From the depths of the sea
From the perilous strait
From the port's ennui
I have, thank God, escaped,
And thus the miseries
I've faced, I can express
And share: and since God has ordained
That I with joyful heart again
Find myself in the Limousin
Which I left in distress,
For the home that I'm blessed
With, for honor, I give thanks to him.

Thank God it was his plan
That I, still strong and healthy,
Should regain this land—
Here a man's more wealthy
With a small orchard than
He'd be with an expanse
Of land and riches elsewhere. For these
Joys of homecoming—gifts that please,
Affectionate words, noble deeds,
The favors my lady grants,
And her sweet countenance—
No other country can exceed.

Ar hai dreg de chantar,
Pos vei joi e deportz,
Solatz e domnejar,
Qar so es vostr'acortz;
E las font e·l riu clar
Fan m'al cor alegransa,
Prat e vergier, qar tot m'es gen!
Q'era non dopti mar ni ven,
Garbi, maïstre ni ponen,
Ni ma naus no·m balansa,
Ni no·m fai mais doptansa
Galea ni corsier corren.

Qi, per Dieu gazaignar,
Pren d'aitals desconortz,
Ni per s'arma salvar,
Ben es dregz, non ges tortz;
Mas cel qi, per raubar
E per mal' acordansa,
Vai per mar, on hom tan mal pren
Em pauc d'ora, s'aven soven
Qe, qan cuj'om pujar, deissen;
Si c'ab desesperansa
Il laissa tot en lansa
L'arm' e lo cors, l'aur e l'argen!

Now I have the right
To sing because I see
What brings joy and delight:
Good friends and gallantry.
My heart warms at the sight
Of fountain and clear river—
Field, orchard, everything pleases—
I no longer fear the sea,
Southwest, northwest, or westerly
    Winds—boats when they shiver—
    I no longer quiver
At menacing corsair or galley.

If to save your soul
Or for love of God you would
Suffer this travail,
That is all to the good:
But if you plan to steal
And evil thoughts are why
You go to sea, to suffer untold
Hardships, you may find that though
You thought you were rising, you're go-
    ing down; so, terrified,
    You pitch over the side
Soul and body, silver and gold.

Robert Kehew

Peire Vidal

> Peire Vidal was . . . one of the craziest men who ever lived, for he believed to be true whatever he liked or wanted. And he . . . recounted the craziest things in matter of arms and of love and in speaking ill of others. . . . And he loved Loba ["She-Wolf"] of Pueinautier . . . and for her sake Peire Vidal took the name of Lop ["Wolf"] and bore wolf arms. And he had shepherds hunt him through the mountains of Cabaret with mastiffs and greyhounds as if he were a wolf. And he dressed in a wolf's skin so the shepherds and dogs would make no mistake about his being one. And the shepherds with their dogs hunted him down and caught him in such a way that he was brought half dead to the house of Loba de Pueinautier. When she saw that it was Peire Vidal, she began to feel great joy for the madness he had committed and to laugh a great deal, and her husband did the same.[1]

It is hard to descend to earth from the fantasy of this *razo*,[2] but this we must do. Peire Vidal was poetically active from around 1180 to 1205. During this period he seems to have traveled everywhere. Peire puts in an appearance at all the troubadour watering holes: Marseilles, Monferrat, Toulouse, Castile, Aragon. The Monge de Montaudon roasts him in his satiric gallery of troubadours. Peire also wanders farther afield: to Hungary, Cyprus, Constantinople, and the Holy Land (with the Fourth Crusade). Peire Vidal is last seen on the island of Malta before he vanishes from sight.

While his medieval biographer is pulling our leg in his *vida*—at one point he also would have us believe that Peire Vidal thought he was the rightful emperor of Constantinople—he is on the mark when he declares that the "great ease" with which the troubadour wrote is one of his charms. Later critics also have remarked on the wide range of emotions that Peire expresses, as well as his refreshing ability to lampoon himself.

In both of the two selections below, longing for a loved one is intermingled with nostalgia for one's homeland. The first poem, "Pos tornatz sui en Proensa" (To Provence I Can Return Now"), also illustrates the troubadours' fascination with (and poetic exploitation of) the paradoxes of *fin' amor*.

While not necessarily denying the nostalgia in the second selection, "Ab l'alen tir vas me l'aire" ("The Song of Breath"), Cheyette offers an alternative reading: he finds that the poem offers an example of how closely politics was intertwined with notions of love in the world of the troubadours. Cheyette points out that the boundaries given in the second stanza ("'Twixt Rhone and the Vensa, / Or from the shut sea to Durensa") are "explicitly political boundaries, the part of Provence ruled by the Barcelonese dynasty as defined by treaty in 1125." In this poem, Cheyette goes on, "the poet declares his allegiance to the Barcelonese. His beloved [Provença] is very much a political lady" (*Ermengard of Narbonne*, 236). Pound—who pioneered such political readings of troubadour lyrics (see chapter on Bertran de Born)—considered this poem to be one of the finest airs to waft out of Provence.

Pos tornatz sui en Proensa

Peire Vidal

Pos tornatz sui en Proensa
Et a ma domna sap bo,
Ben dei far gaia chanso,
Sivals per reconoissensa:
Qu'ab servir et ab honrar
Conquier hom de bon senhor
Don e benfait et honor,
Qui be·l sap tener en car:
Per qu'eu m'en dei esforsar.

Ses peccat pris penedensa
E ses tort fait quis perdo,
E trais de nien gen do
Et ai d'ira benvolensa
E gaug entier de plorar
E d'amar doussa sabor,
E sui arditz per paor
E sai perden gazanhar
E, quan sui vencutz, sobrar.

E quar anc no fis falhensa,
Sui en bona sospeisso
Que·l maltraitz me torn en pro,
Pos lo bes tan gen comensa.
E poiran s'en conortar
En mi tuit l'autr' amador,
Qu'ab sobresforsiu labor
Trac de neu freida foc clar
Et aigua doussa de mar.

To Provence I Can Return Now

Peire Vidal

To Provence I can return now
Since my Lady wills me well,
So the song I make should tell
All my joys are what they were now.
Any man who serves a lord
Seeks rewards and words of grace
For his service and true faith;
Knowing what such gifts are worth,
Let my song's pure joy pour forth.

Lacking fault, I beg for pardon;
Without sinning, I repent;
For my rage, I've merriment
And, for nothing, richest guerdon.
Here's a sweet taste for my sour;
Here is joy for all my tears;
Boldness springs from my worst fears;
Having lost, I've gained much more
And though beaten, won my war.

Since I'm guiltless of offences
I have good hopes that my pain
Can lead back to joy again —
Joy that sweetly now commences
And my case may bring some ease
To sad lovers, since I've drawn
Joy from pains I've undergone —
Clear fire from the snows that freeze
And fresh water from salt seas.

Estiers non agra garensa,
Mas quar sap que vencutz so,
Sec ma domn' aital razo
Que vol que vencutz la vensa;
Qu'aissi deu apoderar
Franc' umilitatz ricor,
E quar no trob valedor
Qu'ab leis me posc' aiudar,
Mas precs e merce clamar.

E pos en sa mantenensa
Aissi del tot m'abando,
Ja no·m deu dire de no;
Que ses tota retenensa
Sui seus per vendr'e per dar.
E totz hom fai gran folor
Que ditz qu'eu me vir alhor;
Mais am ab leis mescabar
Qu'ab autra joi conquistar.

E cel que long' atendensa
Blasma, fai gran falhizo;
Qu'er an Artus li Breto,
On avian lor plevensa.
Et eu per lonc esperar
Ai conquist ab gran doussor
Lo bais que forsa d'amor
Me fetz a mi dons emblar,
Qu'eras lo·m denh' autreiar.

Bels Rainiers, per ma crezensa,
No·us sai par ni companho,
Quar tuit li valen baro
Valon sotz vostra valensa.
E pos Deus vos fetz ses par
E·us det mi per servidor,
Servirai vos de lauzor
E d'als, quant o poirai far,
Bels Rainiers, car etz ses par.

Should hope fail, I'm lost in anguish,
Conquered by her, as she knows,
For my Lady's reasoning goes:
If I'm conquered, then she's vanquished.
So, since true humility
All high powers can overcome
And I've found no champion
That could bend her love to me,
I'll pray for her sympathy.

Now I give myself up wholly
Into her possession, so
She need never tell me No,
Since I'm hers entire and solely,
Hers to give outright or sell.
He's a fool who would declare
I could ever turn elsewhere;
In such pain I'd rather dwell
Than win joy with someone else.

Those who label me a martyr
Since I wait and hope are wrong;
Bretons take pride in their long
Vigil for the good King Arthur.
And in hoping constantly
That I'll win by diligence,
That same kiss love's violence
Made me steal from her, now she
Will vouchsafe me graciously.

Fair Rainier, I find it's true
You've no equal and no mate
Since the lords, however great,
Are all valued less than you.
Since God formed you without par
And assigned me all my days
To your service and your praise,
Lovely Rainier, know you are
Without equal, near or far.

W. D. Snodgrass

Ab l'alen tir vas me l'aire

Peire Vidal

Ab l'alen tir vas me l'aire
Qu'ieu sen venir de Proensa;
Tot quant es de lai m'agensa,
Si que, quan n'aug ben retraire,
Ieu m'o escout en rizen
E·n deman per un mot cen:
Tan m'es bel quan n'aug ben dire.

Qu'om no sap tan dous repaire
Cum de Rozer tro c'a Vensa,
Si com clau mars e Durensa,
Ni on tant fins jois s'esclaire.
Per qu'entre la franca gen
Ai lassat mon cor jauzen
Ab lieis que fa·ls iratz rire.

Qu'om no pot lo jorn mal traire
Qu'aja de lieis sovinensa,
Qu'en lieie nais jois e comensa.
E qui qu'en sia lauzaire,
De ben qu'en diga no·i men;
Que·l mielher es ses conten
E·l genser qu'el mon se mire.

E s'ieu sai ren dir ni faire,
Ilh n'aja·l grat, que sciensa
M'a donat e conoissensa,
Per qu'ieu sui gais e chantaire.
E tot quan fauc d'avinen
Ai del sieu bell cors plazen,
Neis quan de bon cor consire.

The Song of Breath

Peire Vidal

Breathing I draw the air to me
Which I feel coming from Provença,
All that is thence so pleasureth me
That whenever I hear good speech of it
I listen laughing and straightway
Demand for each word an hundred
So fair to me is the hearing.

No man hath known such sweet repair
'Twixt Rhone and the Vensa.
Or from the shut sea to Durcnsa,
Nor any place with such joys
As there are among the French folk[3] where
I left my heart a-laughing in her care,
Who turns the veriest sullen unto laughter.

No man can pass a day in boredom who has remembrance of her, in
whom joy is born and begun. He who would speak her praise to the full,
has no need of skill and lying. One might speak the best, and yet she were
still above the speech.

If I have skill in speech or deed hers is the thanks for it, for she has given
me proficiency and the understanding whereby I am a gay singer, and
every pleasing thing that I do is because of her fair self, and I have all
needful joy of her fair body, even when I with good heart desire it.

Ezra Pound

Peirol

Peirol was a poor knight of Auvergne from a castle named Peirol . . .
in the region of the Dalfin. . . . And he was a courtly man and hand-
some in appearance. And the Dalfin of Auvergne kept Peirol with him
and clothed him and gave him horses and arms.

And the Dalfin had a sister named Sail de Claustra ["escaped from
the cloister"], beautiful and good and well regarded, who was the wife
of . . . a great baron of Auvergne. Lord Peirol loved her truly, and the
Dalfin . . . was very pleased with the songs Peirol composed about his
sister. . . .

And the love of the lady and Peirol grew so much that the Dalfin be-
came jealous of her, for he believed that she accorded the poet more
than was appropriate. And he parted with Peirol and banished him
and did not clothe him or arm him. So Peirol was unable to maintain
himself as a knight and became a minstrel. And he went around the
courts and received clothing and money and horses from the barons.[1]

Peirol was active from around 1185 to 1220. Some thirty-two of his poems
have come down to us. Several of these express enthusiasm for the Crusades,
and in fact Peirol undertook a pilgrimage to the Holy Land. He may have
ended his days in Montpellier.

In his *vida* Peirol is portrayed as a bit of a ladies' man. The Monge de
Montaudon, however, would have none of that. In the satiric gallery of
troubadours that he composed around 1195, the monk observed that Peirol
"has worn the same suit for thirty years and is drier than kindling wood."

Peirol favored the *canso* and was a disciple of the straightforward *trobar leu* school of lyricism. While much of his work is conventional, some originality shines through in his use of simile and metaphor. The poem below displays both the troubadour's simplicity and his deft use of figurative language, with his nod in the opening stanza to the swan song of legend.

Atressi co·l signes fai

Peirol

Atressi co·l signes fai
Quant vol morir, chan,
Quar sai que genseis morrai
Et ab mens d'afan.
Car amors m'a mes en tal latz
Don mains afans ai sofertatz,
Mas pel joi c'aora m'en ve
Non tem mal ni afan en re.

E doncs qual conseill penrai
C'ades muer aman?
Qu'ieu joi non aten de lai
On miei desir van;
Per so no part ma voluntatz,
Si tot m'en sui desesperatz.
Pensiu e consiros mi te
Cella don plus fort mi sove.

Ges melhor dona non sai.
Dieus, per que l'am tan?
Que ja non li ausarai
Dire mon talan.
Gen m'acuoill e·m fai bel solatz,
Mais del plus son desconseillatz,
Car, s'ieu li clamava merce,
Tem que puois se guardes de me.

Preiars, lai on non s'eschai,
Torn' en enuey gran.
Ses parlar la preiarai.
E com? Ab semblan,
Et ill conosca o si·l platz.
C'aissi dobla lo jois e·l gratz
Quant us cors ab autre s'ave,
E quant hom ses querre fai be.

Even as the Swan

Peirol

Even as the swan that knows
    It dies, yet sings, so I
Though suffering sing, thus seeking to
    Relieve distress and die
With greater merit; for Love has fashioned
Such a snare that the joys of passion
Render its torments bearable:
To them I am insensible.

If from love I were to perish
    Would that change my mind?
Some return from her I cherish
    I don't expect to find.
Yet though I do not hope for love,
Still my heart will not be moved
From her: she whom I can't forget
Holds me worried and petulant.

God! I know no finer lady,
    I love her to excess:
But why? The warmth she wakes in me
    I'll never dare confess.
Although I'm welcomed graciously,
I am uncertain how to proceed:
If I begged for her to love me,
That would make her wary of me.

I know that it is tedious to
    Endure unwanted pleading,
So in silence I will woo
    Her—how? With double meanings
That she can understand if she
So wills: for joy is twice as sweet
When favors are, without a word,
Granted; hearts are in such accord.

Robert Kehew

Franquez' ab fin cor verai
Trai amor enan;
Autz paratges la deschai,
Qe·ill ric son truan,
Que tan n'i a de rics malvatz
Per que·l segles n'es sordeiatz.
E domna que bon pretz mante
Non am per ricor, s'als no i ve.

Chansos, vas la bella vai,
Non per ren qe·ill man,
E potz li lo mal qu'ieu trai
Dire ses mon dan.
E di li·m c'a leis es donatz
Mos coratges et autreiatz;
Sieus son e sieus serai jase;
Morir puosc per ma bona fe.

Bona domna, on que siatz,
Jois si' ab vos e joi aiatz,
Qu'eu non vos aus clamar merce
Mas sivals pensar o puosc be.[2]

Raimbaut de Vaqueiras

Raimbaut de Vaqueiras was from a castle called Vaqueiras, and he was the son of a poor knight . . . who was thought to be mad. And Raimbaut became a minstrel. . . . And he came to Montferrat to the Marquis Boniface. And he stayed with him for a long time, and he increased in arms and in [poetic] invention . . . . And the marquis, because of the great worth he recognized in him, made him a knight. . . .

So he fell in love with the sister of the marquis, who was called Lady Beatrice and was the wife of Enrico del Carretto. And he invented many good songs about her. And he called her "Bel Cavalier." And this is why he called her this: Lord Raimbaut had such good fortune that he could see Lady Beatrice whenever he wanted, as long as she was in her room, through a keyhole. Nobody noticed this. And one day the marquis came in from the hunt. And he entered the room and put his sword next to the bed and went out. And Lady Beatrice stayed in the room and took off her mantle and remained in her coat. And she took the sword and girt it in the manner of a knight. And she took it out of its sheath and brandished it up high and swung it in her hand from one side to the other. And she put it back in the sheath, ungirded it, and put it back by the side of the bed. And Lord Raimbaut de Vaqueiras saw everything I told you through the keyhole. So for this reason he afterwards called her "Bel Cavalier" in his songs.[1]

Raimbaut de Vaqueiras's life shows that troubadours could achieve upward mobility: born around 1155–60 in humble circumstances, Raimbaut was eventually knighted, perhaps in 1194. He was active as a poet from around 1180 to 1205. Despite any keyhole-peeping activities he might have indulged in—and there is no reason to believe any of this—Raimbaut remained close to his lord, the marquis of Montferrat, for many years. He apparently joined the marquis in the Fourth Crusade in 1202, but it is not known whether he perished at his lord's side in Salonika in 1207, or lived to return to Provence.

In his work, Raimbaut de Vaqueiras was a bit of a linguistic show-off. Raimbaut did not hesitate, for example, to compose (or engage in) a poetic debate in which his entreaties, made in the courtly *langue d'oc,* were rebuffed by a lady who spoke a Genoese dialect. Similarly Raimbaut penned another poem that is a linguistic tour-de-force: a *descort* in which the stanzas are written successively in Occitan, Italian, French, Gascon, and Galician-Portuguese.[2]

Raimbaut was also renowned for basing certain songs on dance forms— an uncommon practice for troubadours. Page argues that troubadour composition, as exemplified by the rhapsodic *canso,* is essentially a High Style art, where "the idea of the song as the composition of a self-conscious artist is constantly kept in the listener's mind." According to Page, one only encounters the "lower" dance forms at "the very periphery of the troubadour corpus," where "the voice of the singer dissolves into the voices of the dancers (who sing the refrains)" (*Voices and Instruments of the Middle Ages,* 14–23). If the division between High and Low styles was ever that clear-cut, then Raimbaut, more than any other major troubadour, delighted in blurring the distinction. The twenty-six surviving poems that can positively be attributed to his pen range across poetic forms both high and low.

"Kalenda maya" ("May Day"), presented below, is one of only six surviving troubadour *estampidas;* these "stamping songs" are associated with a French dance form, the *retroencha.* Jensen (*Troubadour Lyrics,* 540) points out that melody is the "most prominent feature" of Raimbaut's song. With his "almost obsessive reiteration of rhymes," the poet doggedly pursues form, at the occasional expense of clear meaning. The piece is still performed today with a convincingly driving dance beat and infectious melody.

Kalenda maya

Raimbaut de Vaqueiras

Kalenda maya
Ni fuelhs de faya
Ni chanz d'auzelh   ni flors de glaya
Non es que·m playa,
Pros domna guaya,
Tro qu'un ysnelh   messatgier aya
Del vostre belh   cors, que·m retraya
Plazer novelh   qu'amors m'atraya,
         E iaya,
         E·m traya
Vas vos,   domna veraya;
         E chaya
         De playa
·l gelos,   ans que·m n'estraya.

Ma belh'amia,
Per Dieu no sia
Que ia·l gelos   de mon dan ria;
     Que car vendria
     Sa gelozia,
Si aitals dos   amans partia;
Qu'ieu ia ioyos   mais no seria,
Ni ioys ses vos   pro no·m tenria;
         Tal via
         Faria,
    Qu'om ia   mais no·m veiria;
         Selh dia
         Morria,
Donna   pros, qu'ie·us perdria.

Quom er perduda
Ni m'er renduda
Dona, s'enans   non l'ai aguda?
     Que drutz ni druda
     Non es per cuda;
Mas quant amans   en drut se muda,

May Day

Raimbaut de Vaqueiras

This May Day bringing
   new lilies springing
with songs of birds   through beechwoods ringing
   can scarce delight me
   unless you'd write me
some tender words   that hurry lightly
from your dear form   forbidden to me
to tell me warm   new joys are due me—
   new pleasure
   past measure
whereby   our hearts impel us;
   then let him
   just fret him
then die—   that fool who's jealous.

My lovely Lady,
   if God would aid me
that jealous heart   could not evade me;
   he'd pay full dear
   each frown or sneer
who's dared to part   loves so sincere.
If he could sever   your heart from me
no joy would ever   sooth or calm me—
   I'd wander
   out yonder
where none   could then retrieve me;
   so I
   might die,
dear one,   if you'd bereave me.

If you should leave me [3]
   in scorn, believe me,
My Beauteous Knight,   how deep you'd grieve me.
   Despite my yearning,
   this heart's not turning
to false delights   or loves worth spurning

L'onors es grans   que·ylh n'es creguda;
E·l belhs semblans   fai far tal bruda;
        Que nuda
        Tenguda
    Nou'us ai   ni d'als vencuda;
        Volguda,
        Crezuda
    Vos ai,   ses autr' aiuda.

     Tart m'esiauzira,
     Pus ia·m partira,
Belhs Cavaliers,   de vos ab ira;
     Qu'alhor no·s vira
     Mos cors, ni·m tira
Mos deziriers,   qu'als non dezira;
Qu'a lauzengiers   sai qu'abelhira,
Donna, qu'estiers   non lur garira.
        Tals vira,
        Sentira
    Mos dans,   qui·ls vos grazira,
        Que·us mira,
        Consira
    Cuidans,   don cors sospira.

     Dona grazida,
     Quecx lauz' e crida
Vostra valor,   qu'es abelhida;
     E qui·us oblida,
     Pauc li val vida.
Per qu'ie·us azor   don' eyssernida?
Quar per gensor   vos ai chauzida,
E per melhor   de pretz complida,
        Blandida,
        Servida
    Genses   qu' Erecx Enida.
        Bastida
        Fenida,
    N'Engles,   ai l'estampida.

for then our plight   would please that liar—
he'd have delight,   his full desire.
       He'd know it;
       we'd show it;
My pain—   he'd thank you for that.
       He eyes you
       and spies you,
in vain—   these sighs deplore that.

    What stands at stake, then?
    Am I forsaken
to lose this love   I've never taken?
    How then recover?—
    I've had no lover,
but mere dreams of   love with each other.
When love's embraced   its fame grows grander;
we two stayed chaste   yet came to slander.
       I never
       had ever
undressed you,   drew you toward me;
       I prayed you,
       obeyed you,
nor pressed you   to reward me.

    Lady so gracious,
    the most sagacious
men on this earth   should sing your praises;
    to those not knowing
    your love's bestowing,
life can be worth   naught but foregoing.
Most good and fair   I do assert you;
most noble, rare   and rich in virtue.
       I've sued you
       and wooed you
as young   Eric, Enida;[4]
       Lord Briton,[5]
       I've written
and sung   my estampida.

W. D. Snodgrass

Guillem de Cabestanh

[In Roussillon, Guillem de Cabestanh's birthplace] there lived a woman called my lady Seremonda, wife of En Raimon de Castel-Roussillon. This man was very rich and noble, but also cruel and harsh, fierce and arrogant. Guillem de Cabestanh loved the lady with a great love; he sang of it and wrote his songs for her. And she, young and noble, lovely and charming, loved him above all other creatures. This was told to Raimon de Castel-Roussillon who, in a jealous rage, made inquiries and, finding it was true, had his wife put under guard.

And then one day Raimon de Castel-Roussillon saw Guillem de Cabestanh passing by unescorted and killed him. He had his heart removed from his body and his head cut off. He had the heart cooked and seasoned with pepper, and gave it to his wife to eat. And when this lady had eaten it, Raimon de Castel-Roussillon asked her, "Do you know what you have eaten?" And she answered, "No, I know that it was savory and very good." Then he told her she had eaten the heart of En Guillem de Cabestanh; and in order that she should have no doubts, he had the head brought before her. And when the lady heard and saw this, she lost her sense of sight and hearing. Upon recovering, she said, "Sir you have given me such a fine thing to eat, that I shall never eat again." When he heard this, he leapt at her with sword in hand, intending to strike her on the head, but she ran to a balcony and threw herself down. And so she died.[1]

The reader who is tenderhearted (no pun intended) will be reassured to know that the above narrative is almost certainly fictitious. Enough jealousy, however, apparently smoldered in the breasts of choleric barons regarding the attentions paid to their wives by minstrels to generate similar tales about a Breton harper, a German minnesinger, and a French *trouvère*. This yarn is most widely associated with Guillem de Cabestanh because Boccaccio gave us a version of it. Pound did too, for that matter; see the fourth of his *Cantos*.

This fantastic embroidery patches over a bare spot, for historically we know next to nothing about Guillem de Cabestanh. Someone of this name from the Roussillon fought in the battle of Navas de Tolosa in 1212, and so historians conjecture that the troubadour was poetically active around then. His few surviving poems (seven of positive attribution) all deal with *fin' amor* or related topics, and so there are no topical references to aid in dating him.

The selection below showcases some of Guillem's strengths: simplicity, charm, and lyricism. In stanza 3 of this poem, cynical readers may find Guillem de Cabestanh to be somewhat disingenuous in the way he rationalizes his flirting with other ladies.

Lo jorn qu'ie·us vi, dompna, primeiramen

Guillem de Cabestanh

Lo jorn qu'ie·us vi, dompna, primeiramen,
Quan a vos plac que·us mi laissetz vezer,
Parti del cor tot autre pessamen
E foron ferm en vos tug mey voler:
Qu'aissi·m pauzetz, dompna, el cor l'enveya
Ab un dous ris et ab un simpl' esguar;
Mi e quant q'es mi fezes oblidar.

Que·l grans beutatz e·l solatz d'avinen
E·il cortes dig e l' amoros plazer
Que·m saubetz far m'embleron si mon sen
Qu'anc pueys, dompna gentils, no·l puec aver
A vos l'autrey cuy mos fis cors merceya
Per enantir vostre pretz et honrar;
A vos mi ren, c'om miels non pot amar.

E car vos am, dompna, tan finamen
Que d'autr' amar no·m don' Amors poder,
Mas agrada·m c'ab altra cortey gen,
Don cug de me la greu dolor mover;
Pueis quan cossir de vos cuy jois sopleya,
Tot autr' amor oblit e dezampar:
C'ab vos remanc cuy tenc al cor pus car.

E membre vos, s'a vos plai, del coven
Que me fezetz al departir saber,
Don aic mon cor adoncs guay e jauzen
Pel bon respieit en que·m mandetz tener.
Mout n'ai gran joy, s'era lo mals s'engreya,
Et aurai lo, quan vos plaira, encar,
Bona dompna, qu'ieu suy en l'esperar.

That Day, My Lady, When I First Discovered That You Exist

Guillem de Cabestanh

That day, my lady, when I first discovered
That you exist, that time you first allowed
Me to behold you, the thought of any other
Left my heart, my longings found an abode
In you. Thus, lady, you gave me to know
Longing, with a sweet smile, a simple glance:
You made me forget myself and all existence.

For the great beauty, the gracious presence,
The courteous speech, the pleasures known to lovers
That you granted, deprived me of my sense,
Which I have not been able to recover . . .
Take, lady, this gift my true heart offers—
Let the praise that is your due be rendered:
My love's well placed, to you it is surrendered.

For I love you, lady, and so sincerely
That Love will not give me leave to love another:
Others I court with gracious manners merely,
Attempting to relieve the pain I suffer.
But when I think of you, joy's conqueror,
My love for any other disappears:
My love's constant for you whom I hold dear.

Remember, *s'a vos plai,* the vow that you
Offered to me the day we had to part.
Ah! the joy and happiness I knew
Then, when you commanded me to be of good heart.
I feel it now (though pain also marks
Me), and when it pleases you I'll know it again:
Dearest lady, I live in hope till then.

E ges maltrach no m'en fai espaven,
Sol q'ez ieu cuig e ma vida aver
De vos, dompna, calacom jauzimen;
Anz li maltrag mi son joy e plazer
Sol per aisso quar sai qu'Amors autreya
Que fis amans deu tot tort perdonar
E gen sufrir maltrait per gazaignar.

Ai! si er ja l'ora, dompna, qu'ieu veya
Que per merce me vulhatz tant honrar
Que sol amic me denhetz apelhar!

Suffering thus holds no power to frighten,
So long as I believe I'll win some measure
Of joy from you, lady, before my life ends.
Rather these pains to me are joy and pleasure:
I know that he who truly seeks love's treasure
Must, with courtesy, prepare to withstand
Pain, forgive mistakes; so Love commands.

I live for the day when it will be your pleasure
To show mercy, Lady, and condescend
To honor me by calling me your friend.

Robert Kehew

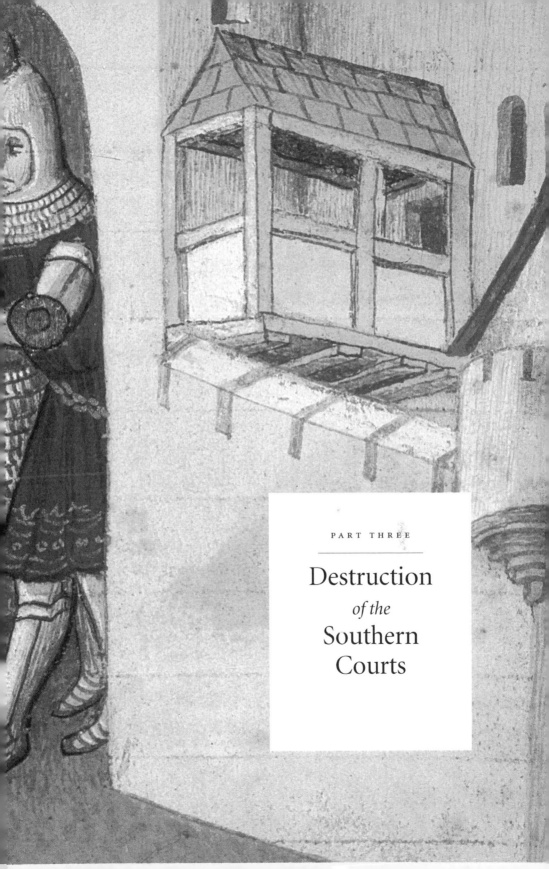

PART THREE

Destruction
of the
Southern
Courts

Folquet de Marseilla

Folquet of Marseilla was the son of a merchant from Genoa. . . . And when the father died, he left Folquet very wealthy. Then Folquet sought fame and merit. And he began to serve the worthy barons. . . . And he was greatly esteemed and honored by King Richard [the Lion-Hearted] and by the count Raimon [V] of Toulouse and by . . . his lord from Marseilla. . . .

He invented poetry very well, and . . . he loved the wife of his lord. . . . And it so happened that the lady died. . . . Because of his sadness over [the death] of his lady and [of] the princes I told you about, he abandoned the world. And he joined the order of Cîteaux with his wife and his two sons. And so he was made abbot of a rich abbey which is in Provence, and which is called Torondet. And later he was made Bishop of Toulouse. And there he died.[1]

Folquet de Marseilla's career as a troubadour began around 1180 and ended before his entrance into the church in the waning years of the twelfth century. While he thus composed at the time when the troubadours were at their apogee, Folquet deserves pride of place in this final part, "Destruction of the Southern Courts," because of the later, much different role that he played in the life (and death) of Occitania—a role only hinted at in the laconic *vida* presented above.

As bishop of Toulouse for the quarter century beginning in 1206, Folquet stood at the stormy center of the Albigensian Crusade. In this position he vigorously aided and abetted the Crusaders. Playing this role stained his hands with blood. Early in this Crusade, while the northern forces were still distant from Toulouse, Folquet organized a gang of thugs from the catholic

Preceding: **Destruction of the Southern Courts.** The expulsion of the Albigensians from Carcasonne. From "The Chronicles of France, from Priam King of Troy until the Crowning of Charles VI," by Boucicaut Master (fl. 1390–1430) and workshop. (British Library, London; the Bridgeman Art Library, London.)

laity in the city. He called this group the White Brotherhood, and rallied them against so-called usurers and heretics. Later he colluded with Simon de Montfort. In 1216, for example, when Simon promised Toulousian rebels that they would receive lenient treatment if they freed some captured crusaders, Bishop Folquet lent his good name and personal prestige to the vow. Then, once the Crusaders were set free, Simon wreaked a terrible vengeance on Toulouse, taking some four hundred citizens prisoner and seizing their property. Further, a contemporary chronicle accused Folquet of having "snuffed out, in body and in soul, the lives of more than fifteen hundred people."[2] This charge, however, cannot be verified.

Folquet lived to witness the decisive humiliation of Raimon of Toulouse. This occurred in April 1229 when, in front of the half-completed Notre Dame cathedral then rising in Paris, a shirt-sleeved Raimon begged for absolution from his sins from the papal legate. Folquet capped his illustrious career by becoming the first chief of the nascent Inquisition in Toulouse.

During his long tenure with the church, Folquet was never able to bury his troubadour past. During a heated debate over the Albigensian Crusade that took place in Rome in 1215, for example, Folquet heard himself derided by an enemy as that "singer of songs whose sound is damnation."[3] A more apocryphal tale is told of Folquet as the elderly bishop of Toulouse, who heard a minstrel singing on the streets of Paris. The bishop subsequently imposed harsh penance on himself, explaining to his bemused brethren that, once upon a time, he himself had penned the offending song.

Dante judged Folquet's conversion from troubadour to priest to be providential. In his *Commedia,* the Catholic poet encounters Folquet de Marseilla in heaven, where he perceives him to be a "bright and precious jewel": one of those whose loving natures originally led them into carnality, but later toward the godhead. Folquet is the only troubadour whom Dante thus assigns to his *Paradiso* (canto IX).

The young Folquet's reputation as a poet is as debatable as are the later bishop's pretensions to a reward in the hereafter. On the one hand, Bonner concludes that Folquet was "one of the half a dozen or so greatest of the troubadours." Among Folquet's virtues, Bonner remarks a "marvelous control over words, rhythms and sounds," a "smooth and effortless" command of intricate sentence structure, and the occasional achievement of a "splendid fabric of conceits" (*Songs of the Troubadours,* 174–75). Jensen, on the other hand, sniffs that Folquet "displays no great originality in his poems, and his style is dry and scholastic" (*Troubadour Lyrics,* 33). In the selection below, where a conventional topic is expressed with a smooth and at-times intricate sentence structure, both critics could find some evidence to support their contending positions.

Tant m'abellis l'amoros pessamens

Folquet de Marseilla

Tant m'abellis l'amoros pessamens
Que s'es vengutz e mon fin cor assire,
Per qe no·i pot nuills autre pes caber,
Ni mais negus no m'es doutz ni plazens,
Qu'adoncs viu sas qand m'aucio·ill cossire,
E fin' amors aleuja mo martire
Qe·m promet joi, mas trop lo·m dona len,
C'ab bel semblan m'a tirat longamen.

Ben sai que tot qant fatz es dreitz niens;
E q'en puosc als, s'amors mi vol aucire?
Qu'a escien m'a donat tal voler
Que ja non er vencutz ni recrezens;
Vencutz si er, qu'aucir m'an li sospire
Tot soavet, pois de lieis cui dezire
Non ai socors, ni d'aillor no l'aten,
Ni d'autr' amor non puosc aver talen.

Bona dona, si·us platz, siatz sufrens
Del ben qu'ie·us vuoill, qu'ieu sui del mal sufrire,
E pois lo mals no·m poira dan tener,
Anz m'er semblan que·l partam egalmens;
E s'a vos platz qu'en autra part me vire,
Ostatz de vos la beutat e·l doutz rire
E·l bel semblan que m'afollis mon sen;
Pois partir m'ai de vos, mon escien.

A totz jorns m'etz plus bell' e plus plazens,
Per qu'ie·n vuoill mal als huoills ab que·us remire,
Car a mon pro no·us poirian vezer
Et a mon dan vezo·us trop sotilmens;
Mos dans non es, so sai, mas no·m n'azire,
Anz es mos pros, domna, per qu' ieu m'albire,
Si m'aucietz, que no·us estara gen,
Car lo mieus dans vostres er eissamen.

So Pleasureth Me the Amorous Thought[4]

Folquet de Marseilla

So pleasureth me the amorous thought
Which has come to beset my true heart
That no other thought can fare there.
Nor is any other thought now sweet and pleasant to me.
For I am hers when the grief of it kills me,
And true love lightens my martyrdom,
Promising me joy; but she gives it to me over-slowly,
And has held me long with fair seeming.

Well I know that all I do is nothing at all,
And what more can I do if Love wish to slay me;
For wittingly he (Love) has given me such desire
As will never be conquered, nor conquer Him.
Thus am I conquered, for the sighs have slain me
So gently, because I have not aid from her whom I desire.
Nor do I expect it from any other,
Nor have I power to wish for another love.

But if you wish me to turn elsewhere,
Part from you the beauty and the sweet laughter,
And the gay pleasure, that had sent mad my wit;
Since, as I ween, I must part me from you,
Every day are you more fair and pleasant to me,
Wherefore I wish ill to the eyes that behold you,
Because they can never see you to my good,
But to my ill they see you subtly (or speedily).

Ezra Pound

Per so, domna, no·us am saviamens
Qu'a vos sui fis et a mos ops trahire;
E·us cug perdre e mi non puosc aver,
E·us pens nozer et a mi sui nozens;
Per so no·us aus mon dan mostrar ni dire,
Mas a l'esgar podetz mon cor devire,
Qu'ar lo·us cuich dir et aras m'en repen
E port n'els huoills vergonh' et ardimen.

Trop vos am mais, domna, qu'ieu no·us sai dire,
E car anc jorn aic d'autr' amor desire
No m'en penet, anz vos am per un cen,
Car ai proat l'autrui chaptenemen.

Vas Nems t'en vai, chanssos, qui qe·is n'azire
Car gaug n'auran, segon lo mieu albire,
Las tres domnas, a cui ieu te presen,
Car ellas tres valon ben d'autras cen.

Peire Cardenal

Peire Cardenal . . . wrote *cansos,* but only a few; however he wrote many *sirventes,* all of which were splendid and beautiful. And in these *sirventes*—or at least for those who understood them—he propounded many fine arguments and examples, for he greatly chastised the folly of this world and greatly vilified false clergymen, as one can see in these poems of his. And . . . En Peire Cardenal, when he passed from this life, was close to a hundred years old.[1]

Peire Cardenal's long life began during the golden age of the troubadours (probably in the 1180s), and ended after the French crown had vanquished the southern forces and annexed the *pays d'oc.* As a witness to the dismemberment of the world of the troubadours, it is not surprising that Peire found *fin' amor* inadequate as a worldview. In the second selection, "Ar me puesc ieu lauzar d'Amor" ("I Dare to Claim, Now, Love Cannot"), for example, note how the author lampoons conventional notions of refined love. Pound (in "Troubadours: Their Sorts and Conditions," 98) advised that "the gentle reader in search of trunk-hose and the light guitar had better go elsewhere," for Peire Cardenal's poetic strengths lie in other areas than the love song.

Peire Cardenal is the lone prophetic figure who, in his own words, "refused this world's mad sanity" (see first selection below). Secure in his moral vision, Peire held the mirror up to the failings and cruelties of his day. He assailed those whom his medieval biographer branded as "false clergymen," and reserved particular wrath for the monastic orders, which he considered hypocritical. Yet this troubadour also was cognizant of life's moral ambiguities. Peire admitted that "the pope and the legate and the cardinal have twisted such a cord that . . . no one can escape committing treachery." At other times, Peire seems to conclude that his words are futile, that the evils of this world cannot be cured. This awareness adds a deeper, tragic resonance to some of his broadsides.

Peire Cardenal was a master at setting off rhetorical fireworks to illuminate his thoughts. In "Ar me puesc ieu lauzar d'Amor," for example, the troubadour deploys *conduplicatio* (repetition of words), *contentio* (contrasting words, such as winners versus losers), and *alliteratio* (alliteration) to drive home his point. The study of such rhetorical devices was well developed in the Middle Ages.[2] At the same time, Peire frequently incorporates legal terminology into his verse. In "Un sirventes novel . . ." ("A New Protest Song"), for example, the troubadour draws upon such lawyerly concepts as *plaideiamen* (plea), *demans* (decree), and *partia* (proposition) to frame his dispute with God as a legal wrangle.[3] Based on such signs of formal training, some have speculated that Peire studied legal science in the canonical school at Le Puy; this hypothesis, however, cannot be verified.

Some have wondered how such an outspoken critic, writing in horrific times, managed to survive into extreme old age. Given the vigor of his denunciation of Rome, some have gone so far as to speculate that Peire Cardenal was actually a Cathar and enjoyed the support of that heretical sect. But the poet's theology, when it does become explicit, appears more Christian than Cathar—he dedicates, for example, a poem to the Virgin Mary who was anathema to the Albigensians—and the Catharist hypothesis has not won widespread endorsement. If Peire was a heretic, his heresy seemed to be of a more humanist strain; see "Un sirventes novel . . ." below.

The cup into which Peire Cardenal poured his bitter draught is the moral *sirventes,* of which he was a master. Pound distinguished Peire's poetic project from that of other troubadours: "the sirventes[es] of Sordello and De Born were directed for the most part against persons, while [Peire Cardenal] drives rather against conditions." Some fifty of Peire's nearly one hundred compositions are *sirventeses*. Poems like our first selection, "Una ciutatz fo . . ." ("There Was a Town"), exemplify the poet's courageous voice and imaginative powers. At the same time Pound justly remarks on "how finely the sound of [Peire's] poems is matched with their meaning. There is a lash and sting in his timbre and in his movement" ("Troubadours: Their Sorts and Conditions," 95–97).

Una ciutatz fo, no sai cals

Peire Cardenal

Una ciutatz fo, no sai cals,
On cazet una plueia tals
Que tug l'ome de la ciutat
Que toquet foron dessenat.

Tug desseneron mas sol us;
Aquel ne escapet, ses plus:
Que era dins una maizo
On dormia, quant aiso fo.

Aquel levet cant ac dormit
E fo se de ploure gequit,
E venc foras entre las gens.
E tug feron dessenamens:

L'uns ac roquet, l'autre fon nus
E l'autre escupi ves sus;
L'uns traïs peira, l'autre astella,
L'autre esquintet sa gonella.

E l'uns ferit e l'autre enpeis,
E l'autre cuget esser reis
E tenc se ricamen pels flancx,
E l'autre sautet per los bancx.

L'uns menasset, l'autre maldis,
L'autre juret e l'autre ris,
L'autre parlet e non saup que,
L'autre fes metolas dese.

E aquel qu'avia son sen
Meravillet se mot fortmen
E vi ben que dessenat son.
E garda aval et amon

There Was a Town

    Peire Cardenal

There was a town, I can't say where;
They had a brief rainshower there
And all on whom drops chanced to fall
Lost their good sense; then, one and all,

They went berserk and there were none
Got off unscathed except just one—
Through the whole time of this mishap
One man was home taking a nap.

As soon as this rainshower was through
And this man's nap was over, too,
He strolled out but it all seemed changed—
His townsfolk's minds must be deranged:

One wore a child's shirt; one went bare;
One spit straight up into the air.
One threw a stick; one heaved a boulder;
One ripped up his own tunic's shoulder.

One hit folks; one shoved them around;
One thought himself a king, new-crowned,
And, hands on hips, would proudly prance;
One on shop-counters stomped a dance;

One growled wild threats; one swore and vowed;
One laughed; one of them cursed out loud;
One chattered without sense or rhyme;
One made fierce faces all the time.

The man who'd kept his wits intact
Stared all around, taken aback
To find his townsfolk brain-bereft,
He looked to right and looked to left

S'i negun savi n'i veira,
E negun savi non i ha.
Granz meravillas ac de lor,
Mas mot l'an il de lui major

Que·l vezon estar suaumen.
Cuidon c'aia perdut son sen
Car so qu'il fan no·l vezon faire,
A cascun de lor es veiaire

Qu'il son savi e ben senat,
Mas lui tenon per dessenat.
Qui·l fer en gauta, qui en col.
El no pot mudar no·s degol.

L'uns l'empenh e l'autre lo bota.
El cuia eusir de la rota;
L'uns esquinta, l'autre l'atrai,
El pren colps e leva e quai.

Cazen levan, a grans scambautz,
S'en fug a sa maizo de sautz,
Fangos e batutz e mieg mortz,
Et ac gaug can lor fon estortz.

Aquist faula es per lo mon:
Semblanz es als homes que i son.
Aquest segles es la ciutatz,
Quez es totz plens de dessenatz.

Que·l majer sens c'om pot aver
Si es amar Dieu e temer
E gardar sos comandamens;
Mas ar es perdutz aquel sens.

Li plueia sai es cazeguda:
Cobeitatz, e si es venguda
Un' erguelhoz' e granz maleza
Que tota la gen a perpreza.

For just one man still sane and sound.
Not one sane man was to be found.
Marveling at them all, he gazed;
They looked back, even more amazed

To see him standing there so calmly.
They thought the poor man must be balmy
Acting in that outlandish way—
Everyone there was certain they

Were *compos mentis,* sound of brain,
So, clearly, he must be insane.
One slapped his face, then clenched his neck;
One knocked him down flat on the deck;

One shoved him; one gave him a kick;
He tried to slip off, stealthy, quick,
But one grabbed, spinning him around.
He got up, slipped, fell to the ground,

Then, lurching, stumbling in his stride,
Crept back to his own house to hide,
Bruised, mud-bespattered and half-dead,
Relieved, though, he'd squirmed loose and fled.

Our world's seen in this parable
And all this wide world's folk, as well;
This earth's the town I have in mind
Where mania's never hard to find.

The best sense mortals here have known
Is to love God, fear Him alone
And always keep the Lord's command.
In our times such good sense is banned.

A Reign of Covetousness fell
Over this world and us as well,
Spreading a huge malicious pride
That preys on humans far and wide,

E si Dieus n'a alcun gardat,
L'autre·l tenon per dessenat
E menon lo de tomp en bilh
Car non es del sen que son ilh.

Que·l sens de Dieu lor par folia,
E l'amix de Dieu, on que sia,
Conois que dessenat son tut,
Car lo sen de Dieu an perdut.

E ilh, an lui per dessenat,
Car lo sen del mon a laissat.

And if one man's preserved by God,
It's clear to all he's sick or odd;
If he has sense they don't all share
They'll leave him wriggling in the air.

God's wisdom is called lunacy,
While the Lord's friend, where'er he be,
Knows they're all mad, the whole damned horde,
Who've lost the good sense of the Lord,

While they know he's just crazy: he
Refused this world's mad sanity.

W. D. Snodgrass

Ar me puesc ieu lauzar d'Amor

Peire Cardenal

Ar me puesc ieu lauzar d'Amor,
Que no·m tol manjar ni dormir;
Ni·n sent freidura ni calor
Ni no·n badail ni no·n sospir
Ni·n vauc de nueg arratge.
Ni·n soi conquistz ni·n soi cochatz,
Ni·n soi dolenz ni·n soi iratz
Ni no·n logui messatge;
Ni·n soi trazitz ni enganatz,
Que partitz m'en soi ab mos datz.

Autre plazer n'ai ieu maior,
Que no·n traïsc ni fauc traïr,
Ni·n tem tracheiris ni trachor
Ni brau gilos que m'en azir;
Ni·n fauc fol vassalatge,
Ni·n soi feritz ni derocatz
Ni no·n soi pres ni deraubatz;
Ni no·n fauc lonc badatge,
Ni dic qu'ieu soi d'amor forsatz
Ni dic que mos cors m'es emblatz.

Ni dic qu'ieu mor per la gensor
Ni dic que·l bella·m fai languir,
Ni non la prec ni non l'azor
Ni la deman ni la dezir.
Ni no·l fas homenatge
Ni no·l m'autrei ni·l me soi datz;
Ni non soi sieus endomenjatz
Ni a mon cor en gatge,
Ni soi sos pres ni sos liatz,
An dic qu'ieu li soi escapatz.

I Dare to Claim, Now, Love Cannot

Peire Cardenal

I dare to claim, now, Love cannot
Rob me of appetite or sleep,
Can't turn me cold, can't turn me hot,
Can't make me yawn or sigh or weep
    Or stay out nights to wander;
Love can't torment or vanquish me—
Now I go grief- and anguish-free,
    I pay no page or pander;
Love can't hoodwink me, can't betray;
I palmed my dice and walked away.

I've found my joy in life's to be
Neither betrayer nor betrayed;
Traitor and traitoress can't scare me
Nor jealous husband's bright sword blade;
    I cut no more mad capers;
I don't get wounded or cast down,
Plundered like some poor captive town;
    Don't stew in brainless vapors;
I don't say I've been Love-oppressed;
Don't claim my heart's ripped from my breast;

Don't say for her sweet self I yearn;
Don't claim that she's so fair I'll die;
Don't say I beg for her and burn;
Don't praise her name and sanctify;
    Don't kneel in her observance;
Don't say my life to her I gave;
Don't claim to be her serf or slave;
    Don't sign on with her servants;
Don't wear Love's chains; far better, I'm
Making my getaway in time.

Mais deu hom lauzar vensedor
Non fai vencut, qui·l ver vol dir,
Car lo vencens porta la flor
E·l vencut vai hom sebelir;
E qui venc son coratge
De las desleials voluntatz
Don ieis lo faitz desmezuratz
E li autre outratge,
D'aquel venser es plus onratz
Que si vensia cent ciutatz.

Pauc pres prim prec de pregador,
Can cre qu'il, cuy quer convertir,
Vir vas sil voler sa valor,
Don dreitz deu dar dan al partir;
Si sec son sen salvatge,
Leu l'er lo larcx laus lag loinhatz;
Plus pres lauzables que lauzatz:
Trop ten estreg ostatge
Dreitz drutz del dart d'amor nafratz.
Pus pauc pres, pus pres es compratz.

Non voilh voler volatge
Que·m volv e·m vir mas voluntatz
Mas lai on mos vols es volatz.

Speaking the truth, men ought to praise
Winners, not losers—victory's head
And brow goes crowned with wreaths of bays;
Losers lie down in graveyards, dead.
    Who's conquered his heart's treachery
And that insane desire that brings
Men to do such outrageous things,
    All foolishness and lechery,
He should find honor in that crown
More than in conquering many a town.

Puerile, these poets that plead, pant, pray
And lure loved ladies toward loose lust;
Who'd warp one's worth to worm his way
Drags all due dignity in dust.
    Who can't rein Love's rash rages,
Will find too fast that fair fame flies;
Praiseworthiness, not praise, I prize.
    Some clods can't quit cramped cages—
Like lovers laid low by Love's lance.
Whatever good gay gifts grace grants,

    I wouldn't want Love's wages.
Nor would I want a wayward will
Whose feigned free flight fails to fulfill.

W. D. Snodgrass

Un sirventes novel vueill comensar

Peire Cardenal

Un sirventes novel vueill comensar,
Que retrairai al jor del jujamen
A sel que·m fes e·m formet de nien.
S'el me cuja de ren arazonar
E s'el me vol metre en la diablia
Ieu li dirai: "Sienher, merce non sia!
Qu'el mal segle tormentiei totz mos ans.
E guardas mi, si·us plas, dels tormentans."

Tota sa cort farai meravillar
Cant auziran lo mieu plaideiamen;
Qu·eu dic qu'el fa ves los sieus faillimen
Si los cuja delir ni enfernar.
Car qui pert so que gazanhar poiria,
Per bon dreg a de viutat carestia,
Qu'el deu esser dous e multiplicans
De retener las armas trespassans.

Los diables degra dezeretar
Et agra mais d'armas e plus soven
E·l dezeretz plagra a tota gen
Et el mezeis pogra s'o perdonar,
Car per mon grat trastotz los destruiria,
Pos tut sabem c'absolver s'en poiria:
"Bels seinhers Dieus! Sias dezeretans
Del enemix enuios e pezans!

Vostra porta non degras ja vedar,
Que sans Peires i pren trop d'aunimen
Que n'es portiers: mas que intres rizen
Tota arma que lai volgues intrar.
Car nuilla cortz non er ja ben complia
Que l'uns en plor e que l'autre en ria;
E sitot ses sobeirans reis poissans,
Si no m'ubres, er vos en fatz demans.

A New Protest Song

Peire Cardenal

I'll now compose a brand new protest song
Which I'll perform on the Last Judgement Day
Telling the Lord who contrived me from clay
That if He's planning to claim I've done wrong
Then stick me down with those devils that scare me,
That I'll just say: "Have a heart, Lord, and spare me!
I had torments in that damned world enough;
If You don't mind, keep Hell's pitchforkers off!"

I'll make the Lord's whole court sit up and stare
When once they've heard the content of my plea,
Saying He treats His own folk wrongfully,
Fixing to torment, then fling them down there.
Whoever chucks out good things he could store
To spare and preserve them, deserves to be poor;
God should be tender and dwell every place
So he could save us from sin and disgrace.

God ought to steal souls from Satan's vast share;
Then He could reap souls more often, more easily;
That's the one theft we'd all witness with glee—
Since He could pardon Himself, then and there.
Wipe out those archtraitors—that's my solution,
Since He could give Himself full absolution:
"Sweet Lord in Heaven, from now on dispossess
None but your foes and their vile sinfulness,

But never turn mortal men from Your door;
That would make Peter, the good saint, feel shame
Keeping the gate; every soul, each the same,
Should just walk in and exult evermore.
Surely no court has been fairly assembled
Where one man laughed while the other man trembled.
Mightiest of all, supreme King though You be,
Open up or You'll get served a decree.

Ieu no me vueill de vos dezesperar:
Anz ai en vos mon bon esperamen,
Que me vaillas a mon trespassamen:
Per que deves m'arma e mon cors salvar.
E farai vos una bella partia:
Que·m tornetz lai don moc lo premier dia
O que·m siatz de mos tortz perdonans.
Qu'ieu no·ls fora si non fos natz enans.

S'ieu ai sai mal et en enfern l'avia,
Segon ma fe tortz e peccatz seria,
Qu'ieu vos puesc ben esser recastenans
Que per un ben ai de mal mil aitans.

Per merce·us prec, donna sancta Maria
C'al vostre fill mi fassas garentia,
Si qu'el prenda lo paire e·ls enfans
E·ls meta lay on esta sans Johans."

Don't make me give up my high hopes of You;
You've always helped me feel free from despair—
You ought to help me escape from sin's snare,
Saving my soul and this poor body, too.
In such a case, here's my best proposition:
Either just pardon my soul from perdition
Or send me back where I was before birth—
How could I sin if I'd not been born first?

Suff'ring here, then suff'ring more in Avernus,
That would be wrongful, a sin of unfairness.
I could reprove You and justly complain
That for each joy I got thousandfold pain."

Mercy, I pray you, St. Mary my Lady,
With your own Son, be my witness and aid me;
May He receive every father and son,
Settling them all in the house of St. John.

W. D. Snodgrass

Guillem Figueira

Guillem Figuera was from Toulouse, the son of a tailor, and he was a tailor also. And when the French took Toulouse, he came to Lombardy.

And he knew how to invent poetry well and how to sing. And he became a minstrel among the citizens. He was not a man who would know how to fit among the barons or among high society. But he was greatly cherished by rogues and harlots and innkeepers and publicans. And if he saw a notable man from the court come where he was, he became sad and afflicted. And at once he would take pains to debase him and exalt the rabble.[1]

Guillem Figueira was unfortunate in his earliest biographer, who seems to have taken an almost personal dislike to the troubadour. Or, what is more likely, the biographer's disaffection sprang not so much from personal as from religious grounds. When this *vida* was penned, Guillem stood on the wrong side of history. In the pious eyes of a medieval Catholic, someone like Guillem was, by definition, fit only to associate with "rogues and harlots and innkeepers"; therefore that is what he surely did. Guillem Figueira affronted good Catholics with his poetic satire. But if Guillem was a fire breather, it was because he had been singed personally by the flames of history. As his *vida* recounts, the troubadour grew up in Toulouse, the city destined to become the storm center of the Albigensian Crusade. He seems in fact to have composed the poem below, "D'un sirventes far en est son que m'agenssa" ("Rome, Where Goodness Declines"), while in Toulouse in early 1229, while the French were menacing that city.

The poem is a broadside. In it Guillem, like any good broadsider, is intent not only on bringing people's ire to a boil but also on funneling that rage into the channel that he deems fit. Guillem holds his tongue with respect to the French soldiers, whom he considers merely pawns in a larger game. Instead he pours out his vitriol onto the Catholic Church. By taking this stance, by no means did Guillem reveal himself to have been a Cathar, the primary target of the Albigensian Crusade. He appears rather to have considered himself a true Christian who, along with his countrymen, has been betrayed by the heirs to the shoes of the fisherman. But Guillem's *sirventes* does not stop at condemning the Albigensian Crusade—it also takes potshots against other missteps by the church and perversions of its founder's teachings. Guillem attacks, for example, the practice of selling indulgences. He was not the first to question this technique for raising money and influencing behavior (nor would he be the last). A century and a half earlier, Humbert of Moyenmoutier put it well when he condemned simony as "the supreme heresy, since it denied the spiritual character of the Church and subordinated the gifts of the Spirit to money and worldly power."[2]

If Guillem intended his poem to stiffen the backbones of the Toulousians against their besiegers, he failed. Later, in 1229, Count Raimon VII finally bowed to French demands. Guillem fled to Italy. The troubadour apparently lived out his final days as an exile in Lombardy. While other sorts of poems also flowed from his pen, it is for the present *sirventes,* poured smoking from the crucible of war, for which he is chiefly remembered.

Vivid as is our present selection, for the noted French critic Jeanroy that immediacy was not enough. Jeanroy dismissed this poem as being "more remarkable for its violence [of expression] than for its talent" (*La poésie lyrique des troubadours,* vol. 2, 219). While this may or may not be the case, the poem nonetheless offers a remarkable window into the events of that time.

D'un sirventes far en est son que m'agenssa *(abridged)*

Guillem Figueira

D'un sirventes far en est son que m'agenssa
No·m vuolh plus tarzar ni far longa bistenssa,
E sai ses doptar qu'ieu n'aurai malvolenssa,
Si far sirventes
Dels fals, d'enjans ples,
De Roma, que es caps de la dechasenssa,
On dechai totz bes.

No·m meravilh ges, Roma, si la gens erra,
Que·l segle avetz mes en trebalh et en guerra,
E pretz e merces mor per vos e sosterra,
Roma trichairitz
E de totz mals guitz
E cima e razitz, que·l bons reis d'Englaterra
Fon per vos trahitz.

. . . .

Roma, als homes pecs rozetz la carn e l'ossa,
E guidatz los secs ab vos inz en la fossa;
Trop passatz los decs de Dieu, car trop es grossa
Vostra cobeitatz,
Car vos perdonatz
Per deniers pechatz. Roma, de gran trasdossa
De mal vos cargatz.

Roma, ben sapchatz que vostra avols barata
E vostra foudatz fetz perdre Damiata.
Malamens renhatz, Roma. Dieus vos abata
En dechazemen,
Car tan falsamen
Renhatz per argen, Roma de mal' escata
Es ab fals coven.

Rome, Where Goodness Declines (abridged)[3]

Guillem Figueira

I don't want to delay or hesitate too long
Before I set this tune to a satiric song
I know without a doubt that some will take it wrong
    If I write scornful lines
    About the treacherous kind
That one is sure to find in decadence's home—
    Rome, where goodness declines.

Rome, it's not to wonder at if people err:
Think how you've plunged the world into torment and war;
Merit and mercy die and by you are interred;
    Your treachery abides
    Of evil you're the guide,
Both base and summit high; by you the good king, lord
    Of England was betrayed.[4]

. . . .

You gnaw the flesh of foolish folk, you chew their bones;
Leading the blind, you usher them to the gravestone;
Your avaricious nature you have clearly shown.
    You flout the Lord's commands;
    For pardon, you demand
That money changes hands.[5] It's quite a load, O Rome,
    Of sins your back must stand.

It was, you know, O Rome, this evil traffic that,
Along with folly caused the fall of Damiette.[6]
Your rule is wicked, Rome; may it please God to let
    You fall into decay—
    For silver you behave
Most falsely and betray. You don't keep covenant,
    O Rome of evil race.

Roma, veramen sabem senes doptanssa
C'ab galiamen de falsa perdonanssa
Liuretz a turmen lo barnatge de Franssa,
Lonh de paradis,
E·l bon rei Loïs,
Roma, avetz aucis, c'ab falsa predicanssa
·l traissetz de Paris.

Roma, als Sarrazis faitz petit de dampnatge,
Mas Grecs e Latis gitatz a carnalatge.
Inz el potz d'abis, Roma, faitz vostre estatge
En perdicion.
Ja Dieus part no·m don,
Roma, del perdon ni del pelegrinatge
Que fetz d'Avinhon.

· ·

Roma, be·s decern lo mals c'om vos deu dire,
Quar faitz per esquern dels crestians martire.
Mas en cal cazern trobatz c'om deia aucire
Roma·ls crestians?
Dieus, qu'es verais pans
E cotidians, me don so qu'eu desire
Vezer dels Romans.

Roma, vers es plans que trop etz angoissosa
Dels prezicx trafans que faitz sobre Tolosa.
Trop rozetz las mans a lei de rabiosa,
Roma descordans.
Mas si·l coms prezans
Viu ancar dos ans, Fransa n'er dolorosa
Dels vostres engans.

· ·

Truly we know, O Rome, it's well within our ken,
The way that you to France's barons did extend
False pardon; thus to torment you delivered them,
    Far from heaven's way;[7]
    And Louis that good *rei,*
You lured him away from Paris—dead by your hand—
    Your preaching made him stray.[8]

Rome, to the Saracens you do little damage,
But Greeks and Latins you deliver up to carnage.[9]
In the abyss of hell, Rome, you dwell in a stage
    Of *perdicion;*
    Of portion give me none,
O Rome, of your pardon, or the pilgrimage
    You made to Avignon.[10]

. . . .

Rome, the evil I point out is easy to see:
You martyr Christians and you do it scornfully.
But tell me where it's written, in what book do you read,
    That man should kill those who
    Believe in Christ? Unto
Him who is the true and daily bread, I plead:
    Give the Romans their due.

Great is your distress, O Rome, it's plain and true,
That those false words you preach against Toulouse bring you
Anguish; you gnaw your hands the way that madmen do,
    O Rome the discordant;
    But if the worthy count[11]
For two more years holds out, then France will come to rue
    Those lies you spread about.

. . . .

Roma, Dieus l'aon e·lh don poder e forsa
Al comte que ton los Frances e·ls escorsa,
E fa·n planca e pon, quand ab lui fan comorsa;
Et a mi platz fort.
Roma, a Dieu recort
Del vostre gran tort, si·l platz; e·l comte estorsa
De vos e de mort.

. . . .

Roma, del malcor, que portatz en la gola,
Nais lo sucx, don mor lo mals e s'estrangola
Ab doussor del cor; per que·l savis tremola,
Quar conois e ve
Lo mortal vere
E de lai on ve (Roma, del cor vos cola),
Don li pieitz son ple.

. . . .

Rom', ab fals sembel tendetz vostra tezura,
E man mal morsel manjatz, qui que l'endura.
Car' avetz d'anhel ab simpla gardadura,
Dedins lops rabatz,
Serpens coronatz
De vibr' engenratz, per que·l diable·us cura
Coma·ls sieus privatz.

May this count, O Rome, who scourges and sheers the French,
Feel the strengthening power of mighty God when they launch
Their sorties; I'm well pleased to see them trampled and trounced.
   May the enormous wrongs
   That they inflict upon
Us be to God well known; may he preserve the count
   From death and you, O Rome.

. . . .

From the maliciousness that in your throat gurgles
Issues the bile that kills the poor wretch—it strangles
All sweetness in the heart, O Rome. The wise man trembles,
   For he sees and knows
   The wellspring from whence flows
This deadly poison, Rome: from your heart it dribbles;
   Men's bosoms bear the load.

. . . .

It's a false bait, O Rome, with which you set your trap.
While others starve to death, there's many a nasty snack
That you've snapped. You're vicious like a wolf in a pack,
   Though outside you're a lamb.
   You're a crowned serpent, and
A viper was your dam. The devil will protect
   You, as he does his friends.

Robert Kehew

Sordel

Sordello came from the region of Mantua [in Italy]. . . . And he was a good singer and a good poet, and also a great lover; but he was very treacherous and false towards women and towards the barons with whom he stayed. . . . [He went] to the castle of the lords of Strasso . . . who were very good friends of his. And he secretly married a sister of theirs called Otha, and he then went to Treviso. And when the lord of Strasso found out about it, he wanted to do him harm. . . . Sordello therefore remained in the house of My Lord Ezzelino, always armed; and when he went out, he rode on a good war horse and had himself accompanied by a great number of knights.

And for fear of those who wanted to do him harm, he left and went to Provence, where he stayed with the Count of Provence.[1]

While Sordel (Sordello in Italian) wrote in the language of the *pays d'oc,* this troubadour was actually born (around 1200) in Italy. He left Italy around 1228, probably fleeing some scandal. After wandering around Spain and southern France, Sordel finally settled in Provence. There he became attached to the court of Raimon Berenguer IV,[2] and then, after the count's death in 1245, to the court of that noble's son-in-law, Charles of Anjou. He seems to have held a position of some importance in both courts. Finally, in 1265, Sordel returned to his homeland. The occasion was the expedition to Italy that resulted in Charles's being crowned king of Naples and Sicily. In 1269, in reward for good service, King Charles awarded Sordel some lands in his homeland. The troubadour seems to have died shortly thereafter.

Despite his notoriety as a seducer (as reflected in his *vida*), Sordel's literary reputation rests, not on love songs, but rather on his political and moral *sirventes*. This is due largely to Dante, who was so impressed by Sordel's satiric gift that he envisioned his fellow Italian as guiding him through a part of *Purgatorio*. In his epic, Dante encounters the morally aloof and majestic Sordel at the entrance to the "valley of the negligent rulers." There the troubadour points out to the Tuscan poet those grief-stricken souls who, although called to high station while on Earth, did not accomplish their appointed tasks before death.

In the present selection, the real-life Sordel precisely anticipated his later, Dantesque reincarnation. While the poem starts out as a *planh* on the lord Blacatz's death (probably in 1237),[3] it quickly morphs into a biting satire of many of the rulers of the day. These lords and kings, in Sordel's view, lacked the necessary mettle to carry out the demanding roles that life had thrust upon them. "Planher vuelh En Blacatz" is not only Sordel's finest work—it also offers a rare historical perspective by an insightful critic on the leading figures of that turbulent period.

Planher vuelh En Blacatz en aquest leugier so
Sordel

Planher vuelh En Blacatz en aquest leugier so
Ab cor trist e marrit, et ai en be razo,
Qu'en luy ai mescabat senhor et amic bo,
E quar tug l'ayp valent en sa mort perdut so.
Tant es mortals lo dans qu'ieu no·y ai sospeisso
Que ja mais si revenha s'en aital guiza no:
Qu'om li traga lo cor, e que·n manjo·l baro
Que vivon descorat: pueys auran de cor pro.

Premiers manje del cor, per so que grans ops l'es,
L'emperaire de Roma, s'elh vol los Milanes
Per forsa conquistar, quar luy tenon conques,
E viu deseretatz, malgrat de sos Tïes.
E deseguentre lui manje·n lo reys frances,
Pueys cobrara Castella que pert per nescïes;
Mas, si pez' a sa maire, elh no·n manjara ges,
Quar ben par, a son pretz, qu'elh non fai ren que·l pes.

Del rey engles me platz, quar es pauc coratjos,
Que manje pro del cor; pueys er valens e bos,
E cobrara la terra, per que viu de pretz blos,
Que·l tol lo reys de Fransa quar lo sap nüalhos.
E lo reys castelas tanh que·n manje per dos,
Quar dos regismes ten e per l'un non es pros;
Mas, s'elh en vol manjar, tanh que·n manj' a rescos,
Que, si·l mair' o sabia, batria·l ab bastos.

Del rey d'Arago vuel del cor deia manjar,
Que aisso lo fara de l'anta descarguar
Que pren sai de Marcella e d'Amilau, qu'onrar
No·s pot estiers per ren que puesca dir ni far.
Et apres vuelh del cor don hom al rey navar
Que valia mais coms que reys, so aug comtar;
Tortz es quan Dieus fai home en gran ricor poiar,
Pus sofracha de cor lo fai de pretz bayssar.

I Want to Mourn Blacatz

Sordel

I want to mourn Blacatz with this simple lament:
My heart is sad and mournful, as makes perfect sense,
For with his passing I have lost a lord and good friend;
All the noble qualities have come to an end.
So deadly is the damage that's been done that I
Hold little hope for any cure except in one way:
Let his heart be cut out, and let the barons feed—
They've no heart now and this will give them what they need.

The first to eat this heart, because his need is great,
Should be Rome's emperor,[4] that is, if he would beat
The Milanese by force; they think that he has been
Defeated, disinherited, despite his friends
From Deutchland. Then the next to eat should be the French king[5]—
He needs it to regain Castile, which he's bungling.
But if his mother[6] disapproves he won't partake—
He never disobeys her, that's what people say.

To grow in strength and valor, I wish the English king[7]
Would gorge on heart—find the courage that he's lacking.
Then he'd regain those lands from which he's being parted—
He's lost his worth, the French king knows that he's faint-hearted.
And he who rules Castile[8] should take a double serving:
He rules two kingdoms—that's two more than he's deserving.
But he should keep it secret if he would be eating—
If his mother[9] found out, she'd take some sticks and beat him!

Some heart I'd like the king of Aragon[10] to eat,
Then he'd be disembarrassed of the shame that he
Inflicts upon himself from Marseille to Millau;
To regain his honor, there's nothing he can do
Or say. Then let the Navarre king[11] eat heart as well—
He was a better count than king, so I've heard tell.
It's wrong for God to raise to lofty power men
Lacking in heart—they'll just decline in worth again.

Al comte de Toloza a ops que·n manje be,
Si·l membra so que sol tener ni so que te,
Quar, si ab autre cor sa perda non reve,
No·m par que la revenha ab aquel qu'a en se.
E·l coms proensals tanh que·n manje, si·l sove
C'oms que deseretatz viu guaire non val re;
E, si tot ab esfors si defen ni·s chapte,
Ops l'es mange del cor pel greu fais qu'el soste.

Li baro·m volran mal de so que ieu dic be,
Mas ben sapchan qu'ie·ls pretz aitan pauc quon ylh me.

Belh Restaur, sol qu'ab vos puesca trobar merce,
A mon dan met quascun que per amic no·m te.[12]

From eating heart the Toulouse count[13] should not refrain,
If he considers what he had and what remains.
He needs a different heart to set his losses right—
That this will happen with his present heart I'm not quite
Convinced. The Provence count[14] should likewise eat if he
Considers that a man who's lost his land is nearly
Worthless. Even if he defends himself and holds
His land, some heart would help him bear this heavy load.

The barons will despise me for putting things so clearly,
But let them know: I hold them low as they do me.

Robert Kehew

Guillelma de Rosers and Lanfranc Cigala

> Lord Lanfranc Cigala was from the city of Genoa. He was a noble and
> learned man. And he was a judge and a knight, but he led the life of a
> judge. And he was a great lover; and he was interested in inventing po-
> etry and was a good inventor, and he composed many good songs.[1]

One of the few generalizations that we can safely make about Guillelma de
Rosers and the other female troubadours is that they were inordinately
drawn to the *tenso* form. For the troubadours as a whole, *tensos* make up less
than 10 percent of their surviving works (194 out of around 2,500 works by
one count). For the *trobairitz,* however, about half of their surviving oeuvre
are *tensos* (24 out of 47 poems by one tally). It is hard to believe that this
differential is due entirely to the fickleness of time, and so it is tempting
to speculate about the reasons for it. Sankovitch hazards that the "situa-
tional aspect" of the *tenso* made this form more accessible to women.
She elaborates: "Social interaction, including conversation, is an aspect
of the patroness/hostess role in which women were accepted, and they
may thus slip unobtrusively from 'ordinary' to 'literary' conversation"
("Troubairitz," 122).

Whether Guillelma was playing hostess to or was the guest of Lanfranc
when they collaborated on the poem below is uncertain. Either arrange-
ment is possible. Lanfranc was from Genoa, and a song records Guillelma's
long sojourn in that city, away from her home in Provence. On the other
hand, a document dating from 1241 records the Genoese lawyer's serving as
envoy to Raimon Berenguer in Occitania. He could have met Guillelma at

this time, although exactly where Guillelma's home (Rosers) was located is not clear.

Other information is scarce on these two. Lanfranc knew and praised Blacatz, who was lamented by Sordel (see his "Planher vuelh En Blacatz"); this association may have brought Lanfranc into contact with other troubadours such as Peirol and Guillem Figueira. Scholars, including Van Vleck ("Lyric Texts," 34), contend that Lanfranc played an important transitional role between the troubadours of southern France on the one hand, and the young Dante and his comrades with their *dolce stil nuovo* ("sweet new style") on the other. Assassins reportedly killed Lanfranc in 1278, in Monaco. Even less is known of Guillelma, for whom not even an unreliable *vida* exists.

Given the paucity of biographical information on these two, we are thrown back on the text of their joint composition. This work supports the contention of Bruckner, Shephard, and White that "the question of hierarchy and the balance of power between lovers and ladies functions as a major issue of troubadour lyric and a matter of dispute between its male and female interpreters" (*Songs of the Women Troubadours,* xlv–xlvi). The *tenso* form proved an ideal field for this (s)wordplay. At the same time, as the present selection shows, even in the hands of a skilled lawyer and an articulate noblewoman, participants in a *tenso* ran the risk of degenerating from rigorous syllogism into nose-thumbing insult.

Na Guilielma, maunt cavalier arratge

Guillelma de Rosers and Lanfranc Cigala

Na Guilielma, maint cavalier arratge
Anan de nueg per mal temps qe fazia,
Si plaignian d'alberc en lur lengatge.
Auziron dui bar qe per drudaria
Se·n anavan vas lur donas non len.
L'us se·n tornet per servir sella gen,
L'autres n'anet vas sa domna corren.
Qals d'aquels dos fes miels zo qe·il taignia?

Amic Lafranc, miels complic son viatge,
Al mieu semblan, cel qi tenc vers s'amia,
E l'autre fes ben, mas son fin coratge
Non poc tam be saber sidonz a tria
Con cil que·l vic devant sos oils presen
Q'a rendut l'a sos cavaliers coven,
Q'eu pres truep mais qi zo qe diz aten
Qe qi en als son coratge cambia.

Domna, si·us plas, tot qan fes d'agradatge
Lo cavalliers qe per sa galiardia
Garda·ls autres de mort e de dampnatge,
E il mouc d'amor, qar ges de cortezia
Non ha nuls hom si d'amor no·il dessen,
Per qe sidonz deu grazir per un cen
Qar deslivret per s'amor de turmen
Tanz cavaliers, qe se vista l'avja.

Lafranc, iamais non razones muzatge
Tan gran con fes aqel qe tenc sa via;
Qe, sapchatz be, mout i fes gran ultratge,
Pueis bel servirs tan de cor li movia,
Qar non servic sidonz premeiramen,
Et agra·n grat de leis e iauzimen,
Pueis per s'amor pogra servir soven
En maintz bos luecs, qe faillir no·il podia.

Which of the Two Behaved Most Fittingly?

Guillelma de Rosers and Lanfranc Cigala

Dame Guillelma, a band of weary knights
Abroad in the dark, in most dismal weather,
Wished aloud in their own tongues that they might
Find shelter. Two lovers happened to over-
Hear while on their way to their ladies who
Lived close at hand; one of them turned back to
Help the knights, the other went to his lady:
Which of the two behaved most fittingly?

Friend Lanfranc, I think that he did best
Who continued on to see his lady.
The other also did well, however his
Loved one couldn't observe in the same way
What the other could see with her own eyes,
Her lover's worth; she waited for him to arrive.
The man who keeps his word is held in much
Higher esteem than he whose plans are in flux.

Pardon, lady, but that brave cavalier
Who saved the rest from death and harm was moved
By affection: there never will appear
A chivalry that doesn't spring from love.
Thus in my opinion, a hundredfold
She ought to thank him, as though she had beheld
The deed in person, for out of love for her
He saved those knights from what might have occurred.

You've never tried to justify such daft
Behavior as this man's, Lanfranc; it's plain
That he handled himself poorly, for if
His heart was moved to serve as you maintain,
Then why didn't he serve his lady first?
Both parties would have equally expressed
Their thanks . . . and opportunities exist
To serve in places where there's much less risk.

Domna, perdon vos qier, s'ieu dic folatge,
Qu'oimais vei zo qe de donas crezia,
Qe no vos platz q'autre pelegrinatge
Fassan li drut mas ves vos tota via,
Pero cavals c'om vol qi biort gen
Deu hom menar ab mesur et ab sen,
Mas car lo drutz cochatz tan malamen
Lur faill poders, don vos sobra feunia.

Lafranc, eu dic qe son malvatz usatge
Degra laissar en aqel meteis dia
Li cavalliers que domna de paratge,
Bella e pros, deu aver en bailia.
Q'en son alberc servis hom largamen,
Ia el no·i fos, mas chascus razon pren,
Qar sai que ha tan de recrezemen
Q'al maior ops poders li failliria.

Domna, poder ai eu et ardimen
Non contra vos, qe·us venzes en iazen,
Per q'eu sui fols car ab vos pris conten,
Mas vencut voil qe m'aiatz, con qe sia.

Lafranc, aitan vos autrei e·us consen,
Qe tant mi sen de cor e d'ardimen
C'ab aital gien con domna si defen
Mi defendri'al plus ardit qe sia.

Forgive me for having uttered foolishness,
I see that my suspicions all were true:
You cannot be content, lady, unless
All lovers' pilgrimages lead to you.
But when you train a horse to joust, you should
Guide it with care, bearing in mind what's good
For it: you drive your lovers so hard that they
Are left debilitated, and you enraged.

I'll say again: not wasting even a day,
That man should change his manner and repent:
He should swear allegiance to a lady
Who's noble, beautiful, and affluent.
They would have eaten well if he had sent
Them to his house in his absence; such men
Make excuses, but he's so sensitive
That in a real crisis he'd lose his nerve.

Lady, I have virility and ardor—
Though not for you, whom I could surely conquer
(Though I was once your fool) . . . I invite you
To try to vanquish me, however you choose.

Lanfranc, I promise and I guarantee
That I possess such heart and tenacity
That with my women's subtlety I'll defend
Myself against the most covetous plans.

Robert Kehew

Guiraut Riquier

It is somehow fitting that no *vida* exists for the so-called Last Troubadour. The act of writing a biography implicitly attaches value or importance to that individual's life, and Guiraut Riquier had the misfortune of outliving the times that appreciated what he had to offer.

While we do not have a *vida* for Guiraut Riquier, we possess something even more valuable: two manuscripts that appear to be very close in origin to—perhaps copied directly from—the author's own compilation. Together these manuscripts offer not only complete texts for some 101 songs, but also dates of composition, melodies for 48 of the pieces, and additional notes including, in one case, performance instructions. One benefit of this treasure trove of information is that we can closely correlate the troubadour's movements with his extensive artistic output.

Guiraut Riquier was born in Narbonne around 1230. His first extant poem dates from 1254, and for sixteen years thereafter he practiced his craft in his hometown, at the court of the viscount of Narbonne. During this period he essayed a variety of forms, and embarked on an interesting series of *pastorelas* that portray a shepherdess aging from saucy girl to wiser older woman. After his patron died, Guiraut struck off for Spain in 1270; there he wound up at the court of one of the age's greatest patrons, Alfonso X of Castile and León. In 1274 we find Guiraut exchanging letters with Alfonso the Wise, wherein the poet protested against the rampant confusion at the court in the use of the terms troubadour and *joglar,* and the king graciously condescended to respond. This was not just a quibble over semantics: rather, the troubadour was trying to protect the status of his profession and, more generally, to shore up a whole way of life that stood in danger of disappearing.

In 1280 Guiraut Riquier left Spain and returned to southern France. There he continued his search for understanding patronage, but the Last Troubadour might just as well have been expecting a unicorn to leap off a medieval tapestry; southern France was no longer the land it had been a century earlier. For a time Guiraut was associated with the court of Henri II of Rodez but, still restless, continued his futile wanderings. Disheartened, he eventually returned to his native Narbonne. His poetic output dwindled and became more religious.

Finally, in 1292, as an old man, a living anachronism, the troubadour wrote his last work, presented below. In this poem, Guiraut Riquier laments what has been lost, confronts the truth that "I was born behind my time," and curses a world that has become "mostly lies." His death marked the passing of an era; the poem serves as an epitaph to the entire troubadour movement.

Be·m degra de chantar tener

Guiraut Riquier

Be·m degra de chantar tener
Quar a chan coven alegriers,
E mi destrenh tant cossiriers
Que·m fa de totas partz doler,
Remembran mon greu temps passat,
Esgardan lo prezent forsat
E cossiran l'avenidor,
Que per totz ai razon que plor.

Per que no·m deu aver sabor
Mos chans, qu'es ses alegretat;
Mas Dieus m'a tal saber donat
Qu'en chantan retrac ma folhor,
Mo sen, mon gauch, mon desplazer
E mon dan e mon pro per ver,
Qu'a penas dic ren ben estiers;
Mas trop suy vengutz als derriers.

Qu'er non es grazitz lunhs mestiers
Menhs en cort que de belh saber
De trobar; qu'auzir e vezer
Hi vol hom mais captenhs leugiers
E critz mesclatz ab dezonor;
Quar tot quan sol donar lauzor,
Es al pus del tot oblidat,
Que·l mons es quays totz en barat.

Per erguelh e per malvestat
Del Christias ditz, luenh d'amor
E dels mans de Nostre Senhor,
Em del sieu sant loc discipat
Ab massa d'autres encombriers,
Don par qu'elh nos es aversiers
Per desadordenat voler
E per outracujat poder.

It Would Be Best If I Refrained from Singing

Guiraut Riquier

It would be best if I refrained
From singing: song should spring from gladness;
But I'm tormented by a sadness
So profound that I'm seized by pain.
Remembering how grim things were,
Considering how hard things *are,*
And pondering the by-and-by,
I have every cause to cry.

Thus my song gives me no pleasure,
Since it of happiness is bare;
But God has granted me such share
Of talent that, through music's measure,
Out flows my wit, my joys and follies;
Both my gains and losses, truly.
If not, I couldn't breathe a line—
For I was born behind my time.

For now no art is less admired
Than the worthy craft of song.
These days the nobles' tastes have run
To entertainments less inspired.
Wailing mingles with disgrace:
All that once engendered praise
From the memory has died:
Now the world is mostly lies.

Through the pride and wicked nature
Of so-called Christians, far removed
From God's commandments, far from love,
We are cast out from his sacred
Place and cursed with encumbrances:
It seems that he is loath to face us,
Given our uncontrolled desire,
And presumptuous grasp at power.

Lo greu perilh devem temer
De dobla mort, qu'es prezentiers:
Que·ns sentam Sarrazis sobriers,
E Dieus que·ns giet a non chaler;
Et entre nos qu'em azirat,
Tost serem del tot aterrat;
E no·s cossiran la part lor,
Segon que·m par, nostre rector.

Selh que crezem en unitat,
Poder, savieza, bontat,
Done a ssas obras lugor,
Don sian mundat peccador.

Dona, maires de caritat,
Acapta nos per pietat
Don ton filh, nostre Redemptor,
Gracia, perdon et amor.

Of gravest peril be forewarned,
A double death over us is looming:
The Saracens are overwhelming,
And our God is unconcerned.
Full of anger, soon we will be
Destroyed, our lives wiped out completely.
Our leaders can't be bothered to
Fulfill their duty, that's my view.

God in your unity and grace,
Wisdom, power we have faith:
Let your works shine out with splendor,
To attract repentant sinners.

Lady, mother of charity,
Pity us, and intercede
With your redeeming son, and win
Blessings, mercy, love from him.

Robert Kehew

When the Soft Wind Turns Bitter
(Quant l'aura doussa s'amarzis; see pp. 36 – 38)

    Cercamon

When the soft wind turns bitter
And the leaf falls from its branch,
And the birds change their songs,
I too, here, sigh and sing
Of Love, which has me bound and confined
Even though I never was in possession of it.

Woe is me! for from Love I have obtained
Nothing but trouble and torment,
And nothing is so difficult to attain
As that which I constantly desire,
Nor does anything cause me such envy
As that which I cannot have.

Because of a fine jewel I am happy,
For never did I love anything so much.
When I am with her I am so dazzled
That I don't know how to tell her of my desire,
And when I leave her, it seems to me
That I totally lose my sense and my wits.

The most beautiful lady one has ever seen
I do not esteem one glove when compared with her;
When all the world darkens,
Where she is, it will be resplendent.
May God protect me until I may touch her
Or see her when she goes to bed.

I shudder all over and shake and tremble
Because of her love, whether I am asleep or awake.
I am so afraid of dying
That I don't dare think of how to plead with her.
But I shall serve her two or three years,
And then perhaps she may perceive the truth.

I neither die nor live nor get well,
Nor feel any sickness, yet I do have a grave one;
Since I cannot foretell her love,
I don't know if or when I may obtain it,
For in her is all the grace
That can elevate or dishearten me.

It pleases me when she drives me insane
And makes me wait and hope in vain;
It pleases me if she scorns me
Or mocks me, to my face or to my back,
Because after the suffering, happiness will come to me
Very soon, if it is her pleasure.

If she doesn't want me, I would have liked to die
The day when she took me into her service.
Oh, God, how softly she killed me
When of her love she made pretense to me,
For she has enclosed me in such a way
That I don't care to see another woman.

Even though I am distraught, I rejoice,
For if I fear her or court her,
Because of her I shall be either false or faithful,
Either loyal or full of deceit,
Either a complete rustic or a complete courtier,
Either anxious or at ease.

But, whomever this may please or not,
She may, if she so desires, retain me.
Cercamon says: "A man can hardly be courtly
If he despairs of love."

Frede Jensen

So Much Does the Anxiety of Love Please Me
(Tant m'abellis l'amoros pessamens; see pp. 266 – 68)

Folquet de Marseilla

So much does the anxiety of love please me,
Which has settled in my loyal heart,
That there is no room there for any other thought,
And no other thought is sweet or pleasant to me any longer,
For I feel good when worries kill me,
And faithful love relieves my torment,
Promising me joy, though dispensing it very slowly,
For it has long attracted me with great beauty.

I know full well that all I do has no value,
But what more can I do if love wants to kill me?
For purposely it has endowed me with a desire
Which will never be conquered nor vanquished;
Though conquered it will be, for the sighs will kill me
Very softly since, from the lady whom I desire,
I receive no relief nor do I expect it from elsewhere,
Nor can I wish for another love.

My good lady, if it pleases you, do accept
The good I wish to do for you, for I feel wretched,
Yet my distress cannot harm me,
But rather it will seem to me that we share it equally;
But if it pleases you that I turn to another lady,
Remove from you the beauty and the sweet smile
And the beautiful appearance which make me lose my mind;
Then truly, I shall separate myself from you.

Every passing day you seem to me more beautiful and gracious,
And therefore I am troubled by my eyes with which I look at you,
For they could never see you for my good,
And it causes me harm that they see you too closely;
For my harm it is not, I know that, at least it does not fill me with grief,
But rather it is for my good, lady, and that is why I believe
That if you kill me, it will not be for your good,
For my harm will also be yours.

I do not love you wisely, my lady,
Because I am faithful to you while to myself a traitor;
And I believe I am losing you, yet I cannot belong to myself,
And I think I am hurting you when it is myself I hurt;
Therefore I do not dare to show you or tell you about my grief,
But from my look can understand my emotions,
For as soon as I am about to tell you, immediately I repent,
And in my eyes I harbor the shame and the audacity.

I love you much more, my lady, than I can tell you,
And although I never desired another love
I do not regret it, but rather I love you hundredfold,
For I have experienced the behavior of others.

"Song, go to Nîmes, whomever this may cause sorrow,
For, in my opinion, the three ladies to whom I present you, will be pleased
with it,
For those three are truly worth more than a hundred others."

Frede Jensen

NOTES

Preface

1. See Bruckner, "The Trobairitz," 203–14. More limited information exists for other *trobairitz*. Rieger (as cited in Paden, "Some Recent Studies of Women," 104) identifies a total of forty-three, while Frazer counts "almost forty" ("Two Contrasting Views of Love," 24). Other women troubadours undoubtedly existed but are now unknown.

2. For transcriptions prepared by W. D. Snodgrass of troubadour songs that he has translated, go to www.hoasm.org, then go to "Research Periods," "Troubadours, Trouvères and Minnesigers," and "Poetry and Prose."

3. Poe, "*Vidas* and *Razos*," 186–96; and Paden, "Manuscripts," 311. For further discussion of the *vidas* and *razos,* see the chapter on Peire Vidal below.

4. William D. Paden, in a personal communication (August 14, 2003), confirmed this decision.

5. As quoted in Sieburth, *Walking Tour in Southern France,* xvi.

6. As quoted in Bonner, *Songs of the Troubadours,* 283.

7. As quoted in McDougal, *Ezra Pound and the Troubadour Tradition,* 20. See this work for a fascinating analysis of Pound's evolution as a translator.

Introduction

1. Quotations from Bernart de Ventadorn's "Pois preyatz me, senhor" ("You've Asked, My Lords, for Song"), translated by W. D. Snodgrass, and the Comtessa de Dia's "Estat ai en greu cossirier" ("Cruel Are the Pains I've Suffered"), translated by Robert Kehew; both poems are included in this collection. While here the sentiments expressed are similar, the *trobairitz'* perspectives on love often differed somewhat from those of their male counterparts. For discussions of the *trobairitz* and their compositions, see the chapters on the Comtessa de Dia, on Maria de Ventadorn (with Gui d'Ussel), and on Guillelma de Rosers (with Lanfranc Cigala). For further information, see Bruckner, "Trobairitz," or Sankovitch, "Trobairitz."

2. The texts of all poems thus cited by name in the introduction can be found in subsequent chapters on individual troubadours.

3. As quoted in Lazar, "*Fin'Amor,*" 62.

4. Some such as Bogin argue that *fin' amor* was a "proto-feminist development" (*Women Troubadours,* 14). Others have followed the lead of Mary Wollstonecraft, who as early as 1792 reviewed the legacy of *fin' amor* and courtly love and concluded that, "while [women] have been stripped of the virtues that should clothe humanity, they have been decked with artificial graces that enable them to exercise a short-lived tyranny." Other positions have also been advanced.

5. While this is the general trend over time, some hints of satire of the cult of refined love can be found even at the dawn of the troubadour era. See "Ab la dolchor del temps novel" ("A New Song for New Days") by Guillem de Peiteus.

6. Some medieval writings distinguish between the terms *vers* and *canso*, and describe certain love songs as fitting into one or the other category. Because present-day scholars have not yet reached consensus on how a *vers* differs from a *canso*, however, my discussion subsumes all love lyrics under the general heading of *canso*.

7. For further discussion of the appeal that this form held for the *trobairitz*, see the chapter on Guillelma and Lanfranc.

8. Pirenne's phrase, as cited in Bonner, *Songs of the Troubadours*, 4.

9. Fulbert of Chartres, *Analecta hymnalogica*, as quoted in Dawson, *Religion and the Rise of Western Culture*, 148.

10. As quoted in Jones and Ereira, *Crusades*, 21.

11. Guillem eventually would make it to Jerusalem before returning home.

12. As translated in Irwin, *Nights and Horses and the Desert*, 252, 255.

13. See ibid., 280.

14. A form consisting of four-line stanzas rhyming *aaab*, where the *a*-rhymes change from stanza to stanza but the *b*-rhyme remains constant throughout. For discussion see Chambers, "Versification," 102–3. The poem by Guillem de Peiteus that is cited is "Pos de chantar m'es pres talenz"; see Jensen, *Troubadour Lyrics*, 80–83.

15. Crocker, *History of Musical Style*, 54. Also see Bond, "Origins," 248.

16. See Marcabru's "Pax in nomine Domini!" ("The Cleansing Place") for a contemporary glimpse into that conflict.

17. It is believed that troubadour Jaufre Rudel sang of his distant love in "Lanquan li jorn" ("A Love Afar") while participating on that Crusade.

18. Weir, *Eleanor of Aquitaine*, 130.

19. See the chapter on Bertran de Born below for more examples of his political mischief-making.

20. Ibid., 233. In 1215, the English barons would wrest the Magna Carta concessions from the hapless King John.

21. The First Crusaders may well have picked up such beliefs on their journeys and brought them back to Europe in the early eleven hundreds. Historians, however, have not decisively established that a direct causal link existed between earlier Manichaeism on the one hand, and later European heresies including Bogomilism and Catharism on the other.

22. Sumption, *Albigensian Crusade*, 49.

23. As quoted in Daniel-Rops, *Cathedral and Crusade*, 299.

24. Raimon VI, as quoted in ibid., 297.

25. As quoted in Sumption, *Albigensian Crusade*, 74.

26. As quoted in ibid., 77.

27. Arnald-Amaury, as quoted in ibid., 93. For Raimon's chastening, see ibid., 83–88.

28. Most scholars accept that the victory of the French following the Albigensian Crusade was a leading cause of the decline of the troubadour culture. William D. Paden, however, offers evidence otherwise; for a summary of his argument, see "Both Borrower and Lender," 5.

Guillem de Peiteus

1. Translated by Bonner, in *Songs of the Troubadours*, 31.

2. Geoffroy de Vigeois, as cited in Jensen, *Troubadour Lyrics*, 24.

3. In the original, *Bon Vezi* ("Good Neighbor") is a *senhal,* or pseudonym, for the lady in question.

4. Jensen (in ibid., 447) finds here a disparaging reference to northerners, seen as lacking the courtly refinements of the south.

5. Some critics identify this work as a *devinalh* or riddle song, with Guillem here challenging a friend to find the *contraclau* or "master key." In seeking to solve this riddle, Bonner (*Songs of the Troubadours,* 243) follows another scholar (Scheludko) in suggesting that the key might be "dreams."

6. The protagonist is traveling along a road to a pilgrimage center, identified by Lejeune as Saint-Léonard-de-Noblat, a village just east of Limoges and the home of a local saint. At the same time, in line 14 we see that the narrator is dressed *a tapi* or with the hooded gown of a pilgrim, here rendered as traveling "on the sly." The ladies thus initially conclude that he is a pilgrim, "just passing through." Jensen, *Troubadour Lyrics,* 450.

7. The original phrase in this stanza, *per amor Deu, l'alberguem,* can be rendered more literally as "for the love of God, let us give him shelter."

Cercamon

1. Translated by Bonner, in *Songs of the Troubadours,* 41.

2. Translated by Jensen, in *Troubadour Lyrics,* 27.

3. Pound departed freely from his base text in his "descant"; see the appendix for a more literal translation of this poem.

Marcabru

1. Translated by Bonner, in *Songs of the Troubadours,* 44.

2. Poem no. XVIII by Marcabru, translated by Topsfield, in *Troubadours and Love,* 80. Topsfield numbers Marcabru's poems according to Dejeanne, J.-M.-L., *Poésies complètes du troubadour Marcabru* (Toulouse: Privat, 1909).

3. Quotations from Marcabru's poems nos. V, XI, and XXXI, respectively. Topsfield, *Troubadours and Love,* 71–83.

4. Stanza 7 of Marcabru's poem "Al son desviat, chantaire," translated by Economou in "Marcabru, Love's Star Witness," 28.

5. The control of the Holy Sepulchre by non-Christians.

6. King Louis VII of France, who launched the Second Crusade in 1146.

7. This line can be translated more literally as, "Thus you would pay me homage" (in a feudal sense).

8. Spain, as opposed to the Holy Land. In 1148, the pope formally proclaimed that the *Reconquista* was a Crusade—a detail that some scholars use to date the present poem to around 1149. This and the following notes are drawn largely from Jensen, *Troubadour Lyrics,* 461. Also to Jensen the translator is indebted for the phrase "the cleansing place" for *lavador.*

9. Some scholars believe that the "Emperor" referred to here is the title promised by God to Crusaders who die in battle; others consider it an allusion to King Alfonso VIII of Castile.

10. Scholars generally believe that the "good marquis" is Raimon Berenguer IV, count of Barcelona and marquis of Provence. The Templars participated with Raimon in the conquests of Tortosa and Lérida, Spain, in 1148–49. Based in part on this reference, Jensen follows Pirot in suggesting that the present poem was written about this time, before the capture of Lérida (ibid., 462–63).

11. Antioch, Aquitaine ("Guyenne"), and Poitou mourned the death of a ruler, which left the settlements of Poitiers and Niort in need of divine protection. Some believe that the personage whose death was thus mourned was Guillem the eighth count of Poitiers, tenth duke of Aquitaine, who died in 1137 while on pilgrimage in Spain. Pirot, however, argues that the poet refers to the death of Guillem's brother Raimon, prince (not count) of Antioch, who died in 1149.

Jaufre Rudel

1. Translated by Bonner, in *Songs of the Troubadours*, 61.

2. Goldin translates the final three lines of this stanza as: "But the path is blocked to my desire, for my godfather gave me this fate: I must love and not be loved." He translates the *tornada,* which Snodgrass elects to pass over, as follows: "But the path is blocked to my desire, a great curse on this godfather who [is] doomed to be unloved" (*Lyrics of the Troubadours,* 106–7). In a gloss on the end to this poem, Jensen observes that "medieval folklore often depicts witches and sorcerers as god-parents" (*Troubadour Lyrics,* 475).

3. *Guiren* would be translated more literally as "witness." The patron that this *senhal* (pseudonym) refers to may be either a woman or, as implied by the present translation, a religious figure.

Bernart de Ventadorn

1. Translated by Bonner, in *Songs of the Troubadours*, 82.

2. An allusion to a proverb about a fool who does not dismount to lead his horse over a bridge; their combined weight broke the flimsy structure (ibid., 261).

3. Goldin translates this stanza as follows: "A lady deserves blame when she makes her lover wait too long, for endless talk of love is a great vexation, and seems like a trick, because one can love, and pretend to everyone else, and nobly lie when there are no witnesses. Sweet lady, if only you would deign to love me, no one will ever catch me when I lie" (*Lyrics of the Troubadours,* 141).

4. *Fachura* means "sorcerer."

Peire d'Alvernhe

1. Translated by Bonner, in *Songs of the Troubadours*, 68. "Clairmon" is apparently Clermont-Ferrand, the capital of the Auvergne.

2. For precision, scholars generally prefer the term *fin' amor* to describe the Occitanian sentiment. For discussion of the relation between these two terms, see Lazar, "*Fin'amor*," 64–65 and 70–72.

3. For a comparison of these two sets of poems, see Macdonald, "Warbled Words," 18–36.

4. Lines from the concluding stanza of Peire's literary *sirventes,* which satirized some of the major troubadours of his day. Translated by Bonner, in *Songs of the Troubadours*, 68.

5. Bonner translates the second *tornada* as follows: "Let that villain Audric know, through this poem, that he of Auvergne says: a man without love's service is no better than a wretched ear of corn" (ibid., 77).

Raimbaut d'Aurenga

1. Translated by Bonner, in *Songs of the Troubadours*, 100, with *chanso'* changed to *cansos*.

2. In the original the three song types cited are *vers*, *sirventes*, and *estribot*. The terms *vers* and *sirventes* are discussed in the general introduction in note 4 and on page 7, respectively. An *estribot* is built on a long succession of alexandrines all on the same rhyme; it is one of the rarest of prosodic fauna in Occitan literature.

Guiraut de Bornelh

1. Translated by Bonner, *Songs of the Troubadours*, 114.

2. Dante, *Purgatorio*, translated by Ciardi, canto XXVI, lines 119–23.

3. Translated by Bonner, *Songs of the Troubadours*, 115.

4. While the base text that Goldin presents stops here at six stanzas, other edited base texts add a final (seventh) stanza. Jensen presents a final stanza as follows: "Bel dous companh, tan sui en ric sojorn, / Qu'eu no volgra mais fos alba ni jorn, / Car la gensor que anc nasques de maire / Tenc et abras, per qu'eu non prezi gaire / Lo fol gilos ni l'alba." Jensen translates this as: "Dear friend, I am in such delightful company that I shall no longer wish that it be dawn nor day, for the most beautiful girl ever born to a mother I hold and embrace; therefore I do not care at all about the jealous fool nor about dawn" (*Troubadour Lyrics*, 212–13).

5. The people of Beziers apparently had a reputation in certain circles for foolishness, possibly for running outside of their walled city if it was attacked (Van Vleck, "Lyric Texts," 46).

6. Jensen translates the *tornada* as follows: "Jongleur, leave now with these your new melodies, and take them quickly to the beautiful lady, in whom nobility is born, and tell her that I am more hers than her own cloak" (*Troubadour Lyrics*, 205).

Peire Bremon lo Tort

1. Translated by Egan, in *Vidas of the Troubadours*, 73.

2. A number of composers apparently followed in the footsteps of Peire Bremon lo Tort to visit Casale during its heyday as a haven for troubadours, including Arnaut de Marueill, Gaucelm Faidit, Peire Vidal, and Raimbaut de Vaqueiras. For Peire Bremon lo Tort's earlier presence, see Keller, "Italian Troubadours," 295–96.

3. Jones and Ereira, *Crusades*, 93, 129–62.

4. "*Pardieu*," or "By God!" "Indeed!"

5. William Longsword, eldest son of William, third marquis of Monferrat, then in Palestine (Keller, "Italian Troubadours," 296).

Bertran de Born

1. Translated by Bonner, in *Songs of the Troubadours*, 149.

2. The "Young King" mentioned in the *razo* was Richard's brother, the son of Henry II. Bertran joined a revolt led by the Young King against Henry II and Richard. The Young King died of dysentery and fever in 1183 at the age of twenty-eight. Bertran laments him in the final selection. Following his capture, then release, at the hands of Richard, Bertran ever after championed Richard's cause.

3. The phrase is from Harvey, "Courtly Culture in Medieval Occitania," 9.

4. Translated by Bonner, in *Songs of the Troubadours*, 136.

5. See *Inferno* XXVIII, lines 113–42. The excerpt is condensed and translated by Pound; a fragment within his poem "Near Perigord."

6. Sieburth (*Ezra Pound among the Troubadours,* 114) cites Makin, as well as Paden, Sankovitch, and Stäblein, as being dismissive of Pound's political reading of "Domna pois . . ." For a not completely dissimilar analysis of a song by another troubadour, however, see the discussion of Peire Vidal's "Al l'alen tir vas me l'aire" ("The Song of Breath") in the chapter on that composer.

7. Lazar, "*Fin' Amor*," 70. For a variation on this theme, see the second stanza of "Non es meravelha s'eu chan" ("No Marvel If My Song's the Best"), by Bernart de Ventadorn.

8. Papiol is a joglar in Bertran's service. *Oc-e-No* is Bertran's stinging *senhal* (pseudonym) for Richard the Lion-hearted.

9. The viscount of Limoges and Richard the Lion-hearted, respectively.

10. The patron saint of prisoners. This and the following notes are largely drawn from Paden, Sankovitch, and Stäblein, *Poems of the Troubadour Bertran de Born,* 123–27.

11. "Elias VI Talairan, count of Périgord, whom Richard beseiged at Périgueux in July 1182 as part of a campaign to establish dominance over Périgord and the Limousin" (ibid.). During the Middle Ages, some Frenchmen apparently sneered at merchants from Lombardy.

12. "Guillem de Gordon . . . has won Bertran's love by ignoring a treaty with the two viscounts, Aimar V of Limoges, and his son Gui, with whom he shared the government. Guillem de Gorden, Aimar, and Gui would all be Bertran's allies in the revolt of 1183" (ibid.).

13. "The name refers to the color bay, or reddish brown, and may allude to the marvelous steed of Renaut de Montauban in the chanson de geste bearing his name" (ibid.).

14. "A follower of the count of Poitiers, Richard" (ibid.).

15. "An allusion to the fable of the peacock and the crow who disguised himself in peacock feathers, only to be stripped and humiliated. Afterwards the peacock said to him . . . : 'He who climbs higher than he should falls from higher than he would like'" (ibid.).

16. "Better than good": a *senhal* for Guischarda de Beaujeu, wife of Archambaud VI of Comborn (Bonner, *Songs of the Troubadours,* 276–77).

17. "Fair Mirror."

18. Goldin translates the *tornada* as follows: "Papiols, you will go for me to tell my Magnet, singing, that love is unrecognized here and fallen from high to low" (*Lyrics of the Troubadours,* 239). As cited in Bonner, Stronski surmised that Bertran de Born and Folquet de Marseilla used "Magnet" as a reciprocal *senhal* (*Songs of the Troubadours,* 293).

19. Following this point in the poem, the base manuscript contains an additional stanza that is not found in most manuscripts and that some critics consider spurious. It is here omitted.

20. Richard the Lion-hearted, king of England.

21. In other words, "they" (the troubadours and *joglars*) have found Death to be a deadly warrior.

Comtessa de Dia

1. Translated by Egan, in *Vidas of the Troubadours,* 28. The spelling of "Peitieus" provided is from the original source.

2. Two of the contenders belonged to a younger branch of the family of the counts of Poitiers (Bonner, *Songs of the Troubadours,* 266).

3. Some, including Goldin (*Lyrics of the Troubadours,* 183), have proposed that the Comtessa is the coauthor of a fifth composition, a *tenso* between Raimbaut d'Aurenga and a

domna who remains unnamed in the manuscripts. Others, such as Bruckner ("Trobairitz," 219), find this attribution doubtful.

4. The allusion is to a French romance, *Floire et Blancheflour.* The tale concerns two children who grow up to love each other and overcome many obstacles that thwart their love. *Mon cor* is "my heart."

5. Seguin and Valensa are lovers in a lost romance, which other troubadours also cite.

Maria de Ventadorn and Gui d'Ussel

1. Translated by Egan, in *Vidas of the Troubadours,* 68–69.

2. For more on the appeal that the *tenso* form held for many of the female troubadours, see the chapter on Guillelma de Rosers and Lanfranc Cigala.

Monge de Montaudon

1. Translated by Bonner, in *Songs of the Troubadours,* 180.

2. Quotations are from the poem "Pos Peire d'Alvernh' a cantat," which is not included in the present anthology. For original text and translation, see Jensen, *Troubadour Lyrics,* 348–55.

3. An allusion to an anecdote about a woman who gave birth soon—perhaps too soon— after marriage (ibid., 555).

4. Weapons used for fighting at a distance, but frowned on for hand-to-hand combat (ibid., 555).

Arnaut Daniel

1. Translated by Bonner, in *Songs of the Troubadours,* 157. Ribairac, now spelled Ribérac, is a town west of Périgueux.

2. Dante, *Purgatorio,* canto XXVI, line 117. Petrarch, *Trionfi.*

3. In its first four stanzas, the original poem exhibits the *capfinida* structure: the root of the end-word of a stanza (here, *broilla*) appears around the middle of the first line of the following stanza.

4. Wribles—warblings [Pound's note].

5. This is nearly as bad in the original [Pound's note].

6. Vivien, strophe 2, *nebotz Sain Guillem,* an allusion to the romance *Enfances Vivien* [Pound's note]. Bonner (*Songs of the Troubadours,* 285) points out that hunger must play a role in the story alluded to here.

7. Longus, centurion in the crucifixion legend [Pound's note].

8. Wilhelm (in *Poetry of Arnaut Daniel,* 51–53) indicates that "all major editors" omit this final *tornada* (although it appears in Pound's published base text). Wilhelm translates this *tornada* as: "Let my Overbody, though great sense overabounds in her (him), just hold on to what she (he) has—if it can't be at all protected." Some emend *sobrecors,* an outer garment, to *Sobretotz,* "Above-All."

9. The *reis de Dobra* in the original text refers to the king of Dover, England, and the next line refers to the king of Estella and Pamplona—Navarre, in Spain.

10. Wilhelm (*Poetry of Arnaut Daniel,* 51–53) indicates that the "Lord of Rome" refers to the king of England.

11. King of the Galicians, Ferdinand II, King of Galicia, 1157–88, son of Berangere, sister

of Raimon Berenguer IV (*"quattro figlie ebbe,"* etc.) of Aragon, Count of Barcelona. His second son, Lieutenant of Provence, 1168 [Pound's note].

12. King [of France] crowned at Etampes, Philippe Auguste, crowned May 29, 1180, at age of sixteen. This poem might date Arnaut's birth as early as 1150 [Pound's note].

13. Call for second throw of the dice [Pound's note].

14. Pre-eminence [Pound's note].

15. Lavaud: *metr'* [Pound's note].

16. Lavaud: *angovencs*. Most probable meaning an angevin, small coin of Anjou, with argot diminutive ending [Pound's note].

17. raik—haste precipitate [Pound's note].

18. Our Lady of Poi de Dome? No definite solution of this reference yet found H. and B. say "town of Perigord." The same? [Pound's note].

19. Mate, fere, companion [Pound's note].

20. Dante cites this poem in the second book of De Vulgari Eloquio with poems of his own, De Born's, and Cino Pistoija's [Pound's note].

21. According to Bonner (*Songs of the Troubadours*, 287), Lucerna (Luserna in original) is most likely a fabled city in northwest Spain in the Middle Ages. According to one legend, possession of the city swung back and forth between Charlemagne and the Saracens until, through the intervention of God and Saint James, the walls came tumbling down and the Christians triumphed.

Arnaut de Marueill

1. Translated by Bonner, in *Songs of the Troubadours*, 133, with Arnaut's place of origin rendered as Marueill for consistency with Akehurst and Davis, *Handbook of the Troubadours*. Marueill (now Mareuil-sur-Belle) is in the Limousin, not far from Ribérac, the birthplace of the "famous" Arnaut, Arnaut Daniel.

2. Translated by Jensen, in *Troubadour Lyrics*, 351.

3. Bonner translates the *tornada* as follows: "Precious Jewel, you need no greater eulogy, and may he who mentions the Marquis of Montferrat praise him no more, for he has done so enough already" (*Songs of the Troubadours*, 135). Bonner identifies the marquis of Montferrat referred to here as Bonifacio I (1188–1207).

4. Jensen translates this final stanza as follows: "She will have mercy on me, if from now on she does not make me wait for a long time; may she give me a kiss as a gift and even more, according to my service! And then we shall make a short trip on a slow and short path, for her beautiful and joyous person has put me in this daze" (*Troubadour Lyrics*, 237).

5. *Alena* here is "inspire" in its primary sense, with the "taste" and "feel" of the wind [Pound's note]. In this note we likely see the influence on Pound of his walking trip in southern France, mentioned in the Foreword.

6. *Frescor del mati* [Pound's note].

Gaucelm Faidit

1. Translated by Egan, in *Vidas of the Troubadours*, 37.

Peire Vidal

1. Translated by Bonner, in *Songs of the Troubadours,* 164–66.

2. Poe points out that this fanciful tale is derived from a *canso* in which Peire, "playing on the name of his lady Loba, claims that he has suffered such scorn at her hands that he might just as well be a wolf chased and beaten by shepherds." Such a source of inspiration and process of transformation is typical of the medieval biographies of the troubadours. In them, in many instances "the figurative language of lyric is interpreted as though it were the literal truth" (*"Vidas* and *Razos,"* 191).

3. "The noble people" in the original; not necessarily French.

Peirol

1. Translated by Egan, in *Vidas of the Troubadours,* 81–82.

2. Jensen (*Troubadour Lyrics,* 367) translates the final two full stanzas and the *tornada* as follows:

"Sincerity with a true and noble heart makes love prosper, while high nobility makes it decline, for the rich are treacherous, since there are so many evil rich people that the world has grown worse. And may a lady who upholds worth not love because of rank, if she sees nothing else there.

"Song, go to the fair lady, not because I am sending her anything, but you can tell her about the torment I am suffering without causing me any harm. Tell her for me that to her I have given and surrendered my heart; hers I am, and I shall be hers forever; I can die because of my good faith.

"Good lady, wherever you may be, may joy be with you, and may you have joy, for I do not dare to plead with you for mercy, but at least I can think of doing it."

Raimbaut de Vaqueiras

1. Translated by Egan, in *Vidas of the Troubadours,* 90–91. *Bel Cavalier* is translated as "beauteous knight," in the selection presented here. Scholars have not succeeded in clearly identifying this sword-brandishing lady.

2. These two poems, not included in the present anthology, are "Domna, tant vos ai preiada," and "Eras quan vey verdeyar."

3. In this translation, W. D. Snodgrass has reversed the order of the third and fourth stanzas so as to "make a convincing English song or poem," since the revised order "seemed more logical" (personal communication, July 22, 2003). The Occitan text presented, however, retains what has come down to us as the original stanzaic order.

4. The main characters of Chrétien de Troyes's romance *Erec y Enide.*

5. Jensen (*Troubadour Lyrics,* 541) reports that Zingarelli has shown that *Engles* is a *senhal* (pseudonym) for the marquis Boniface of Monferrat.

Guillem de Cabestanh

1. Translated by Bonner, in *Songs of the Troubadours,* 188, with the troubadour's name changed to Guillem in accordance with current scholarship. See Akehurst and Davis, *Handbook of the Troubadours.*

Folquet de Marseilla

1. Translated by Egan, in *Vidas of the Troubadours,* 34, with Folquet's place of origin rendered as Marseilla. Folquet, along with his wife and sons, entered Le Thoronet sometime between 1195 and 1200. Folquet became abbot in 1201. The reformed troubadour then became bishop of Toulouse in 1206, and remained in this position until his death in 1231.

2. Bonner, *Songs of the Troubadours,* 173.

3. Raymond-Roger, the count of Foix, speaking at the Fourth Lateran Council (Sumption, *Albigensian Crusade,* 180).

4. While Pound's stanzas 1 and 2 correspond to the first two stanzas of the base text provided, his third stanza may be a composite creation. For an alternate translation of Folquet's entire poem, see the appendix.

Peire Cardenal

1. Translated by Bonner, in *Songs of the Troubadours,* 192, with *chanso* changed to *canso.*
2. See Smith, "Rhetoric," 400–420.

3. For discussion of the use of specialized vocabulary in troubadour songs, see Ghil, "Imagery and Vocabulary," 441–66.

Guillem Figueira

1. Translated by Egan, in *Vidas of the Troubadours,* 56.

2. A quote from 1058, as cited in Dawson, *Religion and the Rise of Western Culture,* 130–31.

3. With twenty-three stanzas, the poem is too long to be conveniently anthologized in its entirety. The present abridged version, consisting of stanzas 1, 2, 4, 5, 6, 7, 9, 10, 12, 21, and 23 of the base text, represents about half of the original. For complete text and translation, see Jensen, *Troubadour Lyrics,* 384–93.

4. John Lackland (1199–1216), who was under an interdict from 1209 to 1214. A possible reference to the sudden desertion of John's Poitevin allies in July 1214. This, along with other developments, gave Simon of Montfort a freer hand to prosecute his war (Sumption, *Albigensian Crusade,* 177).

5. This of course was the medieval practice of selling indulgences—for centuries a point of contention between the Catholic Church and its critics.

6. The Crusaders seized Damiette (or Damietta), located in the Nile Delta, in 1219. Their victory was short-lived, however: in 1221 Sultan Kamel (Al-Kamil) defeated the Christians and forced them to abandon Damiette. The "evil traffic" is the selling of indulgences, mentioned in the previous stanza.

7. To induce the French to participate in the Albigensian Crusade, the church promised them forgiveness of sins—in addition to visions of treasure of a more temporal nature. See Stoyanov, *Hidden Tradition,* 173.

8. Louis VIII of France died in November 1226, probably of dysentery, at the close of a year of campaigning in the Albigensian Crusade.

9. Here Guillem argues that Rome has been misdirecting the energies of the Roman Catholic Church: that while the Muslims are the true enemies of Christianity, the church has been neglecting that threat. With his reference to "Greeks and Latins," the troubadour suggests that the church leadership should regard the Eastern Orthodox as well as Roman Catholics as

Christians. Thus he condemns not only the Albigensian Crusade but also the earlier Fourth Crusade, launched against the Eastern Orthodox Church in 1202.

10. Louis VIII of France captured Avignon in September 1226, after a three-month siege.

11. Raimon VII of Toulouse. This and the stanza that follows (in the present abridged version) appear to indicate that, at the time of composition, the count was still defending his city from the Crusaders. Raimon surrendered in the spring of 1229. Even though the twelve-year-old Louis IX had not fully resumed war following the death of his father in 1226, Raimon sought to forestall another royal attack on Occitania through his capitulation. Sumption, *Albigensian Crusade*, 223.

Sordel

1. Translated by Bonner, in *Songs of the Troubadours*, 204.

2. Sordel mentions this personage in the final stanza of the selection.

3. Blacatz was the lord of Aups near Draguignan in Provence. A composer in his own right, he enjoyed the friendship and praises, and was the subject of the *planhs* of a number of other troubadours, including (to mention only those featured in the present book) Peirol, Guillem Figueira, and Lanfranc Cigala (Van Vleck, "Lyric Texts," 33–34).

4. Frederick II, Holy Roman Emperor. He fought the Milan-based Lombard League with the aid of German mercenaries. Frederick did eventually succeed in defeating the Milanese in November 1237, which suggests that Sordel wrote (or at least began) his satire before then, when the outcome was not yet decided. This and the following notes to the present poem are largely drawn from Jensen, *Troubadour Lyrics*, 579–81.

5. Louis IX (Saint Louis), who was crowned in 1226 at the age of twelve.

6. Blanche of Castile, mother of Louis IX. In between those periods when she directly served as regent (1226–36, and again in 1248–52 when Louis participated in the Seventh Crusade against Egypt), Blanche exerted a strong influence on her son.

7. Henry III. In 1204, Henry's father, John Lackland, lost Normandy, Brittany, Maine, Anjou, Poitou, and Touraine to King Philippe Auguste of France. In 1230, Henry III made an unsuccessful attempt to regain those territories.

8. Ferdinando III. He became king of Castile in 1217, and King of Galicia and León in 1230 when his father, Alfonso IX, died.

9. Berenguera, sister of Blanche of Castile, another strong-willed woman.

10. Jaime I. He lost Millau in 1229, and attempted (but failed) to recover it in 1237. His cousin, Raimon Berenguer, ruled Marseille, but lost it in 1230 during a rebellion.

11. Thibaut I, who was crowned King of Navarra in 1234. He previously ruled as the fourth count of Champagne. He organized a failed rebellion against Louis IX in 1236.

12. Jensen translates the final *tornada* as follows: "Beautiful Restaur, if only with you I may find mercy, I scorn anyone who does not hold me as a friend" (ibid., 409).

13. Raimon VII of Toulouse, who capitulated to King Louis in 1229.

14. Raimon Berenguer IV. Sordel was probably at this lord's court when he wrote the present *planh;* therefore he pulls his punches.

Guillelma de Rosers and Lanfranc Cigala

1. Translated by Egan, in *Vidas of The Troubadours*, 64, with the troubadour's name changed to Lanfranc per Akehurst and Davis, *Handbook of the Troubadours*.

ACKNOWLEDGMENTS

Guillem de Peiteus

Selection from *vida* translated by Anthony Bonner, *Songs of the Troubadours* (New York: Schocken Books, 1972), 31; reprinted by permission of the author.

"Ab la dolchor del temps novel," edited by Frederick Goldin, *Lyrics of the Troubadours and Trouveres* (Garden City, NY: Anchor Press/Doubleday, 1973), 46–48. Translated as "A New Song for New Days," by W. D. Snodgrass; originally published in W. D. Snodgrass, *Six Troubadour Songs* (Providence: Burning Deck, 1977); reprinted, with changes, from W. D. Snodgrass, *Selected Translations* (Rochester: BOA Editions, 1998), 99, by permission of the author and the publisher.

"Farai un vers de dreyt nien," edited by Goldin, *Lyrics of the Troubadours*, 24–26. Translated as "The Nothing Song," by W. D. Snodgrass; originally published in Snodgrass, *Six Troubadour Songs*; reprinted, with changes, from Snodgrass, *Selected Translations*, 103–4, by permission of the author and the publisher.

"Farai un vers, pos mi somelh," edited by Goldin, *Lyrics of the Troubadours*, 26–32. Translated as "The Ladies with the Cat," by W. D. Snodgrass; originally published in Snodgrass, *Six Troubadour Songs*; reprinted, with changes, from Snodgrass, *Selected Translations*, 100–102, by permission of the author and the publisher.

Cercamon

Selection from *vida* translated by Bonner, *Songs of the Troubadours*, 41; reprinted by permission of the author.

"Quant l'aura doussa s'amarzis," edited by Frede Jensen, *Troubadour Lyrics* (New York: Peter Lang Publishing, 1998), 102–4. Rendered as "When the Sweet Air Goes Bitter (Descant on a Theme by Cercamon)," by Ezra Pound; originally published in 1919; reprinted from Ezra Pound, *Translations* (New York: New Directions Books, 1963), 428–31. Translated as "When the Soft Wind Turns Bitter," by Frede Jensen; reprinted from Jensen, *Troubadour Lyrics*, 103–5, by permission of the publisher.

Marcabru

Selection from *vida* translated by Bonner, *Songs of the Troubadours*, 44; reprinted by permission of the author.

"A la fontana del vergier," edited by Jensen, *Troubadour Lyrics,* 90–92. Translated as "By the Bank," by Robert Kehew.

"L'autrier jost' una sebissa," edited by Goldin, *Lyrics of the Troubadours,* 70–76. Translated as "The Peasant Lassie," by W. D. Snodgrass; originally published in Snodgrass, *Six Troubadour Songs;* reprinted, with changes, from Snodgrass, *Selected Translations,* 105–7, by permission of the author and the publisher.

"Pax in nomine Domini!," edited by Jensen, *Troubadour Lyrics,* 94–96. Translated as "The Cleansing Place," by Robert Kehew.

Jaufre Rudel

Selection from *vida* translated by Bonner, *Songs of the Troubadours,* 61; reprinted by permission of the author.

"Lanquan li jorn," edited by Goldin, *Lyrics of the Troubadours,* 104–6. Translated as "A Love Afar," by W. D. Snodgrass; reprinted, with changes, from Snodgrass, *Selected Translations,* 108–9, by permission of the author and the publisher.

"Can lo rossinhol el fulhos," edited by Rupert T. Pickens, *The Songs of Jaufré Rudel* (Toronto: Pontifical Institute of Mediaeval Studies, 1978), 78–86. (Version 3-a, except for lines 20–21, 34, and 36–42, which are from version 3.) Translated as "The Nightingale," by W. D. Snodgrass; originally published in *The Southern Review* (forthcoming); reprinted, with changes, by permission of the author.

Bernart de Ventadorn

Selection from *vida* translated by Bonner, *Songs of the Troubadours,* 82; reprinted by permission of the author.

"Can vei la lauzeta mover," edited by Goldin, *Lyrics of the Troubadours,* 144–48. Translated as "The Skylark," by W. D. Snodgrass; reprinted, with changes, from Snodgrass, *Selected Translations,* 110–11, by permission of the author and the publisher.

"Can l'erba fresch'" edited by Goldin, *Lyrics of the Troubadours,* 136–40. Translated as "When Tender Grass and Leaves Appear," by W. D. Snodgrass; originally published in *The Southern Review* (forthcoming); reprinted by permission of the author.

"Pois preyatz me, senhor," edited by Ronnie Apter, in *A Bilingual Edition of the Love Songs of Bernart de Ventadorn in Occitan and English: Sugar and Salt* (Lewiston: The Edwin Mellen Press, 1999), 220–22. Translated as "You've Asked, My Lords, for Song," by W. D. Snodgrass; originally published as liner notes to the compact disc by Martin Best, *The Testament of Tristan* (London: Hyperion Records, 1986) [CD-A662110]; reprinted, with changes, by permission of the author.

"Lancan vei la folha," edited by Goldin, *Lyrics of the Troubadours,* 148–54. Translated as "Now the Birds are Leaving," by W. D. Snodgrass; first published in *The Kenyon Review*—New Series, vol. XXVI, no. 2 (Spring 2004); reprinted by permission of the author.

"Be m'an perdut lai enves Ventadorn," edited by Goldin, *Lyrics of the Troubadours*, 134–36. Translated as "Farewell to Ventadorn," by W. D. Snodgrass; first published in *Shenandoah*, vol. 52, no. 1 (Spring 2002): 75–77; reprinted by permission of the author.

"Non es meravelha s'eu chan," edited by Goldin, *Lyrics of the Troubadours*, 126–28. Translated as "No Marvel If My Song's the Best," by W. D. Snodgrass; originally published in *The Southern Review*, vol. 38, no. 1 (Winter 2002): 75–77; reprinted by permission of the author.

Peire d'Alvernhe

Selection from *vida* translated by Bonner, *Songs of the Troubadours*, 68; reprinted by permission of the author.

"Rossinhol, el seu repaire," edited by Jensen, *Troubadour Lyrics*, 142–48. Translated as "Nightingale, for Me Take Flight," by Robert Kehew.

"Deiosta·ls breus iorns e·ls loncs sers," edited by Aniello Fratta, *Peire d'Alvernhe: Poesie* (Rome: Vecchiarelli Editore, 1996), 93–98. Translated as "When Days Grow Short and Night Advances," by Robert Kehew.

Raimbaut d'Aurenga

Selection from *vida* translated by Bonner, *Songs of the Troubadours*, 100; reprinted by permission of the author.

"Er resplan la flors enversa," edited by Jensen, *Troubadour Lyrics*, 190–92. Translated as "Splendid Are the Flowers Reversed," by Robert Kehew.

"Escotatz, mas no say que s'es," edited by Goldin, *Lyrics of the Troubadours*, 178–80. Translated as "Beg Pardon, Lords," by W. D. Snodgrass; originally published in Snodgrass, *Six Troubadour Songs;* reprinted, with changes, from Snodgrass, *Selected Translations*, by permission of the author and the publisher.

Guiraut de Bornelh

Selection from *vida* translated by Bonner, *Songs of the Troubadours*, 114; reprinted by permission of the author.

"Reis glorios," edited by Goldin, *Lyrics of the Troubadours*, 194–96. Translated as "Day's Glorious Lord," by W. D. Snodgrass; used by permission of the author.

"Can lo freitz e·l glatz e la neus," edited by Jensen, *Troubadour Lyrics*, 202–4. Translated as "When the Ice and Cold and Snow Retreat," by Robert Kehew.

Peire Bremon lo Tort

Vida translated by Margarita Egan, *The Vidas of the Troubadours* (New York: Garland Publishing, 1984), 73. Copyright © 1984 by Margarita Egan. Reproduced by permission of Routledge/Taylor & Francis Books, Inc.

"En abril, quan vey verdeyar," edited by Carl Appel, *Provenzalische chrestomathie* (Leipzig: O. R. Reisland, 1902), 62–63. Translated as "From Syria," by Ezra Pound; originally published in 1909; reprinted from Ezra Pound, *Collected Early Poems of Ezra Pound,* edited by Michael John King (New York: New Directions Books, 1982), 92–93.

Bertran de Born

Translation from *razo* by Bonner, *Songs of the Troubadours,* 149; reprinted by permission of the author.

"Be·m platz lo gais temps de pascor," edited by Jensen, 256–58. Translated as "A War Song," by Ezra Pound; originally published in 1910; reprinted from Ezra Pound, *The Spirit of Romance* (New York: New Directions Books, 1968), 47–48.

"Un sirventes on motz no falh," edited by Charlotte Ward, in Ezra Pound, *Ezra Pound: Forked Branches,* edited by Charlotte Ward (Iowa City: The Windhover Press, 1985), 10–12. Used by permission of New Directions Publishing Corporation. Translated as "Un sirventes on motz no falh" (or "Quarrels Where Words Don't Miss Fire"), by Ezra Pound, in ibid., 11–13. Used by permission of New Directions Publishing Corporation.

"Domna, puois de me no·us chal," edited by Goldin, *Lyrics of the Troubadours,* 234–38. Translated as "Dompna pois de me no'us cal" (or "Lady, Since You Care Nothing for Me"), by Ezra Pound; first published in 1913–15; reprinted from Ezra Pound, *Personae: The Shorter Poems of Ezra Pound,* edited by Lea Baechler and A. Walton Litz (New York: New Directions Books, 1990), 107–9.

"Ieu m'escondisc, domna, que mal no mier," edited by Jensen, *Troubadour Lyrics,* 260–62. Translated as "He Protests His Innocence to a Lady," by Robert Kehew

"Belh m'es, quan vey camjar lo senhoratge," edited by Jensen, *Troubadour Lyrics,* 252–54. Translated as "The Secret to Staying Young," by Robert Kehew.

"Si tuit li dol e·il plor e·il marrimen," edited by Jensen, *Troubadour Lyrics,* 244–46. Translated as "Planh for the Young English King," by Ezra Pound; originally published in 1909; reprinted from Pound, *Collected Early Poems of Ezra Pound,* 123–24.

Comtessa de Dia

Vida translated by Egan, *Vidas of the Troubadours,* 28. Copyright © 1984 by Margarita Egan. Reproduced by permission of Routledge/Taylor & Francis Books, Inc.

"Estat ai en greu cossirier," edited by Jensen, *Troubadour Lyrics,* 272. Translated as "Cruel Are the Pains I've Suffered," by Robert Kehew.

"A chantar m'er de so q'ieu no volria," edited by Jensen, *Troubadour Lyrics*, 274–76. Translated as "I'm Forced to Sing," by Robert Kehew.

Maria de Ventadorn and Gui d'Ussel

Selection from *vida* translated by Egan, *Vidas of the Troubadours*, 68–69. Copyright © 1984 by Margarita Egan. Reproduced by permission of Routledge/Taylor & Francis Books, Inc.

"Gui d'Ussel be·m pesa de vos," edited by Matilda Tomaryn Bruckner, Laurie Shephard, and Sarah White, in *Songs of the Women Troubadours* (New York & London: Garland Publishing, 1995), 38–40. Translated as "When a Lady Loves," by Robert Kehew.

Monge de Montaudon

Selection from *vida* translated by Bonner, *Songs of the Troubadours*, 180; reprinted by permission of the author.

"Mout me platz deportz e gaieza," edited by Jensen, *Troubadour Lyrics*, 336. Translated as "What I Like," by Robert Kehew.

"Be m'enueia, s'o auzes dire," edited by Jensen, *Troubadour Lyrics*, 338–42. Translated as "What I Don't Like," by Robert Kehew.

Arnaut Daniel

Selection from *vida* translated by Bonner, *Songs of the Troubadours*, 157; reprinted by permission of the author.

"Chansson do·il mot son plan e prim," edited by James J. Wilhelm, *The Poetry of Arnaut Daniel* (New York: Garland Publishing, 1981), 6–8. Translated as "I'll Make a Song," by Ezra Pound; originally published in 1911; reprinted from Pound, *Translations*, 416–18.

"Autet e bas entrels prims fuoills," edited by Ezra Pound, in "Arnaut Daniel," in *Literary Essays of Ezra Pound*, edited by T. S. Eliot (New York: New Directions Books, 1968), 125–27. Translated as "Now High and Low, Where Leaves Renew," by Ezra Pound; originally published in 1920; reprinted from ibid., 124–25.

"Doutz brais e critz," edited by Pound, *Translations*, 172–74. Translated as "Sweet Cries and Cracks," by Ezra Pound; originally published in 1920; reprinted from ibid., 173–75.

"Chan chai la fueilla," edited by Pound, "Arnaut Daniel," 118–19. Translated as "When Sere Leaf Falleth," by Ezra Pound; originally published in 1920; reprinted from ibid., 116–17.

"L'aura amara," edited by Pound, "Arnaut Daniel," 130–33. Translated as "The Bitter Air," by Ezra Pound; originally published in 1920; reprinted from ibid., 127–30.

"En cest sonet coind'e leri," edited by Wilhelm, *Poetry of Arnaut Daniel*, 40–42 (with some variations accepted). Translated as "Canzon: of the Trades and Love," by Ezra Pound; originally published in 1912; reprinted from Pound, *Translations*, 421–23.

Arnaut de Marueill

Selection from *vida* translated by Bonner, *Songs of the Troubadours*, 133; reprinted by permission of the author.

"Si·m destreignetz, dompna, vos et Amors," edited by R. C. Johnston, *Les poésies lyriques du troubadour Arnaut de Mareuil* (Paris: Librairie E. Droz, 1935), 134–37. Translated as "Lady, by You and Love I Am So Swayed," by Robert Kehew.

"Belh m'es quan lo vens m'alena," edited by Jensen, *Troubadour Lyrics*, 236. Translated as "Fair Is It to Me," by Ezra Pound; originally published in 1910; reprinted from Pound, *Spirit of Romance*, 57.

Gaucelm Faidit

Selection from *vida* translated by Egan, *Vidas of the Troubadours*, 37. Copyright © 1984 by Margarita Egan. Reproduced by permission of Routledge / Taylor & Francis Books, Inc.

"Del gran golfe de mar," edited by R. T. Hill and T. G. Bergin, *Anthology of the Provençal Troubadours* (New Haven: Yale University Press, 1973), 128–29. Translated as "From the Depths of the Sea," by Robert Kehew.

Peire Vidal

Selection from *vida* translated by Bonner, *Songs of the Troubadours*, 164–66; reprinted by permission of the author.

"Pos tornatz sui en Proensa," edited by Joseph Anglade, in *Les poésies de Peire Vidal* (Paris: Librairie Ancienne Honoré Champion, 1913), 89–92. Translated as "To Provence I Can Return Now," by W. D. Snodgrass; used by permission of the author.

"Ab l'alen tir vas me l'aire," edited by Jensen, *Troubadour Lyrics*, 300. Translated as "The Song of Breath," by Ezra Pound; originally published in 1910; reprinted from Pound, *Spirit of Romance*, 57.

Peirol

Selection from *vida* translated by Egan, *Vidas of the Troubadours*, 81–82. Copyright © 1984 by Margarita Egan. Reproduced by permission of Routledge / Taylor & Francis Books, Inc.

"Atressi co·l signes fai," edited by Jensen, *Troubadour Lyrics*, 364–66. Translated as "Even As the Swan," by Robert Kehew.

Raimbaut de Vaqueiras

Selection from *vida* translated by Egan, *Vidas of the Troubadours*, 90–91. Copyright © 1984 by Margarita Egan. Reproduced by permission of Routledge/Taylor & Francis Books, Inc.

"Kalenda maya," edited by Hill and Bergin, *Anthology of the Provençal Troubadours*, 151–53. Translated as "May Day," by W. D. Snodgrass; first published in *Southern Review*, vol. 38, no. 1 (Winter 2002): 77–79; reprinted by permission of the author.

Guillem de Cabestanh

Selection from *vida* translated by Bonner, *Songs of the Troubadours*, 188; reprinted by permission of the author.

"Lo jorn qu'ie·us vi, dompna, primeiramen," edited by Jensen, *Troubadour Lyrics*, 360–62. Translated as "That Day, My Lady, When I First Discovered that You Exist," by Robert Kehew.

Folquet de Marseilla

Selection from *vida* translated by Egan, *Vidas of the Troubadours*, 34. Copyright © 1984 by Margarita Egan. Reproduced by permission of Routledge/Taylor & Francis Books, Inc.

"Tant m'abellis l'amoros pessamens," edited by Jensen, *Troubadour Lyrics*, 220–22. Translated as "So Pleasureth Me the Amorous Thought," by Ezra Pound; originally published in 1910; reprinted from Pound, *Spirit of Romance*, 56. Translated as "So Much Does the Anxiety of Love Please Me," by Frede Jensen; reprinted from Jensen, *Troubadour Lyrics*, 221–23 by permission of the publisher.

Peire Cardenal

Selection from *vida* translated by Bonner, *Songs of the Troubadours*, 192; reprinted by permission of the author.

"Una ciutatz fo, no sai cals," edited by Goldin, *Lyrics of the Troubadours*, 302–8. Translated as "There Was a Town," by W. D. Snodgrass; originally published in *Southern Review*, vol. 38, no. 1 (Winter 2002): 79–82; reprinted, with changes, by permission of the author.

"Ar me puesc ieu lauzar d'Amor," edited by Goldin, *Lyrics of the Troubadours*, 286–88. Translated as "I Dare to Claim, Now, Love Cannot," by W. D. Snodgrass; originally published in Snodgrass, *Six Troubadour Songs*; reprinted, with changes, by permission of the author.

"Un sirventes novel vueill comensar," edited by Goldin, *Lyrics of the Troubadours*, 294–96. Translated as "A New Protest Song," by W. D. Snodgrass; used by permission of the author.

Guillem Figueira

Selection from *vida* translated by Egan, *Vidas of the Troubadours,* 56. Copyright © 1984 by Margarita Egan. Reproduced by permission of Routledge/Taylor & Francis Books, Inc.

Excerpts from "D'un sirventes far en est son que m'agenssa," edited by Jensen, *Troubadour Lyrics,* 384–92. Translated as "Rome, Where Goodness Declines," by Robert Kehew.

Sordel

Selection from *vida* translated by Bonner, *Songs of the Troubadours,* 204. Copyright © 1984 by Margarita Egan. Reproduced by permission of Routledge/Taylor & Francis Books, Inc.

"Planher vuelh En Blacatz en aquest leugier so," edited by Jensen, *Troubadour Lyrics,* 406–8. Translated as "I Want to Mourn Blacatz," by Robert Kehew.

Guillelma de Rosers and Lanfranc Cigala

Selection from *vida* translated by Egan, *Vidas of the Troubadours,* 64. Copyright © 1984 by Margarita Egan. Reproduced by permission of Routledge/Taylor & Francis Books, Inc.

"Na Guilielma, maunt cavalier arratge," edited by Bruckner, Shephard, and White, *Songs of the Women Troubadours,* 74–76. Translated as "Which of the Two Behaved Most Fittingly?," by Robert Kehew.

Guiraut Riquier

"Be·m degra de chantar tener," edited by Jensen, *Troubadour Lyrics,* 436–38. Translated as "It Would be Best if I Refrained from Singing," by Robert Kehew.

BIBLIOGRAPHY

Adams, Henry. *Mont-Saint-Michel and Chartres.* 1905; Princeton: Princeton University Press, 1981.

Akehurst, F. R. P., and Judith M. Davis, eds. *A Handbook of the Troubadours.* Berkeley: University of California Press, 1995.

Anglade, Joseph, ed. *Les poésies de Peire Vidal.* Paris: Librairie Ancienne Honoré Champion, 1913.

Appel, Carl. *Provenzalische Chrestomathie.* Leipzig: O. R. Reisland, 1902.

Apter, Ronnie, ed. and trans. *A Bilingual Edition of the Love Songs of Bernart de Ventadorn in Occitan and English: Sugar and Salt.* Lewiston: Edwin Mellen Press, 1999.

Bogin, Meg. *The Women Troubadours.* New York: Paddington Press, 1976.

Bond, Gerald A. "Origins." In Akehurst and Davis, *Handbook of the Troubadours.*

Bonner, Anthony. *Songs of the Troubadours.* New York: Schocken Books, 1972.

Bruckner, Matilda Tomaryn. "The Trobairitz." In Akehurst and Davis, *Handbook of the Troubadours.*

Bruckner, Matilda Tomaryn, Laurie Shephard, and Sarah White, eds. and trans. *Songs of the Women Troubadours.* New York: Garland Publishing, 1995.

Camille, Michael. *The Medieval Art of Love.* London: Calmann and King, 1998.

Chambers, Frank M. "Versification." In Akehurst and Davis, *Handbook of the Troubadours.*

Cherchi, Paolo. *Andreas and the Ambiguity of Courtly Love.* Toronto: University of Toronto Press, 1994.

Cheyette, Fredric L. *Ermengard of Narbonne and the World of the Troubadours.* Ithaca: Cornell University Press, 2001.

Crocker, Richard L. *A History of Musical Style.* 1966; New York: Dover Publications, 1986.

Daniel-Rops, Henri. *Cathedral and Crusade.* Vol. 1. Garden City, NY: Image Books, 1963.

Dante Alighieri. *The Inferno of Dante.* Translated by Robert Pinsky. 1994; New York: Farrar, Straus and Giroux, 1998.

———. *The Paradiso.* Translated by John Ciardi. New York: Mentor Books, 1970.

———. *The Purgatorio.* Translated by John Ciardi. New York: Mentor Books, 1961.

Dawson, Christopher. *Religion and the Rise of Western Culture.* 1950; New York: AMS Press, 1979.

Denomy, A. J. "Courtly Love and Courtliness." *Speculum* 28 (1953): 44–63.

[Dersin, Denise.] *What Life Was Like in the Age of Chivalry.* Alexandria: Time-Life Books, 1997.

Dronke, Peter. *Medieval Latin and the Rise of European Love-Lyric.* Vol. 1. 1965; Oxford: Clarendon Press, 1968.

———. *The Medieval Lyric.* 1968; New York: Cambridge University Press, 1977.

Duby, Georges, ed. *A History of Private Life: Revelations of the Medieval World.* Vol. 2. Translated by Arthur Goldhammer. Cambridge, MA: Belknap Press of Harvard University Press, 1988. (Originally published in France, 1986.)

Economou, George D. "Marcabru, Love's Star Witness: For and Against." *Tenso: Bulletin of the Société Guilhem IX* 7, no. 1 (Autumn 1991): 23–39.

Egan, Margarita, trans. *The Vidas of the Troubadours.* Garland Library of Medieval Literature 6, series B. New York: Garland Publishing, 1984.

Foss, Michael. *People of the First Crusade.* 1997; London: Caxton Publishing Group, 2000.

Fraser, Veronica. "Two Contrasting Views of Love in the Songs of the Troubadours and the Trobairitz." *Tenso: Bulletin of the Société Guilhem IX* 13, no. 1 (Fall 1997): 24–47.

Fratta, Aniello. *Peire d'Alvernhe: Poésie.* Rome: Vecchiarelli Editore, 1996.

Gallo, F. Alberto. *Music in the Castle.* Translated by Anna Herklotz. Chicago: University of Chicago Press, 1995. (Originally published in Italy, 1992.)

Gaunt, Simon, Ruth Harvey, and Linda Paterson. *Marcabru: A Critical Edition.* Cambridge, UK: D. S. Brewer, 2000.

Gaunt, Simon; and Sarah Kay. *The Troubadours: An Introduction.* Cambridge, UK: Cambridge University Press, 1999.

Ghil, Eliza Miruna. "Imagery and Vocabulary." In Akehurst and Davis, *Handbook of the Troubadours.*

Gold, Penny Schine. *The Lady and the Virgin: Image, Attitude, and Experience in Twelfth-Century France.* Chicago: University of Chicago Press, 1985.

Goldin, Frederick. *Lyrics of the Troubadours and Trouveres.* Garden City, NY: Anchor Press / Doubleday, 1973.

Harvey, Ruth. "Courtly Culture in Medieval Occitania." In Akehurst and Davis, *Handbook of the Troubadours.*

Hill, R. T., and T. G. Bergin. *Anthology of the Provençal Troubadours.* New Haven: Yale University Press, 1973.

Hopkins, Andrea. *The Book of Courtly Love: The Passionate Code of the Troubadours.* [San Francisco]: HarperSanFrancisco, 1994.

Huizinga, Johan. *The Autumn of the Middle Ages.* Translated by Rodney J. Payton and Ulrich Mammitzsch. Chicago: University of Chicago Press, 1996. (Originally published in Holland, 1919.)

Irwin, Robert, ed. *Nights and Horses and the Desert: An Anthology of Classical Arabic Literature.* Woodstock, NY: Overlook Press, 2000.

Jackson, W. T. H. *The Literature of the Middle Ages.* New York: Columbia University Press, 1960.

Jeanroy, Alfred. *La poésie lyrique des troubadours.* 2 vols. Paris: Privat, 1934.

Jensen, Frede, ed. and trans. *Troubadour Lyrics.* Studies in the Humanities 39. New York: Peter Lang Publishing, 1998.

Jewers, Caroline. "The Poetics of (S) Cat-Ology in Guilhem VII, Count of Poitiers, IX Duke of Aquitaine's *Canso V.*" *Tenso: Bulletin of the Société Guilhem IX* 11, no. 1 (Fall 1995): 38–63.

Johnston, R. C., ed. and trans. *Les poésies lyriques du troubadour Arnaut de Mareuil.* Paris: Librairie E. Droz, 1935.

Jones, Colin. *The Cambridge Illustrated History of France.* Cambridge, UK: Cambridge University Press, 1994.

Jones, Terry, and Alan Ereira. *Crusades.* New York: Facts on File / BBC Books, 1995.

Kay, Sarah. "Desire and Subjectivity." In Gaunt and Kay, *Troubadours.*

Keller, Hans-Erich. "Italian Troubadours." In Akehurst and Davis, *Handbook of the Troubadours.*

Lazar, Moshé. *Bernard de Ventadour, troubadour du XIIe siècle: Chansons d'amour*. Paris: Librairie C. Klincksieck, 1966.

———. *"Fin'Amor."* In Akehurst and Davis, *Handbook of the Troubadours*.

Le Goff, Jacques. *Intellectuals in the Middle Ages*. Translated by Teresa Lavender Fagan. Cambridge, MA: Blackwell Publishers, 1993. (Originally published in France, 1957.)

Le Roy Ladurie, Emmanuel. *Montaillou, the Promised Land of Error*. Translated by Barbara Bray. New York: Vintage Books, 1979. (Originally published in France, 1975.)

Lewis, C. S. *The Allegory of Love*. 1936; London: Oxford University Press, 1953.

Maalouf, Amin. *The Crusades through Arab Eyes*. Translated by Jon Rothschild. New York: Schocken Books, 1985. (Originally published in France, 1983.)

Macdonald, Aileen. "Warbled Words: The 'Starling' and 'Nightingale' Poems." *Tenso: Bulletin of the Société Guilhem IX* 10, no. 1 (Fall 1994): 18–36.

Marks, Claude. *Pilgrims, Heretics, and Lovers: A Medieval Journey*. New York: Macmillan, 1975.

McDougal, Stuart Y. *Ezra Pound and the Troubadour Tradition*. Princeton: Princeton University Press, 1972.

Meade, Marion. *Eleanor of Aquitaine: A Biography*. New York: Hawthorn Books, 1977.

Merwin, W. S. *The Mays of Ventadorn*. Washington, DC: National Geographic Society, 2002.

Monson, Don A. "The Troubadours at Play: Irony, Parody, and Burlesque." In Gaunt and Kay, *Troubadours*.

Morris, Colin. *The Discovery of the Individual, 1050–1200*. Toronto: University of Toronto Press, 1972.

Paden, William D., Jr. "Both Borrower and Lender: Cultural Exchange in the World of the Troubadours." *Tenso: Bulletin of the Société Guilhem IX* 13, no. 2 (Spring 1998): 3–17.

———. "Manuscripts." In Akehurst and Davis, *Handbook of the Troubadours*.

———. "Some Recent Studies of Women in the Middle Ages, Especially in Southern France." *Tenso: Bulletin of the Société Guilhem IX* 7, no. 2 (Spring 1992): 94–124.

Paden, William D., Jr., Tilde Sankovitch, and Patricia H. Stäblein. *The Poems of the Troubadour Bertran de Born*. Berkeley: University of California Press, 1986.

Page, Christopher. *Voices and Instruments of the Middle Ages: Instrumental Practice and Songs in France 1100–1300*. Berkeley: University of California Press, 1986.

Paterson, Linda. "Development of the Courtly *Canso*." In Akehurst and Davis, *Handbook of the Troubadours*.

Pickens, Rupert T., ed. *The Songs of Jaufré Rudel*. Toronto: Pontifical Institute of Mediaeval Studies, 1978.

Poe, Elizabeth W. "The *Vidas* and *Razos*." In Akehurst and Davis, *Handbook of the Troubadours*.

Pound, Ezra. "Arnaut Daniel." 1920. In *Literary Essays of Ezra Pound*, edited by T. S. Eliot. New York: New Directions Books, 1968.

———. *Collected Early Poems of Ezra Pound*. Edited by Michael John King. New York: New Directions Books, 1976.

———. *Ezra Pound: Forked Branches*. Edited by Charlotte Ward. Iowa City: Windhover Press, 1985.

———. *Ezra Pound From Syria: The Worksheets, Proofs, and Text*. Edited by Robin Skelton. Port Townsend: Copper Canyon Press, 1981.

———. *Literary Essays of Ezra Pound*. Edited by T. S. Eliot. 1935; New York: New Directions Books, 1968.

———. *Personae: The Shorter Poems of Ezra Pound*. Edited by Lea Baechler and A. Walton Litz. 1926; New York: New Directions Books, 1990.

———. *The Spirit of Romance*. 1910; New York: New Directions Books, 1968.

———. *Translations.* New York: New Directions Books, 1963.

———. "The Troubadours: Their Sorts and Conditions." 1913. In *A Walking Tour in Southern France: Ezra Pound Among the Troubadours,* edited by Richard Sieburth. New York: New Directions Books, 1992.

Press, Alan R. *Anthology of Troubadour Lyric Poetry.* Edinburgh: Edinburgh University Press, 1971.

Sankovitch, Tilde. "The Trobairitz." In Gaunt and Kay, *Troubadours.*

Schulze-Busacker, Elisabeth. "Topoi." In Akehurst and Davis, *Handbook of the Troubadours.*

Seward, Desmond. *The Monks of War: The Military Religious Orders.* 1972; London: Penguin Books, 1995.

Sieburth, Richard, ed. *A Walking Tour in Southern France: Ezra Pound among the Troubadours.* New York: New Directions Books, 1992.

Smith, Nathaniel B. "Rhetoric." In Akehurst and Davis, *Handbook of the Troubadours.*

Snodgrass, W. D. *Selected Translations.* Rochester: BOA Editions, 1998.

———. *Six Troubadour Songs.* Providence: Burning Deck, 1977.

Stoyanov, Yuri. *The Hidden Tradition in Europe: The Secret History of Medieval Christian Heresy.* London: Penguin Group, 1994.

Sumption, Jonathan. *The Albigensian Crusade.* 1978; London: Faber and Faber, 1999.

Topsfield, L. T. *Troubadours and Love.* Cambridge, MA: Cambridge University Press, 1975.

Turco, Lewis. *The New Book of Forms: A Handbook of Poetics.* 1968; Hanover: University Press of New England, 1986.

Van Vleck, Amelia E. "The Lyric Texts." In Akehurst and Davis, *Handbook of the Troubadours.*

Weir, Alison. *Eleanor of Aquitaine: A Life.* 1999; New York: Ballantine Books, 2001.

Wilhelm, James J. *The Poetry of Arnaut Daniel.* New York: Garland Publishing, 1981.

Zink, Michel. *Medieval French Literature: An Introduction.* Translated by Jeff Rider. Binghamton: Pegasus Paperbooks, 1995. (Originally published in France, 1990.)

INDEX OF TITLES AND FIRST LINES